THE
TERRORIST PERSPECTIVES
PROJECT

STRATEGIC AND OPERATIONAL VIEWS OF
AL QAIDA AND ASSOCIATED MOVEMENTS

Mark E. Stout, Jessica M. Huckabey, John R. Schindler
with Jim Lacey

NAVAL INSTITUTE PRESS
Annapolis, Maryland

Naval Institute Press
291 Wood Road
Annapolis, MD 21402

Library of Congress Cataloging-in-Publication Data
Stout, Mark, 1964–
  The Terrorist Perspectives Project : strategic and operational
views of Al Qaida and associated movements / Mark E. Stout,
Jessica M. Huckabey, John R. Schindler with Jim Lacey.
     p. cm.
  Includes bibliographical references and index.
  ISBN 978-1-59114-463-2 (alk. paper)
  1. Qaida (Organization) 2. Terrorism—Religious aspects—
Islam. 3. Jihad. 4. Salafiyah. 5. Wahhabiyah. 6. Islam and
politics. 7. Terrorism—Government policy—United States.
I. Huckabey, Jessica M. II. Schindler, John R. III. Terrorist
Perspectives Project. IV. Title. V. Title: Al Qaida and associ-
ated movements.
HV6431.S747 2008
363.325—dc22

                              2007046137

Printed in the United States of America on acid-free paper

14 13 12 11 10 09 08   9 8 7 6 5 4 3 2
First printing

Contents

Acknowledgments

The Institute for Defense Analyses prepared this report under task order AJ-8-2743(03) for the U.S. Joint Forces Command. The report helps address the task order's objective of mining the words of terrorist enemies of the United States in order to identify what the United States may be getting right or wrong in combating such enemies.

Mark Stout led the study team, but many people from the Institute for Defense Analyses (IDA)—primarily its Joint Advanced Warfighting Division (JAWD)—contributed as well. Aside from the authors, Adrienne Janetti; Jeff Jaworski; Mary Kathryn Keegin; Ambassador John Limbert; Michael Pease; Cdr. Randall Peck, USN; and Joel Resnick made significant contributions to this work.

Paul Anir; Col. James Ayers, USAF; Ens. Jacqueline Bengfort, USN; Lauren Burns; Terry Heuring; Thomas Holaday; Drew Lewis; Elizabeth Nathan; Cdr. Doug Pfeifle, USN; Stanley Riveles; Christine Shoemaker; Jagjot Singh; and Lucy Williams spent time on the team as well.

We would like to thank Karl Lowe, JAWD director, and James Kurtz, assistant director, for their leadership and support. Mary Habeck of Johns Hopkins University offered valuable draft language at two critical points in the manuscript. Maj. Gen. Waldo Freeman, USA (Ret.), and Col. Chester Arnold, USMC, brought to bear their perspectives both as analysts and as operators to provide similarly useful comments. James Thomason was kind enough to review a very early version of this work. We are deeply grateful to Laila Sabara and Ayeh Bandeh-Ahmadi, who put their language skills at our disposal. Rob Johnston provided indispensable suggestions early on that put us on the right track. Col. Tex deAtkine, USA (Ret.);

William Simpkins; Caroline Ziemke; and Michael Keleher also gave useful input, as did Col. Pat Lang, USA (Ret.), and Joseph McMillan from the National Defense University. Numerous dedicated officers of the U.S. intelligence community critiqued our ideas and pointed us toward sources of which we would otherwise have been unaware. Similarly, we benefited from the sage council of several members of the academic community who must remain anonymous, aside from Jeffrey Cozzens, who kindly shared with us the central idea of his forthcoming doctoral dissertation.

Many people outside the study group have offered comments and recommendations; however, they are not responsible for any errors that may exist within this work. Blame for any such shortcomings belongs to the lead author.

Needless to say, this project could not have been completed without JAWD's outstanding editorial and support personnel, including Carolyn Leonard, Aundra Campbell, Heidrun Elder, and Carrie Wilkerson.

JAWD was established at IDA to serve as a catalyst for stimulating innovation and breakthrough change. It is co-sponsored by the Under Secretary of Defense for Acquisition, Technology and Logistics; the Under Secretary of Defense for Policy; the Vice Chairman of the Joint Chiefs of Staff; and the Commander, U.S. Joint Forces Command (JFCOM). JAWD includes military personnel on joint assignments from each service and civilian specialists from IDA. JAWD is located in Alexandria, Virginia, and includes an office in Norfolk, Virginia, to facilitate coordination with JFCOM.

This book does not necessarily reflect the views of IDA or the sponsors of JAWD. Our intent is to stimulate ideas, discussion, and, ultimately, the discovery and innovation that must fuel success.

Preface

This book on the strategic and operational perspectives of al Qaida and associated movements (AQAM) draws together the findings to date of the Terrorist Perspectives Project. The Institute for Defense Analyses (IDA) began this project in the fall of 2004 under the sponsorship of the Joint Center for Operational Analysis and U.S. Joint Forces Command (JFCOM) after JFCOM perceived a pressing need within the policy community for a comprehensive study of AQAM's strategic thought. The primary objective is to know the enemy as he knows himself in terms that he would recognize.

This work focuses on Salafi jihadism, the theology that defines AQAM and its strategic and operational manifestations; it is not concerned with "radical Islam" in general or with all Muslim-associated terrorist threats. We discuss only the Salafi jihadist movement's intellectual leadership—its "strategists"—and a representative sampling of their followers—the "foot soldiers"—who together comprise the self-proclaimed vanguard of the global jihad. AQAM's jihadists have demonstrated a global reach, share a common theological outlook, and have declared the United States to be their primary enemy. All other groups are outside the scope of this study.

In the immediate aftermath of 9/11, observations that the attacks "changed everything" were common. That is untrue. The enemy's perspective changed very little. For Osama bin Laden and his fellow Salafi jihadists, September 11, 2001, was not the beginning of a new war; it was the continuation of a decades-long conflict. AQAM has fought campaigns in Egypt, Algeria, Syria, Saudi Arabia, Iraq, Afghanistan, Tajikistan, Somalia, Bosnia, Indonesia, and Chechnya, among other places. Along the way, its leaders learned many lessons that have shaped their strategy and conduct of the war. This book synthesizes these lessons for U.S. civilian and military policy makers and planners as well as for educators at the professional military educational institutions.

As the study team conducted this research, the extent of what Americans, even those directly involved in the "war on terrorism," did not know about the nature and strategy of al Qaida became clear. The national media initially pursued questions such as, Who is Osama bin Laden? What is al Qaida? What do they want? and Why do they hate us?[1] Many analysts offered answers—some superficial or simply incorrect—without considering the enemy's perspective. Their analyses conformed to preexisting notions of how terrorists behave and what they believe. In particular, it is still a common practice, though not usually a correct one, to frame discussions of AQAM solely in terms of the movement's secular outlook.

The 9/11 Commission Report attributes the success of the attacks, in part, to a "failure of imagination" by those whose responsibility it was to study and anticipate al Qaida's motives and intentions.[2] The September 11, 2001, attacks were indeed the most horrific manifestation to date of a much broader al Qaida strategy a decade in the making—the "evil" tip of a larger and more ominous iceberg. While difficult to fathom for those unaccustomed to the milieu of Salafism and violent jihad, the strategy is not at all impossible to comprehend. It is imperative that we understand our enemy if we are to avoid future catastrophes such as 9/11, let alone if the United States and its allies are to prevail in the war on terrorism.

The data and tools necessary to understand AQAM's intellectual world exist, though it is often difficult for government officials, even in the intelligence community, to find the time to undertake such projects. Nevertheless, Americans have done this kind of work before. During the Cold War, for example, scholars such as RAND's Nathan Leites pioneered the work of understanding the Soviet political leadership and military through analyzing their journals and public statements.[3] IDA's Iraqi Perspectives Project (also sponsored by JFCOM), which used interviews with former Iraqi generals and ministers and access to captured Iraqi documents to provide an unprecedented inside picture of Saddam Hussein's national security state, inspired this book.

The two major sources of data underpinning this work are captured documents and open source materials. The study team had access to a government database called "Harmony" that contains many thousands of captured terrorist documents and is an extremely rich source of the enemy's private thoughts. Many of the documents deal with tactical matters that fall below the threshold of this book: specific plots, small-unit tactics, discussions of weapons, and so on. Others, however, discuss strategy, politics, political philosophy, theology, and other high-level topics. Many of these captured documents were found in al Qaida training camps and safe houses in Afghanistan. A great number of documents came from the late Abu Musab al-Zarqawi's organization in Iraq.

Open source information, largely available through the Director of National Intelligence's Open Source Center (OSC, formerly the Foreign Broadcast Information Service, or FBIS), also proved extremely valuable. Much of the business that AQAM conducts—strategy development, military education, and so on, which the U.S. government would conduct in classified channels or at least in the relative privacy of government conference rooms—must be conducted in the open, especially on the Internet, where it becomes available to the OSC as well as to journalists and academic researchers. Other nongovernmental organizations such as the Search for International Terrorist Entities (SITE) Institute, the International Centre for Political Violence and Terrorism Research in Singapore, and the Middle East Media Research Institute (MEMRI) provided useful primary source information based on the monitoring and translating of jihadist media disseminated through Web sites and other outlets. The quality of the translations of the original documents varies greatly, and we have only sparingly corrected the spelling and grammar of the translations. When needed, we used in-house translators on a limited basis to clarify meanings or interpretations.

Members of the study team are sometimes asked whether we can trust open source material the enemy has produced or whether it is disinformation aimed either at gullible Muslim recruits or at "infidel" analysts. With regard to the first objection, we simply observe that the enemy's public discourse matches its private discourse as revealed in captured documents. The Salafi jihadist movement is quite different from the communist movement of an earlier era, which offered idealistic rhetoric to the masses but subscribed to a substantially different and deeply cynical code among the leadership. With regard to the second objection, we note that in attempting to mislead "infidel" analysts the enemy will inevitably mislead its own members. In this connection, we can do no better than to quote the words of terrorism analyst Reuven Paz: "In the final analysis

[the] global Jihad must use open indoctrination in order to sustain and broaden its audience in general, and its younger generations in particular. Open indoctrination is incompatible with disinformation. . . . The Jihadist instigators cannot allow themselves to mislead . . . the future pioneering Jihadi generations."[4]

There is no single AQAM perspective on any question. Within what appears to outsiders to be the narrow confines of the enemy's worldview, debate and dissent are common. While we cannot cite every dissenting view, we have tried to note areas of significant disagreement within the enemy community. AQAM tends to use a relatively few prolific writers (e.g., Abu Ubayd al-Qurashi, Abu Musab al-Suri, and Abu Bakr Naji) to illustrate the main points, and the members of the movement seem to regard them as its intellectual elite. We have also drawn on the enemy's foundational documents, such as the works of Sayyid Qutb, Mohammad Abdul Salam al-Faraj, and Abdullah Azzam, which are in print in many languages and are readily available around the globe in hard copy and on the Internet. As for the voices of AQAM's foot soldiers, the study team selected what appeared to be the most relevant and representative of their views.

Most academic literature on terrorism looks at the subject from the outside, from what anthropologists call the "etic" perspective. As the originator of the term put it, "the etic view is an alien view—the structuring of an outsider."[5] The etic view applies concepts and categories that are meaningful to scientists and may allow objective determination of fact, but which may have no standing within the culture they are being used to describe. Anthropologists therefore evaluate social phenomena from a second, "emic," perspective—that is, from the point of view of the people being studied. An emic perspective allows an anthropologist to focus on the beliefs and phenomena that are meaningful within a given culture, without regard to the question of whether they are objectively "true" or "correct."

Analyses that conclude that the "youth bulge" is causing (or will cause) Salafi jihadist terrorism are examples of etic knowledge. Even assuming that these analyses are sound in their methodologies and conclusions, they bear no resemblance to how Salafi jihadists understand their jihad. Salafi jihadists believe—perhaps *know* would be a better word—that they fight not because they are part of a population boom, but because they recognize that "infidels," "apostates," and "hypocrites" are doing violence to Islam, and God has directed them to fight a defensive war in response.

This book looks at the social phenomena of Salafi jihadism from both the emic and etic perspectives. Because the literature on terrorism is so heavily weighted in the direction of etic analyses, most of it is self-consciously, if imperfectly, emic in its approach. (Chapter 9, which discusses U.S. policy options, is the main exception.) We are trying to let the enemy speak for himself, literally in his own words and on his own terms.

Indeed, AQAM has a rich vocabulary to describe both itself and its enemies. The U.S. government has policy concerns about adopting jihadist terminology when discussing the enemy: in particular, it is concerned that such usage may validate or lend credibility to the enemy's moral or religious claims. Nevertheless, a project of this nature requires us to use the enemy's idiom if we are to understand him. We must follow Sun Tzu's dictum to "know your enemy"—we must not simply construct an artificial enemy that is to our own liking. The enemy's message is inextricably tied to its language and conscious choices of words, and thus we must use such freighted terms as *jihad, mujahideen, infidel,* and *Crusader.*

One term deserves special attention. Throughout this work (aside from quoted, translated materials, which we left unaltered) we refer to the enemy's belief in "God," not "Allah." In Arabic, the word *allah* means "god," be it the one living God or false gods such as Zeus. Muslims believe that they worship the same God that Jews and Christians do, though some Muslims, particularly the Salafi jihadists, believe that Judaism and Christianity are hopelessly corrupt versions of God's word. We understand that many Jews and Christians do not believe that they worship the same God as the Muslims, but we are trying to portray the enemy's view of the world, and the connotations to an English speaker of the word *God* come closest to the connotations to an Arabic speaker of *Allah.*

Notes

1. Much of the initial response to al Qaida was grounded in decades of traditional "counterterrorism speak" and was used to provide context and sense to an otherwise incomprehensible act of inhumanity. Historian Walter Laqueur wrote in the *The Political Psychology of Appeasement: Finlandization and Other Unpopular Essays* (New Brunswick: Transaction Books, 1980) that, "as a rule of thumb, one learns more about a terrorist group by looking at its victims than at its manifestos" (11). The conclusions of this book will modify that rule and emphasize that the group's "manifestos" tell us a great deal about the group.
2. *The 9/11 Commission Report: Final Report of the National Commission on Terrorist Attacks upon the United States* (Washington, D.C.: U.S. Government Printing Office, 2004), 339–48.

3. Nathan Leites's work for RAND (Santa Monica, CA) includes *Kremlin Thoughts: Yielding, Rebuffing, Provoking, Retreating* (1963); *The Kremlin Horizon* (1963); *What Soviet Commanders Fear from Their Own Forces* (1978); *Soviet Style in Management* (1984); and *Soviet Style in War* (1992).

4. Reuven Paz, "Reading Their Lips: The Credibility of Jihadi Web Sites in Arabic as a Source for Information" (Herzliya, Israel: Project for the Research of Islamist Movements, 2006), http://www.e-prism.org/images/Read_Their_Lips.doc, accessed September 23, 2007.

5. The authors are grateful to our colleague Andrea Jackson for bringing this important concept to our attention. See Kenneth L. Pike, "A Stereoscopic Window on the World (Language and Life, Part 1)," *Bibliotheca Sacra* 114 (1957): 141–56; James Lett, "Emic/Etic Distinctions," in *Encyclopedia of Cultural Anthropology*, ed. David Levinson and Melvin Ember (New York: Henry Holt, 1996); Michael Morris et al., "Views from Inside and Outside: Integrating Emic and Etic Insights about Culture and Justice Judgment," *Academy of Management Review* 24, no. 4 (1999): 781–96.

THE
TERRORIST PERSPECTIVES
PROJECT

STRATEGIC AND OPERATIONAL VIEWS OF
AL QAIDA AND ASSOCIATED MOVEMENTS

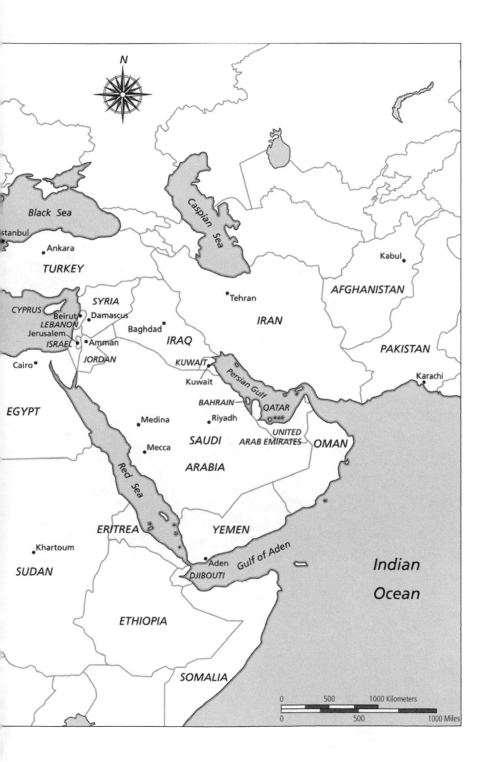

CHAPTER 1

Salafi Jihadist Theology and the Making of a Movement

The enemies of the Believers may wish to change this struggle into an economic or political or racial struggle, so that the Believers become confused concerning the true nature of the struggle and the flame of belief in their hearts becomes extinguished. The Believers must not be deceived, and must understand that this is a trick. The enemy, by changing the nature of the struggle, intends to deprive them of their weapon of true victory.

SAYYID QUTB, *MILESTONES*, 1964[1]

Proof or no proof, it is hard to imagine that a knowledgeable and successful man like Osama bin Laden is unaware of the connection between the terror he directs and the world economy. Such an assumption would be foolish. An unscrupulous businessman of terror like he would never miss such an easy and profitable opportunity. . . . Naked crime is being coated in Islamic religion and sold as an act of liberation from the so-called corrupt and colonialist Western World.

MICHAEL WOLFFSOHN,
"A GERMAN VIEW ON MIDDLE EASTERN TRANSFORMATION"[2]

Who Are the Salafis?

Al Qaida and its associated movements (AQAM) perceive themselves as the base for a Salafi-led Islamic revival and as the vanguard of the global jihad. The true makers of today's Salafi jihadist movement were the reform-minded Islamic thinkers who preceded the formation of al Qaida by many years, if not centuries.[3] Foremost among them was Sayyid Qutb, whose writings still find a receptive and growing audience among those grappling with "apostate" governments and looking for an acceptable, Islamic-based solution. The Salafis who began the global jihad, such as Abdullah Azzam, Osama bin Laden, and Ayman al-Zawahiri, added the swords to concepts that existed long before, such as *tawhid* (oneness or unity of God) and *jahiliyya* (ignorance).

To be a Salafi generally means to follow the ways of the *salaf al-salihin* (pious forefathers), and originally the use of the term implied little about any particular understanding of Islamic law. During the nineteenth century, the term began to take on a somewhat different connotation and became associated with men such as Muhammad Abduh and Jamal al-Din al-Afghani, who argued that Islam needed a revival that could come only by reopening the gates of *ijtihad*, or independent interpretation of the texts. This Salafi movement led to the "Islamic Awakening" of the twentieth century, a much broader trend that tried in various ways to return to the ways of the *salaf*. During the late twentieth century, the followers of Sayyid Qutb (see below) and the Wahhabis (see text box titled "Wahhabism" below) increasingly began to appropriate the term for themselves, claiming that their very narrow interpretation of Islam was the closest to that of the *salaf*. It was this version of Salafism that inspired the development of Salafi jihadism.[4]

Salafis today prefer to base their understanding of Islamic law only on the Qur'an and the Sunnah, the "way of the Prophet," and are, in Marc Sageman's words, "in this regard . . . much more conservative than most other Muslims."[5] Salafis also believe that innovations have corrupted the practice of Islam and that only by stripping away these innovations can the *ummah*—the worldwide community of Muslims—return to the glorious days of Islam's golden age in the seventh century CE. Ultimately, they seek a return to the Islam practiced by the Prophet Muhammed and his companions, the *salaf al-salihin*.[6] Abu Musab al-Zarqawi summarized this view: "We have made a covenant with God that we will revive the ancient principles and adhere to the tradition of the wise [or rightly guided] caliphs."[7]

To be a Salafi is to be literal, even simplistic, in understanding the sacred texts of Islam. For example, Muslims are required to pray five times a day. Any Muslim who prays more often than that, according to Salafi thinking, is engaged in unsound religious "innovation" (in essence heresy) no matter what his motivation.[8] Salafis also firmly reject all forms of idolatry (as they rigidly define it) such as the worship of saints or tombs common among Shia and Sufi Muslims. It is important to note that the adjective *fundamentalist*, commonly used—especially by non-Muslims— to describe Salafis, is a Western (specifically Protestant) term without specific meaning in an Islamic context; Salafis themselves rarely use it.

Despite their agreement on revivalist goals, Salafis differ in their prescriptions for how to return to the lost "golden age." While the theological differences between mainstream Salafis and AQAM (i.e., violent Salafis, or jihadists) are few and easily summarized, they are hugely important to the two communities. Scholars Quintan Wiktorowicz and John Kaltner noted that "non-violent Salafis, who make up the vast majority of the [Salafi] movement, often vehemently reject the use of the Salafi label to describe the violent or jihadi elements. The latter, however, identify themselves as Salafis and dismiss the other groups as misguided, ignorant . . . or corrupt."[9]

Wahhabism

In recent years Westerners have increasingly used the terms *Wahhabi* and Salafi interchangeably. While technically Wahhabism and Salafism are distinct ideologies, the differences between them have always been modest and have decreased over the past thirty to forty years. Today the two streams of thought have all but merged.[10] Wahhabism, which follows the thinking of Muhammad bin Abd al-Wahhab (1703–91), has its roots in the eighteenth century in what is now Saudi Arabia. Wahhabis tend to avoid using that name to describe themselves because they believe it suggests that al-Wahhab merely set up another school of Islamic jurisprudence, whereas they reject the division of Islam into any schools of jurisprudence at all. They prefer to refer to themselves as *muwahhidun*, a word that refers to the importance of their monotheism. Al-Wahhab allied himself with Muhammed Ibn Sa'ud, the founder of the present house of Saud, and Wahhab's understanding of the faith thus became the state religion of the Kingdom of Saudi Arabia when it came into existence after World War I.

Al-Wahhab was not a particularly original thinker, but he would probably have acknowledged that fact and been proud of it, believing as he did that originality in religious thought was harmful.[11] Like Qutb, al-Wahhab drew directly from the writings of Ibn Taymiyya and made monotheism (tawhid) in all its implications a centerpiece of his theology. This included a very hard line against idolatry and any hint of the existence of any intermediaries, such as saints or shrines, between man and God.

After Egyptian President Gamal Abdel Nasser's crackdown on Sayyid Qutb and his intellectual brethren, many of the Salafi jihadists, including Qutb's brother, went to Saudi Arabia, where they took teaching positions that eventually gave them broad influence over the educational system and the minds of young Saudis, including Osama bin Laden.[12] The common experience of the jihad against the Soviet Union probably also helped converge the two streams of thought, at least among their more militant adherents. Today, Wahhabis—jihadists or not—will often say, as Prince Turki al-Faisal, the Saudi ambassador to the United Kingdom, told PBS, "I am a Salafi, and proud to be a Salafi."[13] By the same token, Salafi jihadists sometimes refer approvingly to the works of Muhammad bin Abd al-Wahhab.[14]

Salafis, in other words, are diverse. Although they may have the "same roots," they have "different branches": the purists (Tablighi Jamaat), the politicos/reformists (Muslim Brotherhood), and the jihadists (AQAM).[15] At one end of the Salafi spectrum are the members of the Tablighi Jamaat, a worldwide group founded in India during the 1920s. Operating at the grassroots level, Tablighi Jamaat emphasizes the *dawah* (call), or individual proselytizing, as the proper way to spread the faith and bring other Muslims and non-Muslims to the "true" Islam.[16] The millions of Tablighi Jamaat members are part of a group that Quintan Wiktorowicz labeled "purists."[17] They try to educate others and purify Islam from corruptive influences that include not just Western secularism and popular culture but also its terminology, which they believe represents the "thin end of the wedge," as Wiktorowicz put it, of the whole Western system of meaning, epistomology, and ontology. Purists likewise reject involvement in politics, let alone political violence, as an innovation that implies unacceptable divisions within the *ummah*. Divisions are precisely the opposite of what all Salafis are trying to accomplish: a unified *ummah*.[18] For the Tablighis—noted for their nonviolent tendencies—the oaths of allegiance to a leader that so often accompany membership in a terrorist organization are themselves a form of idolatry.[19] A comment posted on the British Blogistan Web site in 2005 called Tablighis "the most docile group of brothers you will ever come across."[20] A less sympathetic portrait of a group of Tablighis in Pakistan describes them as having "vacant, sleepy eyes" and babbling inanities to the action-oriented author: "Oh no, brother, they would tell me. *Jihad* means love."[21] Tablighis use the pejorative term *hizbiyah*—meaning "partisan" or "party-like," in reference to political parties—to refer to Muslims who pursue political Islam. The Web site www.Salafipublications.com contains a stark discussion of *hizbiyah*: "And how damaging—O seeker of unity—has . . . Partisianship [sic] (*Hizbiyah*) been in destroying the very fabric of comprehensive brotherhood."[22]

One group that members of Tablighi Jamaat and like-minded Muslims often label *hizbiyah* is the Muslim Brotherhood, which is more in the middle spectrum of Salafi thought. The pervasive and powerful Muslim Brotherhood is the most prominent example of what Wiktorowicz called the "politicos" of Salafism.[23] Founded in Egypt in 1928 by Hasan al-Banna, the Muslim Brotherhood (al-Ikhwan al-Muslimin) follows a Salafi theology and seeks the creation of an Islamic state under sharia (Islamic law). Its members believe that science and technology are useful tools, and its members are involved in political parties, labor unions, schools, hospitals, banks, and many other civil institutions. Traditionally, members of the Muslim Brotherhood, which from the outset had a conspiratorial flavor, believed that violent jihad was a permissible but not mandatory tool to use against colonial powers.[24]

For members of the Muslim Brotherhood, as for many Salafis, killing the leader of a Muslim country—or even revolting against him—is theologically problematic. Such actions threaten *fitna*, a term that is hard to define precisely but that suggests upheaval, anarchy, and civil war. Moreover, Muslims should rebel or attack Muslim rulers only if the latter are guilty of the capital crime of apostasy (i.e., abandoning Islam). Traditionally, however, the standards of proof for demonstrating apostasy are extremely high.[25]

Salafi Jihadism

Politically, AQAM resides at the opposite end of the spectrum from the Tablighi Jamaat. AQAM makes no secret of its contemptuous view of other Salafis, let alone non-Salafi Muslims. "As for the Reformist, Sufi, and Tablighi groups, they have increased in absurdity and distance from Muslims' reality," one leading jihadist scoffed.[26] Abu Bakr Ba'asyir, the reputed head of Jemaah Islamiyah in Southeast Asia, dismisses "soft-line" Islamic groups, saying they have "received strong rebuke from Almighty Allah. Soft-line Islam groups [are] people who have compromised His law. Soft-line Islam[ic] groups follow the wishes of polytheists hostile to Islam. . . . They are still enjoying what they regard as pleasure simply because of Allah's compassion."[27]

The various components of AQAM share a theology that many scholars and government officials call Salafi jihadism.[28] Salafi jihadists can rightly be said to be Salafis because they, like the Tablighi Jamaat and the Muslim Brotherhood, believe that all jurisprudence should rest solely on the Qur'an and the Sunnah. Abd Samad Moussaoui, for example, the brother of convicted terrorist Zacarias Moussaoui, wrote about an incident illustrating these beliefs. Although not a jihadist himself, Abd Samad introduced Zacarias, who at that time was a theological novice newly attracted to jihadist thought, to a mainstream Sunni imam and asked the man to tell Zacarias how to learn the science of religion. Zacarias interrupted, saying, "Personally, all I need is the Koran and the Sunna to learn about religion." Abd Samad remembered the imam replying, "If you are prepared to spend ten years finding out how to do your minor ablutions in the Sunna or the Koran, good luck!"[29]

The parting of Salafi ways is most obvious in the application of violence. Salafi jihadists believe that what sets their "true Islam" apart from the beliefs of others, including the Muslim Brotherhood and other Salafis, is their acknowledgment that jihad by the sword is mandatory. For them, violent jihad is essentially another pillar of Islam and involves the duty of overthrowing "apostate" Muslim governments. According to Abu Bakr Ba'asyir, for instance, "the highest deed in Islam is jihad."[30] "If we commit to jihad," he said, "we can neglect other deeds." (Salafi jihadists reject as inauthentic the hadith in which Muhammed said that violent jihad is the "lesser jihad" while the "greater jihad" is the inner struggle to be a better Muslim.)[31] Faris al-Zahrani, a leading al Qaida thinker, explained that "a man cannot be a Salafi in his religious doctrine, as they allege, and an adherent of the Ikhwan [the Muslim Brotherhood] in his way of acting. Also, he cannot be a Salafi in his religious doctrine and a Sufi in his way of acting."[32]

> We have a Cause
> Thank God about every thing and we priey
> for our ~~~~~ priss Mohmmed Bin Abdullah
>
> My brother how fight the enemy ~~~~ you had
> a Cause and your cause is very great.
> and the word of b God will happen in our
> world and what he washed.
> If all our group is dead it is a great
> thing and ~~~ we would gone to priads.
> This is all for our relgin We want our relgi
> in leader we don't care about money our

An al Qaida notebook captured in Iraq. *Source:* Harmony document folder MNFV-2005-000106, Al-Qaida handbook captured in Iraq, July 2005.

Speaking bluntly, "Khalid Kelly," an Irish-born convert to Islam, told a reporter in London a few days after the July 7, 2005, bombings, "Some of the people tell you Islam is a religion of peace because they think that then you'll want to convert. But you cannot possibly say Islam is a religion of peace; jihad is not an internal struggle."[33] Similarly, the Indonesian al-Mujahirun Web site, as of early 2006, included an article entitled "Whoever Denies that Terrorism Is Part of Islam Is an Infidel."[34]

The Roots of Salafi Jihadism

Mawlana Abul A'la Mawdudi, in colonial India (later Pakistan), took the first twentieth-century step toward promoting the view among some Salafis of the centrality of violent jihad within Islam. Mawdudi, in turn, drew upon the work of Ibn Taymiyya, an Islamic scholar of the late thirteenth and early fourteenth centuries. Ibn Taymiyya lived in a time when the question of revolting against Muslim leaders was particularly salient. In his day, the Mongols had recently conquered Mesopotamia and established their own dynasty. Though they arrived as non-Muslims, the Mongols soon converted, thereby leaving the local Arabs to chafe under a foreign occupation while apparently prevented from revolting by the fact that their oppressors were their co-religionists.[35]

Ibn Taymiyya argued for the concept of *tawhid*, the unity of God. *Tawhid* means that God is not only the sole sovereign of the universe (Islam being an intensely monotheistic religion), but also that he is the only object of worship and obedience.[36] Thus, obeying man-made laws is an act of *kufr* (unbelief or apostasy), the well-attested punishment for which is death. This means that the traditional prohibition against revolt applies only if the ruler is a Muslim and if he also governs according to sharia. The Mongol rulers did not meet this latter condition and were declared *takfir* (not Muslims). Thus, revolt against them—jihad—was legitimate.[37]

Mawdudi built upon Ibn Taymiyya's work, and in the 1930s and 1940s enunciated the concept of "modern *jahiliyya*." *Jahiliyya* is an Islamic term referring to the state of barbarism or ignorance of the Arabs before Muhammed arrived in the seventh century. In Mawdudi's view, this new *jahiliyya* resulted from pernicious non-Islamic influences and other deviations, including the use of non-Islamic law. Despite the evident implications of his writings, however, Mawdudi personally eschewed violent revolution against Muslims.[38]

Hasan al-Banna, the founder of the Muslim Brotherhood, was another important intellectual in the years preceding Salafi jihadism. Living at a time when the British occupied Egypt, al-Banna agreed with Muhammad bin Abd al-Wahhab that the *ummah* had fallen away from true Islam. In his mind, the infidels had corrupted Islam, led Muslims astray, and imposed foreign legal systems upon them rather than allowing them to be governed by Islamic law. The correct response was to lead the flock gently back to the right path rather than to use violence against them. The Muslim Brotherhood was al-Banna's way of doing this. Through social programs, preaching, and example, the Muslim Brotherhood would correct the errors of the past and set right the evil done by the British. Muslims came to Egypt from around the world to study Islam at the prestigious Al-Azhar University. While in Egypt, many of these people were exposed to al-Banna's ideas and took them back to their home countries, where they set up chapters of the Brotherhood.

The Brotherhood also had a secret armed section intended eventually to take on the British occupiers in a just jihad, expel them from Islamic lands, and oversee the imposition of Islamic law. As it happened, however, the British left Egypt peacefully. Al-Banna turned to the new Egyptian government, expecting to work with it to implement his vision of Islamic law. But the Egyptian regime rejected his peaceful overture and decided to retain British and French laws, convincing al-Banna that the new rulers of Egypt were not true Muslims, despite their profession of faith. Rather, they were agents of the West, the "puppets" of the British, left in place to ensure that Islam would never be practiced correctly in Egypt. Al-Banna soon turned his armed section against the Egyptian government, which had him assassinated in 1948.[39]

The Influence of Sayyid Qutb

It was left to another Islamic scholar to take Mawdudi's work to its logical conclusions. Mawdudi's more influential works, most notably *Islam and Jahiliyya*, were translated into Arabic in the 1950s and read by Sayyid Qutb, a bookish Egyptian educator and a member of the Muslim Brotherhood who would become the seminal thinker of the modern Salafi jihadist movement.[40]

It is difficult to overstate the importance of Qutb's influence; it has penetrated every corner of the Salafi jihadist movement. Most of the Salafi jihadist leaders are on record as followers of Qutb.[41] Mullah Krekar, for example, the onetime leader of the Kurdish group Ansar al-Islam (now known as Ansar al-Sunnah), was so taken with Qutb's work that he named his eldest son Sayyid Qutb and named his next two sons after Qutb's two most famous books.[42] Fascination with Qutb's works is not an attribute solely of AQAM's leadership. A peripheral actor in the global jihad movement, Mohammed Bouyeri, the Moroccan-Dutch vigilante who murdered filmmaker Theo van Gogh, translated texts from Mawdudi and Qutb into Dutch to disseminate on the Internet.[43]

Though most Salafi jihadist scholars suffer from what Wiktorowicz and Kaltner called a "reputation deficit" compared with the leading mainstream Salafi scholars, few people can doubt the intellectual power of Sayyid Qutb.[44] His best-known book is *Milestones* (1964), a thin volume that Gilles Kepel aptly described as "the Islamic equivalent of Lenin's *What Is to Be Done?*"[45] *Milestones* rests on an impressive twenty-year body of work, most notably *Social Justice and Islam*, written in the 1940s, and the multivolume commentary on the Qur'an, *In the Shade of the Qur'an*, written during Qutb's imprisonment in the 1960s.[46]

Qutb began with the premise that Islam, as manifested in the Qur'an and the Sunnah, contains all the answers mankind needs; all other ideologies are oppressive and corrupt.

> Islam, then, is the only Divine way of life that brings out the noblest human characteristics, developing and using them for the construction of human society. Islam has remained unique in this respect to this day. Those who deviate from this system and want some other system, whether it be based on nationalism, color and race, class struggle, or similar corrupt theories, are truly enemies of mankind! They do not want man to develop those noble characteristics which have been given to him by his Creator nor do they wish to see a human society benefit from the harmonious blending of all those capabilities, experiences and characteristics which have been developed among the various races of mankind.[47]

Furthermore, Qutb longed for a future when men would be free to worship the sovereign Lord of the Universe as he wants to be worshipped. Islam, he wrote, "is really a universal declaration of the freedom of man from servitude to other men and from servitude to his own desires. . . . [I]t is a declaration that sovereignty belongs to God alone and that He is the Lord of all the worlds."[48]

Building on this intellectual base, Qutb brought together the ideas of *tawhid* and *jahiliyya* and declared that the *ummah* was essentially extinct, and had been so for centuries. Virtually everyone had retreated into a state of *jahiliyya* due to the repressive effects of democracy, communism, and various other non-Islamic influences. "The *jahili* society," he said, "is any society other than the Muslim society; and if we want a more specific definition, we may say that any society is a *jahili* society which does not dedicate itself to submission to God alone, in its beliefs and ideas, in its observances of worship, and in its legal regulations. According to this definition, all the societies existing in the world today are *jahili*."[49]

Apparently swayed by a jarring sojourn in late-1940s America that cemented his theological-cum-political hatred of the West, Qutb saw these pernicious non-Islamic influences as an attack on the faith. In such circumstances, jihad is necessary. "If we insist on calling Islamic jihad a defensive movement," he wrote, "then we must change the meaning of the word 'defense' and mean by it the 'defense of man' against those elements which limit his freedom. These elements take the form of beliefs and concepts, as well as of political systems, based on economic, racial or class distinctions."[50]

Faced with these theological conclusions, Qutb proclaimed jihad by the sword a legitimate and, more important, a necessary action against so-called Muslim leaders who did not rule by sharia. Such leaders were not Muslims; they were apostates, idolaters who put man's law above God's law, thereby violating the principle of *tawhid*.[51] "The foremost duty of Islam in this world," Qutb wrote, "is to depose *Jahiliyyah* from the leadership of man, and to take the leadership into its own hands and enforce the particular way of life which is its permanent feature."[52]

This profound idea, a radical fusion of the *takfir*-ism espoused by Ibn Taymiyya and the *jahiliyya* of Mawdudi, has in recent decades become a defining characteristic of Salafi jihadists and is accepted throughout the movement. Al-Zahrani, for example, wrote that "the rulers of the countries of Islam in this age are all apostate, unbelieving tyrants who have departed in every way from Islam. Muslims who proclaim God's unity have no other choice than iron and fire, jihad in the way of God, to restore the Caliphate according to the Prophet's teachings."[53]

By emphasizing that God's law should prevail, Qutb meant that man-made laws must be abolished and replaced with the sharia. In his view, the West's artificial separation of religion and state represented a "hideous schizophrenia" that Muslims must not allow to infect the Islamic world.[54] The idea that God's law should prevail is an article of faith throughout the movement. The belief extends from the Abu Sayyaf Group in the Philippines—which complains that rulers today are "worshipping humans instead of God"[55]—to the Turkish Salafist group in Germany called the Caliphate State, one of whose members stated in court: "When a legal determination agrees with sharia then it is followed, when not, it is not followed. The Koran is the measure of all things, because the Koran contains God's law! All other laws are only made by man! . . . Our goal is that (this) court treat the Koran with respect when we do not adhere to your law!"[56] By the same token, Yusuf al-Ayiri, a leading al Qaida ideologue, wrote shortly before his death, "One of the worst products of secularism is democracy, which abolishes the authority of the sharia over society and opposes it in form and in content. The Most High said, 'the command is for none but Allah' [12:40]. Democracy says that the command is for none but the majority of the people."[57]

The same logic applies to international law and international institutions. Qutb's line of reasoning echoes, for example, in Osama bin Laden's

comments to Mullah Omar in April 2001, shortly after the Taliban
destroyed the ancient statues of the Buddha at Bamiyan:

> Among the most important . . . false gods in our time is the United
> Nations, which has become a new religion that is worshipped to the exclu-
> sion of God. The prophets of this religion are present in the UN General
> Assembly . . . the UN imposes all sorts of penalties on all those who contra-
> dict its religion. It issues documents and statements that openly contradict
> Islamic belief, such as the International Declaration for Human Rights,
> considering all religions are equal, and considering that the destruction [of
> the Buddhas] constitutes a crime.[58]

Similarly, four Islamic scholars wrote a defense of the May 2003 bombings in Riyadh that was recovered from a personal computer in Bosnia. The
document includes the following passage: "The pact is illegal because it
depends on Saudi Arabia being a member of the United Nations, which is an
idolatrous organization, and therefore no Islamic state could belong to it."[59]

While jihadists today often feel compelled to explain the rationale
behind their violence, Qutb himself was unapologetic about the violent
implications of his analysis:

> When writers with defeatist and apologetic mentalities write about "Jihad
> in Islam," trying to remove this "blot" from Islam, then they are mixing
> up two things: first, that this religion forbids the imposition of its belief
> by force, as is clear from the verse, "There is no compulsion in religion"
> (2:256), while on the other hand it tries to annihilate all those political and
> material powers which stand between people and Islam, which force one
> people to bow before another people and prevent them from accepting the
> sovereignty of God. These two principles have no relation to one another
> nor is there room to mix them. In spite of this, these defeatist-type people
> try to mix the two aspects and want to confine Jihad to what today is
> called "defensive war."[60]

While Qutb placed a major emphasis on violent jihad, he also believed
that *dawah*, "the call," or proselytizing, was vital if the Muslim community was to be "restored to its original form."[61] This movement, he wrote,
"uses the methods of preaching and persuasion for reforming ideas and
beliefs and it uses physical power and Jihad for abolishing the organizations and authorities of the *Jahili* system which prevents people from
reforming their ideas. . . . This movement does not confine itself to mere
preaching to confront physical power, as it also does not use compulsion

for changing the ideas of people. These two principles are equally important in the method of this religion."[62]

Thus are the sword and the word complementary instruments of
violent jihad. The *Al-Qaeda Manual*, recovered in Birmingham, England,
puts the issue bluntly: "Islamic governments have never and will never
be established through peaceful solutions and cooperative councils. They
are established as they [always] have been: by pen and gun; by word and
bullet; and by tongue and teeth."[63] A document captured in Afghanistan
contains a testimonial by one Al Abd Azizu al Haq about what he knows
of a particular Bangladeshi organization: "The Islamic Jihad Movement
in Bangladesh, is a Jihadi Dawaa organization."[64] Even Abu Musab al-
Zarqawi, best known in the West for his ruthless violence, said in 2004
that "the sword and the word will complement one another."[65]

In conducting *dawah* Qutb recommended the soft sell: "The correct
procedure is to mix with discretion, give and take with dignity, speak the
truth with love, and show the superiority of the Faith with humility."[66]
This rule, more often honored in the breach, shines through in a pragmatic
self-critique by some of the Arab fighters who fought in Bosnia during the
1990s: "Some [of us] tried to turn the Bosnians into pious men of God
overnight. Actually, when you wish to call to the faith, you do not act in
this way. These people broke bottles of liquor in a barbarous way without
first using friendly argument as God instructs us to do."[67]

The Global Jihad after Qutb

In 1966, Egyptian President Gamal Abdel Nasser ordered Sayyid Qutb
hanged as part of a broader crackdown on Islamists. Qutb's brother
and intellectual ally, Mohammed Qutb (author of *The Jahiliyya of the
Twentieth Century* [1964]), fled Egypt and took a position on the faculty
of a Saudi Arabian university where a young Osama bin Laden was among
his students.[68]

Nasser did not succeed in exterminating the Muslim Brotherhood and
its Salafi jihadist offshoot movements, among whom the works of Sayyid
Qutb remained widely read and highly influential. In the 1970s, small
groups of Salafi jihadists started to form in Egypt. One participant recalled
that his group "began in the mid-70s with nine people in Minya reading the
works of Ibn Taymiyya, Abu Ala al-Mawdudi, Sayyid Qutb, Sayyid Sabiq,
and others."[69] By the late 1970s, some of these groups had coalesced into

the Tanzim al-Jihad (Jihad Organization). The leader of the Cairo branch of
the Jihad Organization was Mohammed Abd al-Salam Faraj. Faraj wrote a
highly influential pamphlet outlining his views that drew heavily on the
arguments of Ibn Taymiyya and Sayyid Qutb and ultimately served as the
justification for the assassination of President Anwar Sadat in 1981.[70] Faraj
believed that Sadat deserved his fate because the punishment for apostasy
is death, and all "the rulers of this age are in apostasy from Islam . . . they
carry nothing from Islam but their names."[71]

Faraj's book translated into French.
Note the image of an American soldier
superimposed upon, and thus symbol-
ically occupying, the Grand Mosque in
Mecca. *Source: Al Mourabitine.com Publications, www.ribaat.org/obl_abs.pdf,
accessed December 23, 2006.*

Faraj pointedly called his pamphlet *The Neglected Duty*, a reference
to jihad by the sword. Echoing Qutb's views, he argued that jihad was
incumbent upon all Muslims because Islam was under attack: "The laws
by which the Muslims are ruled today are the laws of Unbelief. They are
actually codes of law that were made by infidels who then subject the
Muslims to [them]."[72] By this logic, which Qutb would have endorsed, an

attack on the "apostate" state was actually a defensive jihad, and therefore obligatory for right-believing Muslims. The book's title, sometimes rendered in English as *The Forgotten Duty*, soon became a catchphrase of the Salafi jihadist movement. One of the London bombers of July 2005, Mohammed Siddiq, certainly no Islamic scholar, reflected this thinking on duty in his recorded "last will": "I am directly responsible for protecting and avenging my Muslim brothers and sisters."[73]

In essence, Faraj argued that jihad by the sword is the sixth pillar of Islam, alongside prayer, the hajj, and others. This analysis, too, caught on widely in the Salafi jihadist world; it is now common for jihadists to argue, contrary to traditional interpretations of Islamic law, that jihad is in fact the most important obligation of every Muslim. The Islamic scholar Abu Bakr Ba'asyir made this point in an August 2005 interview. Citing evidence from "one of the most revered *ulema*, Ibn Taymiyya," he argued that "there is no better deed than jihad. None. The highest deed in Islam is jihad. If we commit to jihad, we can neglect other deeds."[74]

The Egyptian government executed Faraj in 1982 for his role in the assassination of Sadat. Most of the Jihad Organization members ended up in prison, where disagreements emerged among them over whether an Islamic state could best be established in Egypt through a coup d'état or a broad-based insurgency. The government released most of these men after they had served only three years. They soon formed two related, yet separate and often jealously competitive, groups: the Egyptian Islamic Jihad (EIJ) under Ayman al-Zawahiri and the Egyptian Islamic Group (EIG) under a collective leadership.[75]

After his release from prison in 1984, al-Zawahiri and many other members of EIJ and EIG went to Afghanistan, where they met Muslims converging from all over the world to fight the Soviet invaders. Abdullah Azzam, a Palestinian devotee of Qutb and a former university professor in Saudi Arabia, formed the Maktab al-Khidmat (Service Bureau) to provide practical assistance and direction to the Arab volunteers (mujahideen) coming to Afghanistan. Osama bin Laden was Azzam's assistant. Through these connections and their wartime experiences as "Afghan Arabs," al-Zawahiri and bin Laden became fast friends and close associates.[76]

Azzam's Service Bureau lived on after the Soviets pulled out of Afghanistan, but the question arose as to what to do with the talents and energy of the mujahideen. Some fighters, essentially following Faraj's footsteps, wanted to go back to their home countries to overthrow the local "apostate" regimes. Azzam argued for a more global approach that entailed freeing Muslim lands such as the Philippines, Kashmir, and the Soviet Central Asian republics that were threatened or had been conquered by non-Muslims.[77]

Azzam laid out his views on jihad in *Join the Caravan*—another term that has become common in jihadist circles—in which he used Qutb's work to bolster his contention that

> Jihad and emigration to Jihad have a deep-rooted role which cannot be separated from the constitution of this religion. A religion, which does not have Jihad, cannot become established in any land, nor can it strengthen its frame. The steadfast Jihad, which is one of the innermost constituents of this religion and which has its weight in the scales of the Lord of the Worlds, is not a contingent phenomenon peculiar to the period in which the Qur'an was revealed; it is in fact a necessity accompanying the caravan which this religion guides.[78]

Azzam's work had a profound influence on AQAM strategists such as Osama bin Laden, and his views became established throughout Salafi jihadist circles. The wife of one of the jihadists involved in the May 2003 Riyadh bombings, when asked in 2005 by a journalist to name the sheikhs who most influenced her late husband, replied, "Mostly Sa'ad Al Boraiek and Abdullah Azzam, who opened new horizons for the issue of jihad." Azzam's influence has reached as far as Indonesia, where Imam Samudra cited Azzam's work in his book *Aku Melawan Terroris* (I Fight Terrorists), which justifies the 2002 Bali bombing that he masterminded.[79]

Azzam died in 1989, assassinated under mysterious circumstances. As his heir apparent, Osama bin Laden picked up the burden of guiding the global jihad under the new name al Qaida (the Base; AQ). In the late 1990s, the EIJ under Ayman al-Zawahiri effectively merged with al Qaida, although some EIJ members rejected this shift to a global agenda and preferred to maintain their focus on overthrowing the Egyptian regime. Though they dissented on issues of strategy, they remained part of the broader Salafi jihadist movement, as did many other groups and individuals. As such, they comprise what the U.S. Department of Defense calls AQAM.[80]

The *Ulema*'s Role in Global Jihad

Al Qaida clearly expected that Salafist scholars, the *ulema*, would do their part in supporting AQ's call to global jihad and mobilizing the *ummah*, especially by providing religious justification for the jihad through their fatwas (pronouncements). This did not happen, however, either before or after the 9/11 attacks. Numerous examples occur throughout AQAM literature of al Qaida leaders railing against the *ulema's* failure to speak the "truth."[81] A 2003 publication from the Center for Islamic Studies and Research (CISR) pleads: "We appeal to our brothers who are ulema, scholars, and preachers not to abandon them and to stand by them and explain the facts about them to the people. They cannot be silent while their brothers are being fought in this way. This is not a favor on their part; it is their duty."[82] Al-Zarqawi, ever mindful of any whiff of betrayal, complained in 2004 that the *ulema* were doing the exact opposite of initiating an awakening: "The Sunnis are asleep due to lies told by their so-called wise men and ulema that drugged the nation and let it down. They were the bridge, which the enemies crossed to kill the nation. Whenever the nation wanted to wake up and avenge for the humiliation of its religion and honor, they told it: Stay asleep and don't wake up."[83]

This failure of the *ulema* to join the jihad is a long-standing concern. In 1988, Abdullah Azzam observed, "Our learned brethren and mature propagators have not come to us [in Afghanistan]. On the contrary, some of them advise those who come forward to sit complacently in their own countries, even if they could not say a word against the injustice of the oppressors and the tyranny of the occupiers."[84] A captured document by Abu Musab al-Suri on the "lessons learned in Syria" paints a picture of outright betrayal by the *ulema*: "The worst of those informers were the low life scholars. . . . [S]ome of those scholars sided with the apostate regime, they glorified it and described it as an Islamic regime, their shameful misdeeds misguided simple minded Moslems . . . they went as far as declaring the mujahideen as apostate infidels."[85] Salafi jidahists thus regard preachers as a suspect class, dissolute, dishonest, unwilling to support the jihad, and even in league with al Qaida's enemies. "Except for a small number," explained an al Qaida member in 2004, "the *ulema* have generally been the first who have disappointed the mujahideen, not only in the Arabian Peninsula but elsewhere."[86]

The AQAM-affiliated CISR lamented the role of the "apostate" regimes in the corruption of the *ulema*, castigating "hired media and mercenary journalists . . . harping on the theme of ignorance. They have made the mujahidin out to be ignorant," and assailing "the tyrants' untiring efforts to monopolize the *ulema*, until no one can give a fatwa except someone whom the tyrant selects and appoints, whose fatwas he approves, and whose statements he finds congenial."[87]

The Goal: Restore the Caliphate

For most of Islamic history a Caliphate, ruled by a caliph, was responsible for defending the faith. In 1924, in an act that still resonates within AQAM and its pronouncements, the founder of modern Turkey, Kemal Ataturk, formally abolished the Caliphate, which by then was in its dotage after long centuries of co-optation by the Ottoman emperors. The restoration of the Caliphate has always been a goal of the modern jihadist movement. Once again, Sayyid Qutb pointed the way: "The beauty of this new [Islamic] system cannot be appreciated unless it takes a concrete form. . . . In order to bring this about, we need to initiate the movement of Islamic revival in some Muslim country."[88] Qutb realized that it would be a long time before the restored Caliphate could assume the mantle of world leadership; nonetheless, he did not accept this as an excuse for inaction:

> I am aware that between the attempt at "revival" and the attainment of "leadership" there is a great distance, as . . . the leadership of mankind has long since passed to other ideologies and other nations, other concepts and other systems. This was the era during which Europe's genius created its marvelous works in science, culture, law and material production, due to which mankind has progressed to great heights of creativity and material comfort. It is not easy to find fault with the inventors of such marvelous things, especially since what we call the "world of Islam" is completely devoid of all this beauty. But in spite of all this, it is necessary to revive Islam. The distance between the revival of Islam and the attainment of world leadership may be vast, and there may be great difficulties on the way; but the first step must be taken.[89]

The idea that Islam must assume global leadership through reestablishing the Caliphate has become increasingly popular since Qutb's time. Mohammed al-Faraj followed Qutb's footsteps, writing in 1981:

> The establishment of an Islamic State and the reintroduction of the Caliphate were (not only) already predicted by the Apostle of God—God's peace be upon him—(but) (they) are, moreover, part of the Command of

the Lord—majestic and exalted He is—for which every Muslim should exert every conceivable effort in order to execute. . . . If, moreover, (such a) state cannot be established without war, then war is an obligation as well. Muslims are agreed on the obligatory character of the establishment of an Islamic Caliphate. To announce a Caliphate must be based on the existence of a (territorial) nucleus (from which it can grow). This (nucleus) is the Islamic State.[90]

Ayman al-Zawahiri, having emerged from Faraj's group, had a great influence on al Qaida's views on the Caliphate even before his EIJ officially merged with al Qaida. Therefore, it is not surprising that the al Qaida constitutional charter, a document dating from the 1990s captured in Afghanistan, lists among al Qaida's goals "the victory of the mighty religion of Allah, the establishment of an Islamic Regime and the restoration of the Islamic Caliphate, God willing."[91]

Osama bin Laden described the Caliphate in terms of a global Islamic state: "Today, every member of the Muslim world agrees that all the Muslim countries of the world having geographical boundaries on the basis of nationality, geography, religious discord, color and race, should be merged into one Muslim state, where men do not rule men. There should be one caliph for the whole state whose capital should be Mecca. There should be one currency and defense for this state and the Holy Koran should be its constitution."[92]

It is worth noting that very few jihadists discuss issues of governance in the jihad beyond bin Laden's platitudes, though everyone in the Salafi jihadist movement takes as an article of faith the necessity and inevitability of the Caliphate.[93] In September 2005, the al Qaida–associated Global Islamic Media Front expressed its support for a Caliphate when it launched a radio program (later expanded to Web-based video format as well) that was "especially dedicated to the two shaykhs, Usama bin Ladin and Ayman al-Zawahiri," as well as Mullah Omar and his army, al-Zarqawi, and "all other Islamic armies." The radio program was called *Sawt Al-Khilafa* (The Voice of the Caliphate).[94]

Nabil Sahraoui, then the "commander" of the Salafi Group for Call and Combat in Algeria, expressed similar thoughts in 2004:

The relationship between us and al Qaida and the rest of the jihadist groups in the world is based on two points. First, the actions of the Salafi Group for Call and Combat in the fields of *al-dawah* and jihad are integrated with the rest of the groups. As we said in our charter, our sixth goal asserts that the Salafi Group for Call and Combat is a means at this stage that aims at ultimately establishing the Islamic Caliphate. This is a sacred goal that all Muslims should uphold and seek to realize each according to his abilities.[95]

By the same token, the seminal strategy document of Indonesia's Jemaah Islamiyah states that the group's goal is to establish an Islamic state that could be the basis for building a broader Caliphate.[96] In Iraq, Abu Musab al-Zarqawi announced that "our jihad will continue. It will not distinguish between a 'Western infidel' or 'Arab apostate' until the Caliphate returns to earth, or we die."[97]

Salafi jihadists differ with regard to how and where to carry out the restoration of the Caliphate. Many Arabs argue that the Caliphate should emerge in the "heart of the Islamic world"—near Egypt or Saudi Arabia— and then grow from there. Al-Zawahiri's language in Knights under the Prophet's Banner (2001) is typical of this sentiment: "The jihad movement must adopt its plan on the basis of controlling a piece of land in the heart of the Islamic world on which it could establish and protect the state of Islam and launch its battle to restore the rational Caliphate based on the traditions of the prophet."[98]

As recently as 2005, an intercepted letter from al-Zawahiri to al-Zarqawi suggested that al-Zawahiri envisioned the Caliphate growing from Iraq. "If our intended goal in this age is the establishment of a Caliphate in the manner of the Prophet and if we expect to establish its state predominantly—according to how it appears to us—in the heart of the Islamic world, then your efforts and sacrifices—God permitting—are a large step directly towards that goal."[99] Abu Ayman al-Hilali, writing in 2002, expressed the thought that the starting point should be the Land of the Two Mosques (Saudi Arabia): "'Expel the polytheists from the Arabian Peninsula.' This slogan had been forgotten, but it calls for the unification of all the scattered Muslims and mujahidin to restore the Caliphate and reunite the [ummah]."[100]

Other Salafi jihadists have different views on the seat of the restored Caliphate. The Caliphate State organization in Germany foresaw Turkey as the core of the new Caliphate.[101] By contrast, Jemaah Islamiyah's immediate goal is the establishment of an Islamic state centered in Indonesia, which will then grow into a Southeast Asian Caliphate.[102]

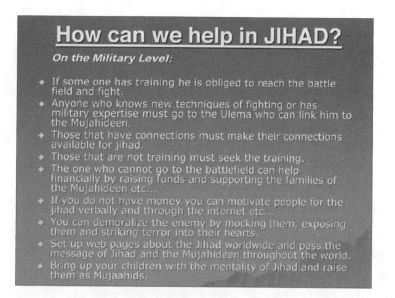

PowerPoint slide on Muslims' obligation to participate in jihad prepared by the Abu Sayyaf Group in the Philippines. *Source: Harmony document folder 500MI-2005-RP-MLA00013,* Slide Presentation on Propaganda Materials for Jihad Influencing Terrorist Acts, *captured in a March 2005 raid on an ASG safe house in Manila, 2005. Though in recent years ASG has succumbed to the lure of banditry, it is Salafi jihadist in its origins and, as this document shows, retains those basic inclinations.*

Dissent in the Salafi Jihadist Community

The al Qaida "organizational charter" written in the 1990s states that the movement's "relation with non-Jihad Islamic groups is one of love and friendship and advice, and bringing out the good in them and correcting their mistakes if the situation requires it."[103] When, as is often the case, al Qaida starts to stray into the territory of theological exclusion, its ideologues try to reel it back. As an illustration, an al Qaida leader outside Africa in 1993 wrote to a colleague in Somalia: "It appears to me that al Qaida's Salafia tendencies have led it to search for a political ally in Somalia with an identical intellectual focus. This is the greatest calamity."[104] Abu Musab al-Suri (al-Suri means "the Syrian"), a leading AQAM military thinker, proudly noted his participation in the Algerian jihad while "they adhered to the straight path" yet was careful to say that after 1996 "I had the honor to disassociate myself from everyone who deviated from the right path and assailed Muslims."[105]

More recently, Abu Musab al-Zarqawi moved in an even more exclusionary direction, arrogating to his authority alone the right to kill Muslims in Iraq who did not hew to his understanding of Islam, whom he had declared *takfir* (excommunicated). Al-Zarqawi's blinding hatred of all Shia and his desire to kill Shiites and foment sectarian war in Iraq took al Qaida's larger global jihad "off script." Al Qaida's leadership strongly dissented from this approach and disapproved of his methods. Abu Muhammed al-Maqdisi, Zarqawi's onetime mentor in Jordan, publicly and sharply criticized this policy:

> When it comes to military decisions, Abu-Mus'ab should not excommunicate people in general. He should know that the masses in the country where we live call themselves Muslims. Thus, he should refrain from shedding the blood of Muslims, even if they are sinners or defiant. . . . Shedding the blood of people who are protected by the laws of vendetta is a critical dilemma on Judgment Day. It is better to leave a thousand atheists than to shed the blood of one Muslim. We hope he is aware of this.[106]

Conclusion

At present, the majority of Muslims across the world say that Salafi jihadism is not "true Islam." While the question is of transcendent importance for Muslims, those outside the *ummah* have no say in the matter, because non-Muslims have no standing to declare bin Laden and his followers (or anybody else) "bad Muslims." In fact, for those outside the *ummah* looking in, the question is no more relevant today than the question whether Stalin, Trotsky, or Bukharin was the "true" heir of Lenin was in the 1920s. Salafi jihadism exists as a global and growing phenomenon that must be dealt with; it cannot be argued out of existence. It is also important to recognize that non-jihadi Salafism as well as other non-Salafi strands of Islam exist and play roles as counterpoints to Salafi jihadist thinking.

What policy makers can and *should* do is understand the situation from the jihadists' own perspective. Beliefs and ideas—in the case of AQAM, theologically based ones—are important because they illuminate the enemy's goals and how he is likely to pursue them. A thorough understanding of the enemy's ideas, at all levels, will also yield critical information about how the nature of the threat is likely to evolve and may point policy makers in the direction of new strategic opportunities.

Furthermore, understanding the conceptual and pragmatic relationships among the various parts of the Islamic theological tradition may allow policy makers to find ways in which those strands of Islam interact (or can be made to interact) to the benefit of the United States and its allies. For example, given that the philosophical differences between nonviolent Salafis and Salafi jihadists are so minor, nonviolent groups such as Tablighi Jamaat often serve as gateways to jihadism; perhaps the flow can be reversed and jihadists can be induced to embrace or revert back to nonviolent Salafi beliefs.

However uncomfortable it may make Americans, if we are truly to understand our enemy we must understand and take seriously his theology. Two conclusions become apparent when one immerses oneself in the enemy's public and private words. First, members at all levels of the enemy community are true believers. Salafi jihadism is not like the Cold War–era communist movement that had one idealistic, albeit warped, discourse among the followers and another far more cynical discourse among its leaders. Second, religion suffuses every aspect of the enemy's behavior; the United States and others ignore that fact at their peril. As discussed in the next chapter, al Qaida views itself as greater than the sum of its parts (groups, networks, cells, etc.) and aims to create a global movement with enough staying power to restore its own perceived lost glory of Islam.

Notes

1. Sayyid Qutb, *Milestones*, 1964, www.youngmuslims.ca/online_library/books/milestones/hold/index_2.asp, accessed September 23, 2007.
2. Michael Wolffsohn, "A German View on Middle Eastern Transformation," June 25, 2005, http://zope06.v.servelocity.net/hjs/sections/greater_europe/document.2005-06-26.1219285640, accessed September 23, 2007.
3. The work of Quintan Wiktorowicz is an indispensable guide to both radical Islam and the Salafi movement and is a good starting point for those unfamiliar with Salafi theological details. See Wiktorowicz, "A Genealogy of Radical Islam," *Studies in Conflict and Terrorism* 28 (2005): 75–97; and "Anatomy of the Salafi Movement," *Studies in Conflict and Terrorism* 29 (2006): 207–39.
4. We are grateful to Mary Habeck for helping us navigate our way through these complex concepts. See her *Knowing the Enemy: Jihadist Ideology and the War on Terror* (New Haven: Yale University Press, 2006), 27–28.
5. Marc Sageman, *Understanding Terror Networks* (Philadelphia: University of Pennsylvania Press, 2004), 4. The Sunnah is known through the hadiths, stories of what the Prophet said or did as told by people who witnessed these events. There are thousands of hadiths. Some are generally recognized among Muslims as being "authentic," some are generally recognized as "inauthentic," and some are disputed.

6. Ibid., 4; Wiktorowicz, "Anatomy of the Salafi Movement," 207, 209.

7. FBIS GMP20040706000164, "Al-Zarqawi Message Defends Executions, Calls for Jihad," FBIS Report in Arabic, July 5, 2004.

8. Wiktorowicz, "Anatomy of the Salafi Movement," 210. It is important to note that *innovation* as used here is a religious term and does not refer to technological progress. Charges of innovation are flung around even within the movement. Omar Nasiri, who trained in al Qaida's camps in Afghanistan during the mid-1990s, said that he and his comrades thought the Taliban were innovators who invented overly strict rules for society that did not have a sound religious basis. Omar Nasiri, *Inside the Jihad: My Life with al Qaeda, a Spy's Story* (New York: Perseus Books Group, 2006), 192, 212.

9. Quintan Wiktorowicz and John Kaltner, "Killing in the Name of Islam: Al-Qaeda's Justification for September 11," *Middle East Policy* 10, no. 2 (2003): 78–79.

10. Except as noted, this section draws on Wiktorowicz, "A Genealogy of Radical Islam," 81–83; Quintan Wiktorowicz, "The Salafi Movement as an Ideological Network: Beliefs, Structures, and Trends," MS dated August 2004; Sageman, *Understanding Terror Networks*, 8–9; and Christopher M. Blanchard, "The Islamic Traditions of Wahhabism and Salafiyya," Congressional Research Service Report RS21695, February 10, 2005, 1–2.

11. Elizabeth Sirriyeh, "Wahhabis, Unbelievers and the Problems of Exclusivism," *Bulletin of the British Society for Middle Eastern Studies* 16, no. 21 (1989): 124–25.

12. Wiktorowicz, "A Genealogy of Radical Islam," 81.

13. Lowell Bergman (correspondent), "Al Qaeda's New Front," PBS *Frontline*, March 12, 2004; transcript online at www.pbs.org/wgbh/pages/frontline/shows/front/etc/script.html, accessed December 30, 2005.

14. See, for example, Harmony document folder ISGM-2005-001834, book titled *The Position of the Scholar Mujahidin in the Event of the Islamic Emirate in Afghanistan*, in which Abu Muhammad al-Maqdisi extensively quoted al-Wahhab.

15. We owe this typology to Quintan Wiktorowicz; see "Anatomy of the Salafi Movement," 207–39.

16. An excellent summary of the history, beliefs, and practices of the Tablighis is in Abdul Aziz, "The Jammah Tabligh Movement in Indonesia: Peaceful Fundamentalist," *Studia Islamika: Indonesian Journal for Islamic Studies* 11, no. 3 (2004): 467–517.

17. Wiktorowicz, "Anatomy of the Salafi Movement," 217.

18. Sageman, *Understanding Terror Networks*, 20–21; Wiktorowicz, "Anatomy of the Salafi Movement," 217.

19. Sageman, *Understanding Terror Networks*, 5; Wiktorowicz, "A Genealogy of Radical Islam," 75; International Crisis Group, "Why Salafism and Terrorism Mostly Don't Mix," *Asia Report*, no. 83, September 13, 2004, Internet, www.crisisgroup.org/home/index.cfm?id=2967&l=1, accessed June 18, 2006. Sufism is a widespread sect of Sunni Islam that emphasizes the mystical experience of religion and involves venerating saints and holy places. Salafis routinely accuse Sufis of polytheism.

20. Blogistan.com, www.blogistan.com.uk/blog/index.php/2005/06/20/us-govt-slanders-tablighi-jamaat/, accessed September 14, 2005. This Web log called itself "an authentic, moderate face of Islam in Britain."

21. Nasiri, *Inside the Jihad*, 111–12.

22. SalafiPublications.com, www.Salafipublications.com/sps/sp.cfm?subsecID=TZ K01&articleID=TZK010003&articlePages=3, accessed September 14, 2005. This Web site described itself as "the need and manhaj of the Salafi US."

23. Wiktorowicz, "Anatomy of the Salafi Movement," 222. Another term is *reformists*.

24. Sageman, *Understanding Terror Networks*, 7; Vincenzo Oliveti, *Terror's Source: The Ideology of Wahhabi-Salafism and Its Consequences* (Birmingham, U.K.: Amadeus Books, 2002), 15–16. According to Ayman al-Zawahiri, the Muslim Brotherhood entered politics and thus "reneged on its history of struggle and what this history contains in terms of the blood of the martyrs, the wounds of the detainees, and the agony of the fugitives. Not only that, the Muslim Brotherhood has also reneged on its principles and creed. The Muslim Brotherhood is drifting away from its history, creating a new generation who only cares about worldly things now and in the future"; FBIS GMP20020108000197, "Al-Sharq al-Awsat Publishes Extracts from al-Jihad Leader al-Zawahiri's New Book," *Al-Sharq al-Awsat*, London in Arabic, December 2, 2001.

25. Sageman, *Understanding Terror Networks*, 7–8; Wiktorowicz, "Genealogy of Radical Islam," 77–78.

26. FEA20060523023251, "Availability of Abu Mus'ab al-Suri's 'The Call to Global Islamic Resistance,'" May 24, 2006; linked to CTC/OTA Translation and Analysis, "Abu Musab al-Suri's 'The Call to Global Islamic Resistance,'" 89–135, February 2006, al-Suri's page 117.

27. SEF20060714031006 Indonesia: "Ba'asyir Book Condemns 'Assassin' Bush, Urges 'Jihad' for Islamic Law," OSC Report in English, July 14, 2006.

28. For recent scholarly usage of the term *Salafi jihadism*, see examples in Gilles Kepel, "The Origins and Development of the Jihadist Movement: From Anticommunism to Terrorism," trans. Peter Clark, *Asian Affairs* 34, no. 2 (2003): 97; statement of Kenneth M. Pollack, Senior Fellow and Director of Research, Saban Center for Middle East Policy, Brookings Institution, Committee on Senate Foreign Relations, July 18, 2005; Alex Alexiev, "Tablighi Jamaat: Jihad's Stealthy Legions," *Middle East Quarterly* 7, no. 1 (2005); Olivier Roy, *Globalized Islam: The Search for a New Ummah* (New York: Columbia University Press, 2004), 234; and Petter Nesser, "Jihad in Europe—A Survey of the Motivations for Sunni Islamist Terrorism in Post-millennium Europe," Norwegian Defence Research Establishment, Kjeller, Norway, 2004, 10.

29. Abd Samad Moussaoui with Florcen Bouquillat, *Zacarias Moussaoui: The Making of a Terrorist*, trans. Simon Pleasance and Fronza Woods (New York: Seven Stories Press, 2003), 95.

30. Scott Atran, "The Emir: An Interview with Abu Bakar Ba'asyir, Alleged Leader of the Southeast Asian Jemaah Islamiyah Organization," *Spotlight on Terror* 3, no. 9 (September 15, 2005).

31. Habeck, *Knowing the Enemy*, 53.

32. FBIS GMP20040820000143, "Ideology of Recently Captured Saudi al-Qa'ida Theoretician al-Zahrani Analyzed," *Al-Hijaz*, London, August 15, 2004.

33. James Brandon and John Thorne, "The Sidewalk Where Terror Breeds," *Christian Science Monitor*, July 22, 2005, www.csmonitor.com/2005/0722/p01s01-woeu. html 22.

34. FBIS SEP20060303311001, "Jihadist Al-Muhajirun Website Promotes 'Terrorism' against US," OSC Report in Indonesian. See also FBIS SEP20040524000077,

"Australia Channel 9 Interviews Bali Bombing Mastermind in Jakarta," an interview with Amrozi, one of the Bali bombers.

35. For Ibn Taymiyya's role in the "crystallization of jihad theory," see David Cook,
Understanding Jihad (Berkeley: University of California Press, 2005), 63–66, an
excellent and concise history of the evolution of the idea of jihad over the centuries. Also see Noor Mohammad, "The Doctrine of Jihad: An Introduction," *Journal
of Law and Religion* 3, no. 2 (1985): 380–81; and Wiktorowicz, "A Genealogy of
Radical Islam," 78.

36. For the centrality of *tawhid* to AQAM thinking, see Habeck, *Knowing the Enemy*,
58–66.

37. Mohammad, "The Doctrine of Jihad," 381; Wiktorowicz, "A Genealogy of Radical
Islam," 78. The act of declaring a Muslim ruler an infidel is *takfir*.

38. Wiktorowicz, "A Genealogy of Radical Islam," 78–79; Mohammad, "The Doctrine
of Jihad," 394–95.

39. We are grateful to Mary Habeck for crafting the first draft of this section on al-
Banna. See also her *Knowing the Enemy*, 27–34.

40. Wiktorowicz, "A Genealogy of Radical Islam," 79.

41. Other examples include FBIS GMP20031113000204, "Book Entitled: '39 Ways to
Serve and Participate in Jihad,'" in Arabic, November 23, 2003, www.almaqdese.
com/a?i=278. Naji mentioned Qutb in his book *The Management of Savagery: The
Most Critical Stage through Which the Umma Will Pass*, trans. William McCants
(Cambridge, Mass.: Harvard University, John M. Olin Institute for Strategic
Studies, 2006), 8. English translation available at the U.S. Military Academy's
Combating Terrorism Center Web site, http://ctc.usma.edu/publications/naji.asp,
accessed September 23, 2007. This book began appearing on jihadist Web sites in
early 2005. All page references to this book use Naji's original pagination. The
Egyptian connection is obvious for former EIJ members, but especially for Ayman
al-Zawahiri (Sageman, *Understanding Terror Networks*, 9). Oddly, however,
Osama bin Laden does not appear to have personally cited Qutb among his inspi-
rations, at least not in public pronouncements.

42. FBIS GMP20050721706001, "Kurdish Islamist Mulla Krekar Interviewed on
Ansar al-Islam, Talabani Hostility," *Al Quds al-Arabi*, July 21, 2005, 4.

43. Petter Nesser, "The Slaying of the Dutch Filmmaker—Religiously Motivated
Violence or Islamist Terrorism in the Name of Global Jihad?" Norwegian Defence
Research Establishment, Kjeller, Norway, FFI/Rapport-2005/00376, 2005, 15;
available at http://rapporter.ffi.no/rapporter/2005/00376.pdf, accessed October
25, 2007.

44. Wiktorowicz and Kaltner, "Killing in the Name of Islam," 81.

45. Gilles Kepel, *Allah in the West: Islamic Movements in America and Europe*
(Stanford: Stanford University Press, 2003), 198–99.

46. Paul Berman gave an excellent layman's introduction to the thoughts of Sayyid
Qutb in "The Philosopher of Islamic Terror," *New York Times Magazine*, March
23, 2003. John C. Zimmerman's "Sayyid Qutb's Influence on the 11 September
Attacks," *Terrorism and Political Violence* 16, no. 2 (2004): 222–52, is a useful
discussion of Qutb's thought and its subsequent influence.

47. Qutb, *Milestones*.

48. Ibid.

49. Quoted in Sageman, *Understanding Terror Networks*, 13.

50. Ibid., 12.

51. Ibid., 13–14.

52. Qutb, *Milestones*.

53. FBIS GMP20040820000143.

54. Berman, "The Philosopher of Islamic Terror," 24. See also Berman's book and the chapter on "Hideous Schizophrenia" in *Terror and Liberalism* (New York: W. W. Norton, 2003), 77. Yusuf al-Ayiri echoed this idea in a book titled *Future of Iraq, Arabian Peninsula after the Fall of Baghdad*, FBIS GMP20030929000003, August 1, 2003, Internet, www.cybcity.com/image33/index.htm: "Secularism is about more than just democracy. Secularism involves the separation of religion and state. It operates on the principle, 'Render therefore unto Caesar the things which are Caesar's; and unto God the things that are God's.' They also call for hateful capitalism, the emancipation of women, equality between men and women, the equality of religions, and no differentiation between people on the basis of religion or creed. Secularism espouses absolute freedom—freedom of belief, freedom of worship, freedom of conduct, utterance, and action, freedom of knowledge, freedom in all things. The human being is transformed from a servant of God into a base animal. We see how they live today in the United States and in Europe—people in decay, unrestrained by any boundaries, serving only their desires, moved only by desire, opportunistic and ugly, driven only by self-interest, even at the cost of millions of human deaths."

55. Harmony document folder 500MI-2005-RP-MLA00011, *Mini Manual of the Urban Mujahideen*, 2004.

56. Harmony document folder NGIC-2002-84001, *Bavarian State Office of the Protection of the German Constitution: Political Activities of Islamic Extremist Groups Operating in the German State of Bavaria*, February 2001. It says that the Kalifatsstaat (Caliphate State) "makes an uncompromising claim to its interpretation of Islam being the sole, true reflection of Islam with world dominance as the ultimate goal. Primary emphasis is put upon the elimination of the secular-Turkish state infrastructure which is to be replaced by an Islamic system. . . . It rejects democracy and party pluralism as being completely incompatible with Islam. Only the Koran and Sunna can . . . serve as a basis for legal decision-making."

57. FBIS GMP20030929000003.

58. Quoted in Alan Cullision, "Inside al-Qaeda's Hard Drive," *Atlantic Monthly*, September 2004, 64.

59. Harmony document folder SFOR-2003-A00842, *Arabic Article that Defends the May 2003 Bombings in Riyadh*, May 25, 2003.

60. Qutb, *Milestones*.

61. Ibid.

62. Ibid.

63. Quoted in Walter Laqueur, *Voices of Terror* (New York: Reed Press, 2004), 403.

64. Harmony document folder AFGP-2002-800928, *10 Letters Supporting the Establishment of Islamic Jihad in Burma*, October 10, 1993.

65. FBIS GMP20040615000107, "Text of Al-Zarqawi's Letter to bin Ladin on Future of Mujahidin in Iraq," in Arabic, June 15, 2004.

66. Qutb, *Milestones*.

67. FBIS GMP20011120000057, "Memorandum Reveals Errors of Arab Fighters in Bosnia-Herzegovina," *Al-Sharq al-Awsat*, London, in Arabic, November 20, 2001.

68. Wiktorowicz, "A Genealogy of Radical Islam," 81.

69. "What Does Gama'a Islamiyya Want? An Interview with Tal'at Fu'ad Qasim," *Middle East Report*, January–March, 1996, 41.

70. Faraj's work was reprinted several times in Egypt and Jordan in the few years immediately after Sadat's assassination. The work was recently printed in a commercial English-language edition with an innovative new subtitle: *The Absent Obligation: And Expel the Jews and Christians from the Arabian Peninsula* (Maktabah al Ansaar, no date).

71. Sageman, *Understanding Terror Networks*, 15, 30. Faraj is quoted in Johannes J. G. Jansen, *The Neglected Duty: The Creed of Sadat's Assassins and Islamic Resurgence in the Middle East* (New York: Macmillan, 1986), 169. Jansen's book reproduces the entire text of Faraj's *Neglected Duty* in English translation.

72. Jansen, *The Neglected Duty*, 167.

73. FBIS GMP20050901535005, "Al-Jazirah Airs 'Will' of London Bomber, al-Zawahiri Speech," Doha Al-Jazirah Satellite Channel Television in Arabic, September 1, 2005. See also FBIS EUP20050206000046, "Freed Guantánamo Briton's 'Autobiography' Admits Volunteering for Suicide Attack," *Sunday Times*, London, February 6, 2005; and FBIS GMP20041013000259, "Confidant Writes on al-Zarqawi's 'Mysteries, Experiences,' Part One," in Arabic, September 9, 2004.

74. Atran, "The Emir." JI was responsible for the 2002 Bali bombings.

75. Sageman, *Understanding Terror Networks*, 33–34.

76. Ibid., 35; Trevor Stanley, "Understanding the Origins of Wahhabism and Salafism," *Jamestown Foundation Terrorism Monitor* 3, no. 14 (2005): 9.

77. Sageman, *Understanding Terror Networks*, 36.

78. Abdullah Azzam, *Join the Caravan*, 1989; www.religioscope.com/info/doc/jihad/azzam_caravan_3_part1.htm, accessed September 19, 2005.

79. Mahfuh Halimi and Muhammad Haniff Hassan, "'License to Kill': Imam Samudra's Justification for Bali Bombing," from Rohan Gunaratna's database at the International Centre for Political Violence and Terrorism Research, www.pvtr.org, ICPVTR document #13753, 2004.

80. Sageman, *Understanding Terror Networks*, 47.

81. For example, FBIS GMP20040420000246, "Saudi Fugitive al-Dakhil Interviewed by al-Qa'ida Affiliated Sawt al-Jihad," Saudi Arabia, April 6, 2004; FBIS GMP20040406000138, "'Text' of al-Zarqawi Message Threatening More Attacks," FBIS report in Arabic, April 6, 2004; FBIS GMP20030214000152, "Islamist Site Posts Translation of Purported bin Ladin Audio Message," Internet, February 14, 2003; FBIS GMP20050518336002, "Al-Zarqawi Justifies Killing of Innocent Muslims, Condemns Shia 'Betrayal' of Sunnis," Jihadist Web sites, May 18, 2005.

82. FBIS GMP20031004000119, "Islamic Research Center Publishes Book on 12 May Riyadh Operation," August 1, 2003, Internet, www.cybcity.com/newss/index.htm.

83. FBIS GMP20040406000138. Al-Zawahiri later reprimanded al-Zarqawi for his continual disparagement of the *ulema*, which al-Zawahiri viewed as counterproductive to their cause: "The *ulema* among the general public are, as well, the symbol of Islam and its emblem. Their disparagement may lead to the general public deeming religion and its adherents as being unimportant. This is a greater injury than the benefit of criticizing a theologian on a heresy or an issue," and "I wish to stress the warning against diminishing the *ulema* before the general public"; FBIS EUP20051012374001 "Report: Complete Text of al-Zawahiri 9 July 2005 Letter to al-Zarqawi," Washington Office of the Director of National Intelligence Web site in English, October 11, 2005.

84. Azzam, *Join the Caravan.*
85. Harmony document folder AFGP-2002-6000080, *Al-Qaeda Captured Document (Part 2) Discusses Lessons Learned from Jihad* in Syria, 2002, http://ctc.usma.edu/aq/pdf/AFGP-2002-600080-Trans.pdf, accessed September 22, 2007. Al-Suri's opinion of the *ulema* has if anything worsened since then. Writing in 2004, he said: "What a pity about those considered the ulema of the Muslims!! In short, the matter disgusts the soul and fills it with pain. The hypocrites among them have become even more hypocritical after September 11, and the silent and cowering among them more silent" (al-Suri, *Call to Global Islamic Resistance*, 81–135; CTC/OTA translation, February 2006, 126 [al-Suri, 38]).
86. FBIS GMP20040420000246, "Saudi Fugitive al-Dakhil Inteviewed al-Qa'ida Affiliated Sawt al-Jihad."
87. FBIS GMP20031004000119, "Islamic Research Center Publishes Book on 12 May Riyadh Operation."
88. Qutb, *Milestones.*
89. Ibid.
90. Jansen, *The Neglected Duty.* Jansen inserted the words in parentheses for clarity.
91. Harmony document folder AFGP-2002-600175, *Al-Qaida: Constitutional Charter, Rules and Regulations,* 2002, http://ctc.usma.edu/aq/pdf/AFGP-2002-600175-Trans.pdf, accessed October 16, 2007.
92. FBIS SAP20010108000072, "Daily Prints Usama bin Laden 'Letter' Calling for 'Global Islamic State.'" *Rawalpindi Nawa-i-Waqt,* in Urdu, January 7, 2001.
93. There are two exceptions. Abu-Bakr Naji discussed some issues of governance in the Caliphate in his 2005 book, *The Management of Savagery,* and Omar Bakri Mohammed's al-Muhajiroun in the United Kingdom published "The First 24 Hours after the Establishment of the Islamic State," a twenty-five-page document, written perhaps in 2003, that discusses in some detail government departments, their policies, and organization in the "Khilafah state." Al-Muhajiroun originally made this document available on the Internet.
94. FBIS GMP20050919371013, "Global Islamic Media Front Announces Plans to Launch New Jihadist Radio Broadcast," Jihadist Web sites, September 19, 2005.
95. FBIS GMP20040109000138, "Interview with Nabil Sahraoui, Leader of Islamic Fundamentalist Salafi Group," *Al-Hayah,* London, in Arabic, January 9, 2004. This was before GSPC's announced formal merger with al Qaida in mid-2006. The group now calls itself al Qaida in the Islamic Maghreb.
96. SEP-2005-1013071001, "Indonesian Weekly: Radical Islamic Groups Divided over Wisdom of Terrorism," *Jakarta Gatra* in Indonesian, October 15, 2005, 68–69.
97. FBIS GMP20040406000138, "Al-Zarqawi Claims Operations in Iraq, Calls for More Attacks."
98. FBIS GMP20020108000197, "Al-Sharq al-Awsat Publishes Extracts from al-Jihad Leader al-Zawahiri's New Book."
99. ODNI News Release, No 2-05, "Letter from al-Zawahiri to al-Zarqawi," October 11, 2005, www.dni.gov/press_releases/letter_in_english.pdf, accessed September 22, 2007.
100. FBIS GMP20031027000226, "Book Commemorates September 11 'Raid,'" September 1, 2002, Internet, www.cybcity.com/newss/index.htm, in Arabic.
101. Harmony document folder NGIC-2002-84001-HT, February 2001.
102. Singapore, Ministry of Home Affairs, "The Jemaah Islamiya Arrests and the Threat of Terrorism," January 7, 2003, 6; International Centre for Political Violence and Terrorism Research, Institute of Defence and Strategic Studies, Singapore, "The

Struggle Guide Series (II), General Guide, Al-Jama'ah al-Islamiyyah (PUPJI), released by the Central Leadership Council of Jemaah Islamiyah," n.d.

103. Harmony document folder AFGP-2002-000080, *Al-Qaida Organizational Charter and Duty Descriptions for All Members and Their Qualifications*, http://ctc. usma.edu/aq/pdf/AFGP-2002-000080-Trans.pdf, accessed September 22, 2007.

104. Harmony folder AFGP-2002-600053, *Letters Discussing Various al-Qaeda Issues and Operations in Somalia, Tajikistan and Afghanistan, Including Key Personnel, and Future Plans and Strategies for Africa and Asia*, also referred to as "Five Letters to the Africa Corps," 1993, http://ctc.usma.edu/aq/pdf/AFGP-2002-600053-Trans-Meta.pdf, accessed September 22, 2007.

105. FBIS GMP20050201000226, "Abu Mu'sab al-Suri Responds to State Department Terrorism Accusations," Jihadist Web sites, in Arabic, January 21, 2005.

106. FBIS GMP20050601712006, "Sixth Part of Serialized Book on al-Zarqawi and al-Qa'ida Published," *Al-Quds al-Arabi*, London, in Arabic, May 19, 2005. Of note, al-Maqdisi, according to the USMA Combating Terrorism Center's *Militant Ideology Atlas* (November 2006), is the most influential (living) jihadi ideologue and the "primary broker" among the three main types of influential jihadist thinkers (conservative scholars, Saudi establishment clerics, and jihadi theorists). His works, available at the Tawhed Web site, proved to be the most cited among all scholarly tracts in CTC's sampling. The Executive Report is available at www. ctc.usma.edu/atlas/Atlas-ExecutiveReport.pdf, accessed September 22, 2007.

CHAPTER 2

Enemy Self-Perceptions

[The infidels] are still fixated on fighting individuals, oblivious to the fact that they are actually fighting an idea, one that has spread across the globe like fire and which is embraced even by those whose faith is a mustard seed.

ANONYMOUS JIHADIST, 2005[1]

Movement versus Network

American analysts generally think about terrorism in terms of sharply defined networks consisting of members (or nodes) and the myriad links among them. This model has worked well for decades, at least since the heyday of the Ku Klux Klan, because most of the terrorism confronting the United States has involved small groups. This has been true domestically in such cases as the Christian Identity Movement (a numerically negligible proportion of the American population, despite its arrogation of the term *movement*), the Symbionese Liberation Army, and the Weather Underground, and abroad in the Abu Nidal organization, the German Red Army Faction (which grew out of the Baader-Meinhof Gang), the Belgian Cellules Communistes Combattantes, the Italian Red Brigades, and others.

Each of these groups made a dubious claim to be the vanguard of a revolutionary movement that would sweep away the old order. In fact, however, most were tiny cliques of angry, alienated individuals who met in basements to spout self-congratulatory rhetoric divorced from the concerns of those for whom they claimed to be fighting. When facing such a threat it is possible through careful network analysis to understand the enemy in something approximating its entirety. Sufficient intelligence effort can locate every link and node. That gradations of membership cannot readily be accommodated in a network diagram is not a problem because membership boundaries are sharp.

These conditions do not prevail for AQAM. By the standards of traditional terrorist organizations, AQAM is enormous, diverse, and widely distributed, and therefore, practically speaking, impossible to map fully. Furthermore, membership in AQAM is not well defined. In fact, one analyst has said that the "jihad movement is more akin to an 'ideological umbrella' than to a homogeneous movement."[2] In its heyday in the 1990s, al Qaida itself could be characterized as those "brothers" who had sworn *bayat* (fealty) to Osama bin Laden. Clearly, that definition does not apply to AQAM in 2007. Today the movement *includes* al Qaida and many other groups and has no single leader to whom one could swear an oath. It is more helpful to view AQAM as consisting of thousands of committed members around the globe, each surrounded by many more people with varying degrees of commitment who provide a supportive environment in which to operate.[3]

Consider the case of Britain. According to the former chief of London's Metropolitan Police, more than three thousand Britons attended al Qaida training camps before September 11, 2001.[4] Furthermore, in 2004 the British Home Office estimated the number of Britons who actively supported al Qaida or similar terrorist groups at ten to fifteen thousand.[5] And where on the network diagram would an analyst put the 58 percent of Indonesians who in 2003 had "confidence" in Osama bin Laden's "ability to do the right thing regarding world affairs"?[6] Surely at least some of them actively supported AQAM, though probably not al Qaida itself, given the proximity of Indonesia's own jihadist group, Jemaah Islamiyah. Considering that AQAM has pretensions to be a force for social change, the rest may contribute to it simply by virtue of taking bin Laden seriously as a major positive actor on the international stage.

Al Qaida recognizes gradations of membership within the movement, as the following quotation from a captured letter probably dating from the 1990s from Abu Hudaifa to bin Laden indicates: "As for the regular cadre, bound by commitment and a contract, he functions by two motives, his belief in the cause and his commitment and contract. Moreover, he acts according to the projections of the Movement and its general strategy, which allows him freedom of action on the tactical level, and which guarantees that no one will try to harm the Movement, contrary to the volunteer who works on the outside framework of the Movement and away from the strategic main principles, and he has no commitment to it."[7]

The second reason Americans typically perceive terrorists as forming networks is the common, though now less so, inclination to approach terrorism as a law enforcement problem. Certainly, terrorists violate American law when they conduct their operations in the United States or when they harm Americans abroad. From a purely legal perspective, this makes terrorists "criminals." Broadly speaking, criminal groups can well be described as networks because their membership is well defined, whereas few if any criminal groups have pretensions to the status of a social movement.

The third reason for the net-centric approach is the influence of John Arquilla and David Ronfeldt's seminal book, *The Advent of Netwar*.[8] While the networks Arquilla and Ronfeldt described had fuzzier boundaries, they would not, unlike the more traditional definition of *network* referred to above, be mistaken for social movements. Since its formulation in the early 1990s, the idea of netwar has garnered significant influence in the U.S. government's discourse on emerging and future modes of war fighting. Many analysts endeavoring to understand nontraditional, particularly nonstate, belligerents adopted this vision of actors employing networks of organization, doctrine, and strategy to pursue their ends. The more deeply we move into the post-9/11 war on terrorism, the more appealing Arquilla and Ronfeldt's ideas have become. Eliot A. Cohen's 2002 review of their book *Networks and Netwars for Foreign Affairs* notes that "before September 11, readers might have been naturally inclined to pooh-pooh such talk of loose networks of terrorists, criminals, and militant subversives. But the peculiar structure of al Qaeda vindicates much of the argument here."[9]

The Enemy's Self-Perception: Movement

While there is much to be said for Arquilla and Ronfeldt's analysis, AQAM simply does not think of itself as a network. Revealingly, when the word *network* does appear in the enemy's discourse, it is usually in a technical, not a self-referential, sense.[10] To the extent that self-perception influences behavior, AQAM is most effectively analyzed as a movement.

Al Qaida and its theological brethren believe that in order to realize a "restored" Caliphate, they must unify the *ummah* under the banner of Salafi jihadism. Central to that objective—almost its defining charac-teristic—is the creation and growth of a movement with a revolutionary vanguard marching at its head. Indeed, "networks" and "cells" are only structural aspects of the vanguard, which is itself the most ideologi-cally evolved element of the overall movement. There is inherent tension between a "movement," which must be primarily an overt and inclusive organization (within the context of the *ummah*), and a "network," which smacks of secrecy and exclusivity. AQAM strategists seldom call them-selves "cells" or "nodes" in a "network," because the creation of these structures is merely a tactical exigency for survival, applicable only at par-ticular times and places.

Unquestionably, many AQAM components are flexible and willing to adapt their organizational structure, particularly its security aspects, to the operating environment. In some situations this malleability may drive them toward network structures at the tactical level, in other cases not. In 1989, strategist Abu Musab al-Suri made precisely this point. After dis-cussing the relative merits and flaws of "pyramid hierarchy," "thread con-nection," and hybrid organizational structures, he confessed: "Structuring an organization requires a lot of thought and foresight, it should take into account the nature and strengths of the enemy, the type and strengths of its security system, the geographical nature of the country, what has worked and what has failed in similar situations. . . . The particular conditions on the ground should determine the best structure for the organization."[11]

Nevertheless, at higher levels—national, regional, global—AQAM nor-mally refers to itself as a movement, and the term appears frequently in self-referential Salafi jihadist discourse. For example, in *Knights under the Prophet's Banner*, al-Zawahiri repeatedly described his group, Egyptian Islamic Jihad, as an "Islamic movement" or "fundamentalist movement." Sayf al-din al-Ansari also talks about the "Islamic movement" and the "world jihad movement" that is confronting the United States.[12] Abu Ayman al-Hilali said in 2002, "Like all jihad movements, al-Qa'ida is based on doctrine, ideas, education, politics, and military action. Its project is a civilization."[13] As of late 2002 or early 2003 there was even a group called the Pashto Islamic Freedom Movement.[14] On at least one occasion,

Osama bin Laden neatly sidestepped the network characterization: "We are the sons of the nation and an indivisible part of it," he somewhat disingenuously answered a reporter who in October 2001 asked about his "wide network."[15] It is worth noting that the enemy seems to prefer the term movement in specifically military contexts as well, as illustrated in a captured document on guerrilla warfare. In January 2004, Abu-Hajar Abd-al-Aziz al-Muqrin, then the head of al Qaida in Saudi Arabia, referred in a military journal to the substantial agreement that existed among "the majority of Islamic movements."[16]

Some al Qaida members will argue that the question of al Qaida's structure is of secondary importance; the true relevance is the idea behind al Qaida. This, of course, is an implicit argument for thinking about al Qaida as a movement, because movements are defined by the ideas they embody, whereas networks are defined by a set of nodes and a set of links.[17] AQAM military analyst Abu Ubayd al-Qurashi, however, provided a partial exception to this preference for the word *movement*. In a captured 2002 document, he referred to the complexity of al Qaida's "international financial network,"[18] but he also said that al Qaida was so strong and could survive the blows struck against it because of its "complex network, decentralized mentality, and concept of a jihad league." Nevertheless, he betrayed some ambivalence on the whole "network" question by continuing in the same passage to say that al Qaida's practices are "worthy of emulation by other Islamic movements."[19] It is relevant to note al-Qurashi's occasional use of the word *movement*; for instance, when he referred to al Qaida as "the standard bearer of the world jihad movement."[20]

If any member of AQAM were to refer to his movement as a "network," one should expect it to be al-Qurashi, because among enemy thinkers, he is probably the most influenced by and cognizant of American military thought. Indeed, he has read and footnoted two works by Arquilla and Ronfeldt: their article "Cyberwar Is Coming!" and a book they coauthored in 1999 with several other RAND analysts, *Countering the New Terrorism*.[21] Al-Qurashi may thus be said to be giving us his reading of America's reading of al Qaida.

Declaring oneself a "movement" does not make it so, of course, and even if the enemy is best described as a movement, it certainly has networks embedded within it. Brinton Milward and Jörg Raab's characterization seems apt in this context.[22] In their discussion of "dark networks"—networks that must operate covertly because other organizations

are seeking to destroy or control them—they observed that "terrorist networks are conventionally divided between a core and periphery," which
may consist of several levels. In the case of al Qaida, the outermost level
"consists of a worldwide jihadist movement that is recognizable from Lyon
to Kuala Lumpur."[23]

Another school of thought among Western social scientists—that of
social movement theory—offers a counterpoint to the network view that
supports the current shape and aims of AQAM. Much of social movement theory is based on the political process model, which itself has three
basic components:
1. Mobilizing structures—vehicles through which collective action grows
2. Political opportunity structures—exterior, positive openings for col-
    lective action such as the Soviet invasion of Afghanistan
3. Cultural framing—the systems of beliefs and practices brought by
    people to address current circumstances, such as the ideas suggested
    by being a Sunni Muslim Egyptian Salafi[24]

Successful movements must address all three, and in particular must
be successful at mobilization to sustain themselves.[25] Not unlike the
various labor, social justice, and liberation movements throughout history
with global aspirations, al Qaida has two main concerns: (1) continued
expansion of the movement into new populations and subsequent generations, and (2) maintaining dynamism and action in already mobilized
sectors of the group.

One important facet of the current problem that social movement
theory does not handle well is AQAM's multigenerational nature. Most
past movements carried out their major goals or met defeat within the
course of a single generation, after a long buildup of grievances. The enemy,
however, looks at the present conflict as one that will take decades or even
centuries to win.[26] These characteristics of a movement, coupled with the
Islamic revivalist agenda described in chapter 1, make the global Salafi
jihadist movement a unique and unprecedented adversary.

America's efforts to defeat this movement must start with an effort
to understand the enemy's strategic self-perception. Network analysis—a
detailed understanding of links and nodes—constitutes a necessary and
powerful tool for detecting, thwarting, and understanding *tactical* terrorist
activities. However, Milward and Raab rightly pointed out that "while it is

important to be able to visualize what the known parts of Al Qaeda look like, it tells us nothing of its strategic plan."[27] Here, focusing on the larger, relatively overt, movement will be more helpful. Moreover, there is considerable value in considering how the enemy views himself because that is the basis on which he makes decisions and communicates his goals. AQAM consciously tries to spread a religious message and to encourage the entire *ummah* of some 1.2 billion people to "join the caravan" that is moving boldly into the future.

AQAM's Quandary: Trying to Centralize a Movement

Beyond superficialities, AQAM does not entirely fit Arquilla and Ronfeldt's description of a networked enemy. The latter wrote: "Netwar differs from modes of conflict and crime in which the protagonists prefer to develop large, formal, stand-alone, hierarchical organizations, doctrines, and strategies as in past efforts, for example, to build centralized movements along Leninist lines."[28] Though AQAM is far from a "centralized movement along Leninist lines," many of its thinkers imagine it that way or at least aspire to make it that way. Arquilla and Ronfeldt saw doctrine as providing "a central ideational, strategic, and operational coherence that allows for tactical decentralization," but that is a looser approach than Mao's maxim that "command must be centralized for strategic purposes and decentralized for tactical purposes."[29] A reading of Abu Hudaifa's letter to bin Laden (quoted above) would be consistent with Ronfeldt and Arquilla's formulation. Al Qaida propagandist Lewis Atiyatallah similarly claimed in 2004 that one of the movement's strengths is that it easily survives the loss of any single member because the work is distributed among the members, all of whom are indoctrinated with the group's strategy.[30]

Not all AQAM members agree that decentralization is the best policy. In 2004, Abu Jandal, bin Laden's former bodyguard, said, "Al Qa'ida pursues a method or principle that calls for 'centralization of decision and decentralization of execution.' The decision was made centrally, but the method of attack and execution was the duty of field commanders."[31] A 1999 document captured in Afghanistan goes even further, saying that when the movement is starting from scratch to destabilize a society, the top leadership must minutely control all attacks. In these circumstances,

it is necessary to subordinate the terrorist war to a specific strategy planned precisely because loss of sight makes the movement flounder when selecting targets. It receives very adverse reactions. . . . This has an effect on the people which leads to an increase in national isolation. The terrorist war must submit to a resolute and disciplined leadership and [be] controlled with an iron fist. . . . Precise intended political objectives must be designated for the act of terrorism. No tactical operations are permitted outside the general strategic plan. No undisciplined initiatives in tactics are allowed. Operation orders and target specifications and timing of strikes come from the general leadership only and not from local leadership in districts and cities.[32]

At about the same time, Abu Hudaifa wrote to Osama bin Laden that the "political section" of al Qaida should have among its duties "continuously maintaining a high degree of sensitivity and transparency with regards to the project of the Movement; establishing regular connections between the Movement's pivotal points: the command, the middle command, and the base."[33] Here Abu Hudaifa was thinking about how to maintain a degree of centralization of command, not how to move toward a networked, decentralized structure. Similarly, Khalid Sheikh Mohammed told interrogators that Hambali, al Qaida's Southeast Asia coordinator and the operational leader of Jemaah Islamiyah, was in touch with four 9/11 plotters when they met in Kuala Lumpur because, as a rule, he had to be informed of al Qaida operative activities in Southeast Asia.[34]

AQAM's goals, as Stephen Lambert correctly noted, are "nothing less than a revolutionary transformation of the status quo."[35] In light of the dim view that Marxism-Leninism took of Islam in general and its political manifestations in particular, it is ironic to see the parallels between Marxism-Leninism and AQAM's thinking. Much as Communists believed that the "scientific laws" of dialectical materialism promised them eventual victory, the Salafi jihadists believe that, though the fight will be long and difficult, God has promised them victory in the end. This is a core conviction throughout the movement, regardless of circumstances. Abu Bakr Ba'asyir, when interviewed from prison in August 2005, bluntly stated that the West "will constantly be enemies. But they'll lose. I say this not because I am able to predict the future but they will lose and Islam will win. That was what the Prophet Muhammad has said. Islam must win and Westerners will be destroyed."[36] A captured document on the jihad in Tajikistan from the early to mid-1990s contains the reassurance that "real Muslims are invincible, and their triumph in any war is guaranteed by God's will."[37] In the aftermath of the defeat in Afghanistan, a document purporting to be bin Laden's last will (allegedly written during the battle of Tora Bora in late 2001) portrays a downcast, even angry bin Laden who nevertheless betrayed no doubt that God and his fighters ultimately will be victorious. "Despite the setback that Allah, praise and glory be to Him, has tried us with, this battle will lead to the disappearance of the United States and the infidel West, even after dozens of years."[38] In early 2003, having regained his equilibrium, bin Laden put a rather less desperate spin on the matter: "I inform you of the good news that our *Ummah* has been promised victory by Allah, but if this victory has become delayed, then it is due to our sins and our sitting back from helping the Religion of Allah."[39] In short, the Salafi jihadists see themselves on the right side of history, and of theology. Indeed, they believe that they are driving history and playing a very particular providential role in bringing about the victory that God has promised.

In a further parallel with communist thought, the organizations within AQAM view themselves as the vanguard of the revolution. Both Mawdudi and his intellectual successor, Qutb, wrote at a time when Marxist-Leninist thought was in the intellectual air. Though both scholars thoroughly rejected atheist Marxism, they absorbed some of its terminology and modes of thought. Most notably, Mawdudi advocated the creation of an Islamic "revolutionary vanguard" composed of ideological leaders who in turn would help to birth a new Islamic state; Qutb picked up on the term, using it in *Milestones*.[40] "How is it possible to start the task of reviving Islam?" Qutb asked. "It is necessary that there should be a vanguard which sets out with this determination and then keeps walking on the path."[41] Numerous AQAM luminaries have publicly used the term, including al-Zawahiri in *Knights under the Prophet's Banner*, bin Laden, and al-Qurashi.[42] Indeed, the Salafi jihadist group that fought alongside the Muslim Brotherhood against the Syrian regime in the late 1970s and early 1980s called itself the "Fighting Vanguard."[43]

Marxism-Leninism held that feelings of national patriotism were the product of "false consciousness," and that the true, meaningful distinctions among people were class distinctions. It further held that the party was an indispensable leadership group that would guide the broader revolutionary masses as they overthrew the existing economic and political order.[44] The party, in its role as the vanguard of the revolution, had to be pragmatic in its approach and had to pay careful attention to "objective conditions" (i.e., those conditions that could not be changed) so that its actions would be effective and decisive. The similarities of those concepts to Sayf al-din al-Ansari's conception of the Islamic vanguard are striking. In a book published on the first anniversary of the 9/11 attacks, al-Ansari wrote that "the Islamic movement is not a substitute for the Islamic community; it is the vanguard that goes ahead of it."[45] In particular, al-Ansari thought that

> the world jihad movement today as represented by al Qaida is a vanguard movement that has succeeded in carving out a place for itself in modern thought. As a movement, it has all the prerequisites for action. As a group, it is close to the community, cutting across borders and nationalities. It embodies the idea that there is no difference between an Arab and a non-Arab. A belief in monotheism is the identity card of the Muslim community. This is why al Qaida cares about the concerns of all. It is not limited by the imaginary borders that colonialism imposed. Its involvement in the community's concerns is practical and effective. It does not limit itself to the rhetoric of condemnatory statements and protest positions. These evaporate quickly in the light of day, especially if they are not tied to forceful action on the ground that makes others recognize your presence on the field.[46]

In carrying out that "forceful action," however, al-Ansari was quick to caution:

> We must not act with confused emotion, but rather with carefully considered movements on the field of battle, presenting an ongoing challenge. This is what moves the issue forward in thought and conscience, generating the necessary vigilance. Yes, local projects may require at certain stages a "slow-cooked" approach that avoids confrontation. This is because the local movement is subject to specific conditions and particular goals that impose minute political calculations. The world jihad movement, on the other hand, moves in open conditions and pursues general goals. It seeks primarily to make use of strategic precepts and views the community as a whole, acting as a vanguard force to confront great dangers.[47]

Sulayman Abu-Ghayth articulated essentially the same idea in December 2002: "The mujahideen are part of this victorious, blessed nation. They are the vanguard, which has taken upon itself to spark off the inevitable confrontation with our enemies. Therefore, it is not fighting on behalf of the nation, but trying to mobilize it against its enemy so that the whole nation will rise in face of the usurper and occupier enemy."[48]

Also in 2002, bin Laden enunciated the concept of revolutionary vanguard organizations using a different metaphor. Summing up the resources available to the Muslims, he said:

> Our nation is rich with many resources and capabilities and the absolutely most important resource is the Muslim person who is the battle's fuel and the conflict's motor. We do not mean by the person here only the scholars and propagators who are committed to and working for Islam and the sons of the Islamic awakening and movements but also the Muslim peoples and all their general and particular groups. If the particular groups have their role that others do not undertake, then the general groups are the real fuel of the battle and the explosive material. The role of the particular groups is that of the detonator and the motor that detonates this material.[49]

Finally, one of the two key components of doctrine that Arquilla and Ronfeldt described as "particularly apt for netwar actors" is the absence of visible leaders or a multiplicity of leaders who use "consultative and consensus-building mechanisms for decision-making." In the United States, the famously elusive environmental terrorist group Earth Liberation Front fits this description perfectly as a "leaderless resistance."[50] In Southeast Asia, Jemaah Islamiyah makes a modest attempt by denying its own existence and thus denying that it has a leader. (Outside analysts unanimously agree, however, that Abu Bakr Ba'asyir is the group's leader.) Yet, most of the individual organizations under the AQAM rubric do not fit this description. Osama bin Laden and Ayman al-Zawahiri are international icons for al Qaida, and at least before 9/11, all formal members of al Qaida swore an oath of allegiance to bin Laden. Abu Musab al-Zarqawi was famous as the leader of "al Qaida in the Land of the Two Rivers" (Iraq), and he, too, swore *bayat* to bin Laden. In early 2005, self-designated mujahideen in the Russian republic of Dagestan, adjacent to Chechnya, did not hesitate to have themselves videotaped swearing *bayat* to their leaders.[51] The longtime leader of the Arab mujahideen in Chechnya, the strikingly charismatic Ibn al-Khattab, attained during his lifetime a celebrity status befitting a rock star. Since the death of Yusuf al-Ayiri in 2003, al Qaida in Saudi Arabia has doggedly kept naming new leaders as the regime has killed each in succession. One witty Saudi journalist was moved to comment that "the leaders of the Al Qa'ida organization have so rapidly succeeded one another that the organization has become leaderless," although this is scarcely what Arquilla and Ronfeldt had in mind.[52]

Strategists and Foot Soldiers

In the West there are, broadly speaking, two different schools of thought about the goals and motivations of AQAM's members. The first says that al Qaida and like-minded groups are pursuing a generally rational strategy in order to achieve a particular desired outcome; for the adherents to this school of thought, AQAM's violence is *instrumental*. The second school of thought sees little or no strategy in AQAM's actions, attributing them instead to blind rage or a simple love of fighting; this group views AQAM's violence as noninstrumental, existential, or expressive.[53]

The first school is probably the majority view. Observers running the political gamut from Victor Davis Hanson to Noam Chomsky saw the events of 9/11 as a rational, instrumental act of war intended to achieve some political objective; that is, as fundamentally Clausewitzian.[54] Michael Scheuer, formerly head of the bin Laden unit in the CIA's Counterterrorist Center, has been among the most ardent proponents of this view. Using military terminology he wrote in 2004, "for nearly a decade now, bin Laden has demonstrated patience, brilliant planning, managerial expertise, sound strategic and tactical sense . . . and focused, limited war aims."[55] A Royal Navy officer portrayed an al Qaida bearing a great resemblance to Donald Rumsfeld's military: "Al-Qaeda has undergone transformational change, shifting emphasis from static resistance to Soviet occupation, to delivery of precise effects throughout the world."[56] RAND's Bruce Hoffman derived his metaphors from the business world but nevertheless portrayed a bin Laden and al Qaida (his definition of which includes "like-minded guerrillas and terrorists") that attempt to fit means to ends in a rational, instrumental way: "Osama bin Laden is perhaps best viewed as a terrorist CEO. He has essentially applied the techniques of business administration and modern management, which he learned both at university and in his family's construction business, to the running of a transnational terrorist organization. In the 1990s he did what the executives of transnational companies did throughout much of the industrialized world—namely, design and implement a flexible new organizational framework and strategy incorporating multiple levels and both top-down and bottom-up approaches."[57]

Ryan Thornton, writing in the *Harvard International Review* in 2005, went so far as to claim that "all of the intelligence gathered thus far in the U.S.-led War on Terror displays a visible strategy and system of attack that Al Qaeda is employing in its terrorist operations." Later in the same article he asserted, "it is undeniable that al Qaeda must have reconsidered its strategy in light of the U.S. War on Terror, specifically in relation to the removal of the Taliban."[58]

The noninstrumental, or existential, explanation is less widely held but has prominent and insightful proponents. Brian Jenkins of the RAND Corporation, for example, argued that for this enemy, "fighting is process, not progress oriented. It provides opportunities to prove conviction, courage and prowess. The jihadists view death not as a sign of defeat, but the pathway to martyrdom. Ultimate victory will come when God wills it."[59] Similarly, journalist Fareed Zakaria saw the enemy engaged in a vicious existential battle, though he emphasized anger rather than the role of religion in the enemy's thinking: "Today's Islamic terrorism is motivated not by a specific policy but by a nihilistic rage against the modern world."[60]

In 2002, Lee Harris wrote an article in the Hoover Institution's *Policy Review* that takes this argument to its purest form, describing the enemy's "fantasy ideology" as "political and ideological symbols and tropes used not for political purposes, but entirely for the benefit of furthering a specific personal or collective fantasy."[61] He suggested that the leaders of fantasy ideologies, among whom he included Hitler and Mussolini, can make their followers believe the fantasy only because they themselves believe it. This belief, however, does not come after a rational examination of the facts at hand; rather, it is "a deliberate form of make-believe, but one in which the make-believe is not an end in itself, but rather the means of making the make-believe become real."[62] Accordingly, in al Qaida's fantasy ideology, suicide in the form of "martyrdom" is an end in itself. Harris concluded that it is a mistake to try to fit such behaviors "into the mold created by our own categories and expectations."

Nowhere is this better illustrated than on the videotape of Osama bin Laden discussing the attack. The tape makes clear that the collapse of the World Trade Center was not part of the original terrorist scheme, which apparently assumed that the twin towers would not lose their structural integrity. But this fact gave to the event—in terms of al Qaida's fantasy ideology—an even greater poignancy: Precisely because it had not been part of the original calculation, it was therefore understood as a manifestation of divine intervention. The nineteen hijackers did not bring down the towers—God did.[63]

Compounding the confusion engendered by these two compelling explanations of the enemy is the fact that the Western intellectual pedigree, anchored in the Enlightenment, obscures the importance of religion and its influence on the enemy's behavior. More recent events such as the flood of Marxist thought through the educated classes during the last hundred years and the American constitutional separation between church and state (to say nothing of official French hostility to religion) have further weakened Westerners' analytic capabilities in this regard.[64] Michael Wolffsohn of the University of the German Armed Forces, for example, believes that all actions must be for an instrumental purpose. When he sees evidence of the sort of existential thought processes that Jenkins described, however, his mind rebels and instead seeks to conjure up instrumental motives in their place. Thus, he argued that bin Laden, the "unscrupulous businessman," is cynically invoking religion to cover his true motivation, which purportedly is to enrich himself.[65] While Wolffsohn was able to make that assertion cogently, he soon found himself in a morass of contradictions:

> Every action requires a will and has an end. What is the terrorists' aim? Terror is not an end in itself, for it is only but a means. Terror is the Strategy, and strategy requires political will. What do the terrorists want? Islamic world domination? . . . Should men like bin Laden and al-Zawahiri, well-trained in scientific thinking, really pursue such an irrational and unrealistic aim as "world domination"? They know as well as the next man that this would be hubris. . . . In January 2005, terrorist leader, al-Zarqawi, proclaimed "a merciless war against the foul principle of democracy and all who follow this wrong ideology." Such an aim is entirely irrational and therefore not a political means. Such terror is not instrumental, it is *existential* (i.e., an end unto itself and therefore useless even to the terrorists). Born and raised in Jordan, al-Zarqawi could have only one real political aim: the fight against Israel and an overthrow of the Hashemite dynasty of Jordan. . . . Existential terror à la Zarqawi can only be fought militarily, not politically.[66] [Emphasis in original]

Wolffsohn's misunderstanding is both commonplace and understandable; the problem is decidedly counterintuitive from the point of view of Westerners schooled in Clausewitz. But there is a solution. Brynjar Lia and Thomas Hegghammer of the Norwegian Defence Research Establishment approached this solution in their assessment of the anonymous document published on the Internet that apparently inspired the March 2004 Madrid bombings.[67] They suggested that "'al Qaida ideology' should not be treated as a homogeneous entity. It no doubt covers a number of intellectual sub-streams with various priorities and various degrees of pragmatism."[68]

Jeffrey Cozzens finally solved the conundrum in 2005 when he observed that "al-Qaeda and its warfare are dualistic."[69] Drawing on the work of Christopher Coker, Cozzens argued that religion, culture, and ideology all shape the violence of al Qaida and the sympathetic groups that occupy its universe. In other words, for members of AQAM, violence expresses who they are: the mujahideen, slaves to God, seekers of martyrdom. For them, as for many others in history, "even suicide can be life affirming."[70] Given this realization, Cozzens believes that understanding the cultural, theological aspects of the "Global Salafi Jihad" is the single most important component of knowing the enemy. In fact, for many but not all members of AQAM, the sole merit of the undertaking is in the fighting, not in the changes it will wreak on the outside world. For those individuals, whom we call foot soldiers, fighting is not *instrumental*. That said, some members of AQAM think in instrumental terms as well, and so it is imperative also to study the functionalist, instrumental side of the enemy.[71]

Cozzens's insight deeply informs this book.[72] We suggest that all members of AQAM share similar noninstrumental tendencies, that they see themselves as mujahideen who thirst for martyrdom. However, some of them have to varying degrees submerged these inclinations in favor of a functionalist, instrumental, strategic approach to the struggle in which they find themselves. We call these jihadists "strategists."

The Dichotomy through the Enemy's Eyes

Some AQAM members recognize the difference between the strategists and foot soldiers in their midst. Jihadists themselves recognize a variety of reasons why their "brothers" fight, including to kill the enemy, to seek martyrdom, to establish an Islamic state, and to gain glory on earth. Al-Suri identified this phenomenon as having been present in Syria in the 1970s and 1980s.[73] Noninstrumentalism was also evident in the jihad against the Soviets in Afghanistan. A captured document written in about 1997 by a veteran of that war makes this clear. During the war against the Soviets, he wrote, "I was one of the minority [of] Arabs who dedicated themselves for the 'Afghani jihad.' . . . [For the rest,] martyrdom was closer to their hearts and many of them won that. I was more looking for the conquest. . . . I did not worry about martyrdom because it comes from

God. . . . Most Arabs surprisingly did not think about victory and they are still not thinking about it. Their interest is limited to martyrdom and the victory is from God."[74]

Sayf al-Adl, a senior al Qaida operations leader and former colonel in the Egyptian Army, noticed the same thing during Operation Enduring Freedom in Afghanistan: "The sweet smell of martyrdom . . . lit the fire of competition to become martyrs. . . . Many times I had to ask the leaders of the groups to restrain the fervor of the youngsters and not let them chase the enemy outside the realm of the set plan."[75] The leaders who attempted to keep their subordinates within "the realm of the set plan" were instrumental strategists; the youngsters competing to become martyrs were the noninstrumental foot soldiers.

The designations we use in this work, calling the instrumental fighters "strategists" and the noninstrumental fighters "foot soldiers," refer to the way these individuals think about their struggle, not to their position in a hierarchy or their degree of centrality in a network diagram. Though many strategists are senior leaders of AQAM, the unknown jihadist's diary from Iraq quoted above indicates the presence of some at the lowest rungs of the jihad who also see the world in instrumental terms. The words of Azmiray al-Maarek underscore this point. In late 2001, Osama bin Laden selected him for a suicide mission, thereby motivating him to write a joyful letter to his wife: "By the time you receive this will, I will be in the craws of birds, God willing, after having performed a martyrdom operation against the country of infidelity. This operation, God willing, will turn the tide for Islam and Muslims."[76]

Moreover, while a "strategist" may have no formal position in any terrorist group and may lead a sedentary life of contemplation, this need not prevent him from being a thought leader: a few are mujahideen of the pen, while others are mujahideen of the sword. Until his capture in late 2005, Abu Musab al-Suri, one of the leading thinkers in the movement, liked to portray himself (albeit probably falsely) as leading a solitary, academic existence writing on important military questions.[77] One highly complimentary observer described al Qaida propagandist Lewis Atiyatallah as unable to "live in the Tora Bora mountain caves separated from his keyboard or his copy of the *Financial Times*."[78]

The anonymous tract "Jihad in Iraq: Hopes and Dangers," which appeared on a popular jihadist Web site in late 2003, also illustrates this issue. Western analysts who discovered the tract debated whether it was an "authoritative" document written by a member of al Qaida.[79] Regardless of its author, the document is worth studying because whoever wrote it clearly was steeped in Salafi jihadist thought and possessed a keen strategic mind. The perpetrators of the 3/11 bombing in Madrid frequented the Web site where the document was posted and may have read it.[80] Others in the community probably read it as well and were in some way influenced by it. In other words, even without any formal al Qaida imprimatur, this document is now part of the AQAM intellectual milieu and its author is at the very least a minor thought leader.

The Foot Soldier's Perspective

Violent jihad is an inextricable, defining part of a foot soldier's life: many of the foot soldiers believe that they were specifically created to fight and die. For many, these feelings were inculcated very early in life. A young Arab, possibly not even in his teens, said on an inspirational video: "We are terrorists, and terror is our way. Let the oppressors . . . and their masters know that we are terrorists and that we frighten. 'Prepare what force and equipment you can to terrorize the enemy of God.' [Qur'anic reference] For terror is an obligation of the religion."[81] Others arrive at these feelings through conversion. "Khalid Kelly," an Irish-born convert, rhetorically asked a reporter in the summer of 2005, "How dare anyone come on television and say suicide bombings are not part of our belief? These [moderates] are the lunatic fringe."[82]

Whatever their personal circumstances, foot soldiers and strategists both understand jihad as a form of worship. The CISR characterizes jihad as "a mass worship religiously and a combat operation militarily."[83] By going on jihad, the foot soldiers are fulfilling their individual obligation to God. "I am directly responsible for protecting and avenging my Muslim brothers and sisters," Muhammad Siddiq, one of the London bombers, said in his "last will" video.[84]

While foot soldiers want Islam to triumph, they do not always perceive a particular connection between their personal actions and the realization of victory. Their military thought rarely rises above the tactical, and often it does not even reach that level. That fact may help explain why jihadists attack certain targets without an apparent rationale. In many cases, the reason may simply be "because they could." While the al Qaida leadership has always given operational commanders a great deal of latitude in target selection, too much indiscriminate targeting can alienate AQAM's base support, the "Muslim on the street."

Foot soldiers thirst for martyrdom—"I pray for death every day," a Pakistani jihadist told an American researcher—and some make attaining death the organizing principle of their lives.[85] They believe that being martyred guarantees them a privileged place in paradise and the company of seventy-two virgins, the *houris* (pure ones), whom they describe as beautiful and doe-eyed. It also allows them to intercede on behalf of relatives and friends, guaranteeing them a place in paradise as well. Amrozi, one of the Bali bombers, became known to the world media as the "smiling bomber" not only for his generally cheerful demeanor but also for his exultation when the court handed down his death sentence.[86] Similarly, jihadists often consider news that a fellow jihadist has died on a mission reason to celebrate because he has entered paradise. Indeed, bestowing wishes of martyrdom can become so ingrained that it becomes almost a reflexive social courtesy. For example, a man calling himself Wayn al-Shahadah posted the following on a Web site in early 2005: "Following is a wonderful research. I ask God to bless the author and bestow martyrdom on him. It is a beautiful research about shooting, written by our fraternal brother, Talut, May God protect him and grant him martyrdom. . . . Some fraternal brothers suggested that we publish the research in a jihadist journal. Thanks to God, we are publishing it in the *Al-Battar School*. We ask God to grant martyrdom to the one who made the suggestion, the author, and everyone. Say Amen."[87]

Though their influence should not be overemphasized, the sexual attractions of the seventy-two virgins who allegedly await a martyr are not lost on many foot soldiers. Documents describe jihadists literally dreaming of how beautiful blond girls will escort them to paradise, where they will revel in the presence of "flirtatious" virgins or even "72 beautiful and sexy celestial nymphs."[88] A captured motivational document approaches the problem from the other direction, pointing out in graphic terms the many shortcomings (both sexual and personal) of a wife. The implicit point is clear: the seventy-two virgins awaiting the mujahid in paradise are far superior, by every standard, to any earthly female.[89]

The majority of AQAM's foot soldiers doubtless live in the Islamic world, but many live in the West, often as the children or grandchildren of immigrants. Despite what might seem to be a vast chasm separating the thinking of these foot soldiers from the everyday life of the Western world, they are often culturally quite integrated into the societies in which they live. For instance, Mohammed Bouyeri, the killer of filmmaker Theo van Gogh, while certainly viewing himself as apart from Dutch society, was sufficiently "Dutch" to write his last will in Dutch in the form of a poem using traditional Dutch poetic structure.[90] That poem indicates that Bouyeri was seeking martyrdom: "This is my last word, felled by bullets, dipped in blood, as I had hoped."[91]

The case of Momin Khawaja is an even more interesting example, though his foot-soldier tendencies were adulterated in some ways by elements of a strategic outlook. Khawaja was a Pakistani-Canadian citizen arrested by authorities in 2004 for his alleged part in a plot to bomb London. He had many of the characteristics of a foot soldier. Two factors in particular appear to have played a major role in his decision to be martyred. The first was the rising anger he felt as he watched television coverage of Operation Enduring Freedom in Afghanistan. The second was his inability to find a wife despite first going to college and subsequently getting a white-collar job. In January 2004 he wrote on his blog site: "I'm going to get married in Janna. Yes, Paradise. Now the only thing left to do is to get there. I'm working on that part, InshaAllah."[92]

Khawaja, in fact, was a computer contractor working for the Canadian Foreign Ministry, and he was sufficiently attuned to local pop culture to have a blog site and to eat crullers ("yumminess factor, very high") at the neighborhood Tim Horton's.[93] Remarkably, his language in e-mails (written under his nickname, "YaS") recovered by the Canadian security services shows the true extent of his integration into North American popular culture while still seeing that culture as the other. "Sis, I just saw your recent blog post, *mashaAllah* that iz awesome!, are u into that kinda stuff too like supporting the Jihad and *Mujahideen*? man, I am so happy that muslim sistaz are into that and supportive cuz u know the way the world is split into two camps . . . one of *Iman* and anotha of *Kufr* (and that's the non-believers). The only solution for the *Ummah* and muslims is the Jihad against the *kuffar*. All out. *Wassalaam*, bro YaS."[94]

The archetypal case of an al Qaida holy warrior plucked directly from American popular culture is Aukai Collins, a blue-eyed, red-haired American who, according to his autobiography, *My Jihad*, was essentially a beach bum. He had a troubled youth marred by domestic violence. After a Samoan drug gang murdered his mother, he turned to crime and eventually found himself in jail, where he converted to Islam. Upon his release, he began attending a Tablighi Jamaat mosque. He soon came to the attention of jihadists, who persuaded him that, as a Muslim, he was obligated to go on jihad. After abortive attempts to get into the fray in Kashmir and Bosnia, he eventually found himself in Chechnya as part of Ibn al-Khattab's band, an appendage of AQAM. He lost a leg in combat and came home to the United States to recover, though he later returned to Chechnya for more fighting. Collins was clearly a dedicated jihadist whose first love was the fighting rather than its outcome. Evidently, the love of danger was in his veins; after he finally gave up the life of a mujahid, he worked as a bounty hunter in Mexico. In 2003, with his days as a jihadist behind him, he told a reporter, "I don't want to sound corny, but I consider myself a warrior."[95]

The Strategists' Perspective

AQAM's strategists subscribe to the same religious beliefs as their foot soldiers. They believe they are individually obligated to go on jihad, and they long to attain martyrdom and reap all the concomitant heavenly rewards. While they are on earth, however, they strive to attain victory, which entails uniting the *ummah* and restoring the Caliphate. Hence, their discourse is quite different from that of the foot soldiers. Abdullah Azzam, the founder of al Qaida, put it well when he wrote, "Undoubtedly, armed Evil must be taken on by armed Good. . . . Falsehood strengthened by numbers must be confronted by Truth garbed with preparation . . . otherwise it would be suicide, or jest not befitting Muslims."[96] Wayn al-Shahadah, at other times expressing strong foot-soldier tendencies, is of one mind with Azzam on this point: "A Muslim should never hesitate to prepare himself. He should not say: My enemy is a coward who fights from fortresses or behind walls. He should not say: I am Muslim. I do not fear death and therefore, I do not need to prepare myself."[97]

Strategists can certainly be found on the battlefield leading other jihadists against the "infidels" and the "apostates," or being led themselves. The most erudite among them, however, can also be found debating the finer points of Clausewitz or Mao, or discussing the influence of the works of Bernard Lewis on Samuel Huntington's *Clash of Civilizations* (see chapter 5).[98]

While most strategists value formal structures and organizations, these have not always been possible since the United States and its allies launched the war on terrorism. In particular, the most learned strategists and those who find themselves in the most senior positions place a premium on executing strategy, namely by controlling, calibrating, and channeling military, political, informational, and theological efforts so as to optimize progress toward their eventual goal.[99]

The raw material with which strategists execute their strategies, however, is mostly manpower: the foot soldiers who fight only to express their obedience to God, not to attain victory per se. Despite the necessity of having them around and the theological imperative of increasing their numbers, foot soldiers are often profoundly annoying to the strategists. This has been a continuing concern for the instrumentalists in AQAM since the days of the jihad against the Soviets in Afghanistan. In those days, Abdullah Azzam complained about the lack of education of the faithful who flocked to the battleground.[100] *The Arab Volunteers in Afghanistan*, published in 1991 by the World Association of Muslim Youth and Committee for Islamic Benevolence, notes quite frankly that the battle of Jaji with the Soviets in April 1987—the battle on which the reputation of the Arab mujahideen rests—was not all that it was cracked up to be: "Arab participation in the battle could not be called serious. The presence of so many of them without them fulfilling any function was a burden upon the mujahideen—and upon themselves. Therefore bin Laden decided to take most of them back."[101]

The book also notes that some of the Arab brothers "could not be easily made to stick to discipline" and that others became impatient during a lengthy period of positional warfare with little or no combat. They had come to fight, and they threatened to go home unless action was forthcoming. In the face of this pressure, the leadership—having first carefully calculated that it was feasible—arranged a battle just to keep the foot soldiers happy.[102] Sometimes, getting into battle is a mixed blessing from the viewpoint of the instrumentalist. A document captured in Abu Hafs's house in Kandahar attributes many casualties when fighting the Soviets to the mujahideen's "ignorance of military tactics [sic] rules or unwillingness to apply these rules."[103]

The nearby jihad in Tajikistan occasioned similar critiques. The same book describes the "two kinds of [Arab] volunteers for [the] Jihad movement in Tajikistan." Some were strong believers, obedient to sharia, brave, and patient. Others, however, were emotionally unstable, disputatious, rebellious, lazy, disorganized, inexperienced, and represented counterintelligence risks.[104] In a similar vein, an after-action report prepared by

Arab jihadists who had fought in Bosnia criticized "brother" foot soldiers for alienating the more secular Bosnian Muslims whom they were trying to help by, among other things, being disrespectful to Bosnian generals, rudely breaking liquor bottles, accosting couples walking down the street, and even seizing brides at gunpoint. Another point of criticism related to war crimes, especially decapitating prisoners. The strategists were not disturbed that the foot soldiers had committed these acts per se, rather that they had allowed themselves to be photographed doing so, thereby handing a potential propaganda victory to the other side.[105]

These complaints persist. Many operational commanders grumble about jihadists who arrive with the desire only to take a bullet in the head. Hence, many of the young volunteers coming to Iraq are considered "an additional burden" because they want to rush forward to martyrdom without considering that they might be able to make a more useful contribution later.[106]

The strategists believe that in order to attain victory they must stave off physical defeat at the hands of their enemy's coercive forces while simultaneously rallying the *ummah* to their banner. Given this, one of the most important measures of merit for AQAM's activities is whether they attract people to the movement or repel them. The strategists tend to have grave concerns that too many of the actions undertaken in the name of AQAM needlessly repel the very people AQAM is trying to attract. They fear that they are losing the battle for the "hearts and minds" of the *ummah* (see chapter 7).[107] Insufficient political savvy and the general tendency to engage in disjointed and ill-considered operations come together to create the particularly toxic problem of killing other Muslims.

Prominent among the ways in which experience has shown AQAM that it can inadvertently "separate from the masses" is by killing co-religionists. Here AQAM is on the horns of a dilemma. Innocent Muslims will from time to time be collateral damage in some terrorist attacks, and the nature of war makes occasional moral costs the price of doing business. Osama bin Laden himself recognized this brutal truth when he said in 1999, "When it becomes apparent that it would be impossible to repel these Americans without assaulting them, even if this involved the killing of Muslims, this is permissible under Islam."[108]

However, the willingness of those prosecuting a war to accept such costs does not lessen them; the bill must still be paid in terms of public support, no less by al Qaida than by the military forces of "infidels." The support of the people is not merely a theological requirement; its presence will bolster the movement; its lack will impede progress on the military track against the enemy's security and military forces. Sometimes political considerations also require forging tactical alliances, another process that can be impeded by the perception of wanton violence.

When the Muslim masses begin to perceive that such collateral damage is being inflicted wantonly (or even deliberately), the results can be catastrophic for the jihad. An al Qaida operative in the early 1990s warned that "a movement that is isolated from its masses, that is suspicious of its people, and whose people are suspicious of it, can achieve nothing but destroy itself."[109] Worse, the people may turn against the jihadists. Thinking along similar lines, Shaykh Abd-al-Aziz bin Rashid al-Anzi observed in 2006 that "the Muslim nation is the strategic depth of the mujahideen in the guerrilla warfare. It provides shelter, refuge, and camouflage during fighting. The Muslim masses are a source of information for the mujahideen. They gather information and help with monitoring and surveillance. Moreover, they provide the mujahideen with fighters and supplies that never end."[110]

Al-Zawahiri urged the movement to "avoid any action that the masses do not understand or approve, if there is no contravention of sharia in such avoidance, and as long as there are other options to resort to."[111] Al-Anzi likewise advised the mujahideen to "take the people's stance into consideration since it is one of the most influential factors in the war not only for support and sympathy but also for averting the reproaches of opponents."[112] Abu Ubayd al-Qurashi perceptively drew on the experiences of leftist Uruguayan urban guerrillas and enunciated the key principle that the insurgents must appear more attractive to the people than the government they are seeking to overthrow. He considered any action that had to be explained to the masses to be a failure.[113] Much to its chagrin, AQAM has repeatedly conducted operations that failed al-Qurashi's test. No event has made this a more pointed issue in the mind of the jihadist community than the horrific civil war in Algeria during the 1990s between an "apostate" regime and a succession of Salafi jihadist groups.

After the Algerian government nullified the 1991 elections, denying the Islamic Salvation Front (Front Islamique du Salut, or FIS) its share of power, the more radical Armed Islamic Group (Groupe Islamique Armé, or GIA) embarked on an orgy of killing Algerian citizens and foreigners in Algeria. The FIS denounced this development, and over time it became clear that the GIA was not only failing to achieve victory but was, in fact, increasingly alienating the fearful and horrified civilian population. A 1996 book on guerrilla warfare recovered in Afghanistan mentions the "negative effects" of attacks on civilians in Algeria and in Egypt, noting the "lack of a legal agreement on that action" and the resulting "political splits and disputes" and the increasing "isolation of the movement."[114]

As he recounted in *Knights under the Prophet's Banner*, Ayman al-Zawahiri also learned the lesson about the dangers of killing Muslims.[115] An unsuccessful assassination attempt by the EIJ on the Egyptian prime minister led to the death of a young girl named Shayma who happened to be standing in front of her nearby school when the bomb detonated. Al-Zawahiri described how the government very effectively spun the event, portraying it to the public as a dastardly attack on the girl. This event led al-Zawahiri to recommend paying blood money to the families of innocent bystanders killed in EIJ attacks.[116]

The May 2003 bombings of American compounds in Riyadh, which killed many Muslims, are a significant example as well. The bombings resulted in a strong backlash among the Saudi populace and forced the al Qaida–associated CISR to publish a book that tried "to explain the demands of jihadi activity in the Arabian Peninsula and to remove some of the ambiguities from the religious and military standpoints."[117]

Abu Musab al-Zarqawi, who posed a serious threat in this regard, was forced to talk a good line: "The American Muslim is our beloved brother and the infidel Arab is our dire enemy. . . . Every Muslim is our brother, whom we defend. Let Muslims everywhere know that we have not and will not kill a Muslim, whose life is protected, or spill forbidden blood, God forbid!"[118] Yet from the point of view of other leaders of the movement, al-Zarqawi filled his protestations with too many "weasel" words. Al-Zarqawi's former mentor, al-Maqdisi, criticized using car bombs and mortar explosions in Iraqi "streets and markets packed with Muslims" and attacks on Shiite mosques, and warned that the "pure hands of [the] mujahideen should not be stained by shedding inviolable blood." Such deeds "tarnished" the image of jihad. "The acts of ultra extremist groups are fresh in memory," al-Maqdisi wrote in a probable reference to Algeria; "beware of repeating these acts."[119]

Al-Zarqawi was unable or unwilling to take al-Maqdisi's advice. His attacks on hotels in Amman, Jordan, in November 2005 sharply divided the Salafi jihadist movement and horrified much of the *ummah* worldwide.

Popular demonstrations against al-Zarqawi ensued in Jordan, and contributors to extremist Web sites took him to task as well. One posting urged al-Zarqawi not to harm any more innocent Muslims. "This is both a [religious] task and a pragmatic tactic," the author wrote. "Acts where many innocent Muslims lose their lives make us lose a lot of popular support." "I swear to God it was a big mistake in which al Qaida will pay a heavy price," wrote another.[120] Similarly, an alarmed jihadist in Iraq wrote, probably in early 2006, that al Qaida in Iraq should be more discriminating in its violence: "Stop the killing of people unless they are spying, military, or police officers. We have to find a secure method because if we continue using the same method, people will start fighting us in the streets."[121]

Conclusion

In the final analysis, AQAM represents a large number of individuals united by a common theology, albeit with differing ethnic backgrounds, experiences, and perspectives on jihad. Such variances inevitably lead to different perspectives on organizational and strategic questions. Among Salafi jihadists who reflect on such questions, however, the view of AQAM as a global movement with a revolutionary vanguard at its head is the dominant perspective. That vision leads the thoughtful members of AQAM to be greatly frustrated with the foot soldiers, including even leaders such as Abu Musab al-Zarqawi, who exhibit strong just-do-it, nonstrategic tendencies and do not bother to act with due deference to these considerations. This tension between the instrumentalist strategists and the existentialist foot soldiers may be one of the greatest potentially exploitable seams within AQAM.

Notes

1. Quoted in Stephen Ulph, "Testimony to the Open Hearing of the Senate Select Committee on Intelligence," May 24, 2007, intelligence.senate.gov/070612/ulph. pdf, accessed July 24, 2007.
2. Paz, "Reading Their Lips," 2. See more on the discussion of amorphous AQ "membership" in chapter 8.
3. For a discussion of one al Qaida view of the typology of their supporters, see chapter 8.
4. FBIS EUP20050710031003, "Former Metropolitan Police Chief Says Britons Probably Planned London Attacks," *Sunday Times*, London, July 10, 2005.
5. FBIS EUP20040530000088, "Leaked Plans Outline Government's Agenda to Tackle Roots of UK-Islamic Terrorism," *Sunday Times*, London, May 30, 2004.

6. Pew Research Center, *Views of a Changing World: War with Iraq Further Divides Global Politics*, Washington, D.C., June 2003, 3, available at http://people-press. org/reports/display.php3?ReportID=185, accessed September 23, 2007.

7. Harmony document folder AFGP-2002-003251, *Abu Hudaifa Advises Usama bin Laden to Publicize al-Qaeda's Goals and Accomplishments through Effective Informational Media in Order to Rally Public Support and Invigorate al-Qaeda's Mission in Saudi Arabia*, July 20, 2000.

8. John Arquilla and David Ronfeldt, *The Advent of Netwar* (Santa Monica, Calif.: RAND, 1996).

9. Based on John Arquilla and David Ronfeldt, *Networks and Netwars: The Future of Terror, Crime, and Militancy* (Santa Monica, Calif.: RAND, 2001).

10. Hence, Imam Samudra, a convicted Bali bomber, talked about the need for Muslim hackers "to attack US computer networks"; FBIS SEP20041222000085, "Indonesia: Convicted Terrorist Calls for Computer Hacking, Jihad against US," Indonesia, FBIS Report in English, December 22, 2004. Other "jihadists" mention electrical power and television networks: FBIS GMP20041202000294, "Bahrain Group Posts New Threat; Brigade Threatens Iraqi Parties in Election," Jihadist Websites, FBIS Report in Arabic, December 2, 2004; Harmony document folder AFGP-2002-002883, *Abu Massab al-Soory's Computer Disks, PGP Program, Information about Taliban, and Computer Program, and a Discussion of Intelligence Collection Refers to a "Network of Agents."* See also Harmony document folder AFGP-2002-600172, *Intelligence Agent Recruitment, Training, and Testing. Target Selection. Operational Techniques*, no date, found at Abu Hafs's house in Kandahar. This document is substantially the same as a discussion of tactical intelligence by Sayf al-Adl published in *Al-Battar Camp* and disseminated by FBIS as FBIS GMP20041018000218, "Al-Qa'ida's Sayf al-Adl Defines 'Intelligence,'" Jihadist Websites, FBIS Report in Arabic, October 12, 2004.

11. Harmony document folder AFGP-2002-6000080.

12. FBIS GMP20031027000226.

13. Ibid.

14. Harmony document folder AFGP-2004-002509, *Islamic Freedom Movement Propaganda Letter*, late 2002–early 2003.

15. FBIS GMP20040209000243, "Compilation of Usama Bin Ladin Statements 1994—January 2004," in English, February 9, 2004.

16. FBIS GMP20040121000214, "Al-Qa'ida-Affiliated Magazine Analyzes Guerrilla Warfare," FBIS Report in Arabic, January 15, 2004.

17. Ulph, "Testimony to the Open Hearing of the Senate Select Committee on Intelligence."

18. FBIS GMP20031027000226.

19. Ibid.

20. Ibid.

21. FBIS GMP20021126000154, "Commentator Analyzes Recent bin Ladin Tapes, Sees US as Losing 'Information War' against al-Qa'ida," (Internet) *Al-Ansar*, November 20, 2002. See also FBIS GMP20020614000107, "Pro-al-Qa'ida Writer Expects Failure of US 'Crusade' against Jihad Movements," (Internet) *Al-Ansar*, June 12, 2002.

22. H. Brinton Milward and Jörg Raab, "Dark Networks as Problems Revisited: Adaptation and Transformation of Islamic Terror Organizations since 9/11," paper presented at the Eighth Public Management Research Conference at the School of Policy, Planning and Development at the University of Southern California, Los

Angeles, September 29–October 1, 2005; "Complexity and Social Networks Blog," www.iq.harvard.edu/blog/netgov/2006/03/brinto_milward_on_dark_network. html, accessed March 20, 2006.

23. Milward and Raab, "Dark Networks," 11–12.
24. Originally devised by several sociologists in the late 1970s and early 1980s; more recently, Aldon Morris offered an expanded process model; see Aldon Morris, "Reflections on Social Movement Theory: Criticisms and Proposals," *Contemporary Sociology* 29, no. 3 (2000): 445–54. A more dynamic model put forth by Doug McAdam, Sidney Tarrow, and Charles Tilly in 2001 is in *Dynamics of Contention* (Cambridge: Cambridge University Press, 2001).
25. See chapter 8 for more on the importance of mobilization to al Qaida.
26. This discussion on social movement theory was adapted from an unpublished research paper by Ens. Jacquelyn Bengfort, USN, "A Movement of Martyrs: Social Movement Theory and the Terrorist Threat," completed while she was a JAWD intern in 2006.
27. Milward and Raab, "Dark Networks," 29.
28. Arquilla and Ronfeld, *Networks and Netwar.*
29. Ibid.
30. FBIS GMP20040217000209, "Lewis Atiyatallah Predicts US Attack on Arab Peninsula," Saudi Arabia, in Arabic, January 23, 2004.
31. Harmony document folder AFGP-2002-000026, *Excerpt from a Book Entitled Introduction to Guerrilla Warfare,* November 1, 1999.
32. Ibid.
33. Harmony document folder AFGP-2002-003251.
34. "Substitution for the Testimony of Khalid Sheikh Mohammed," Defendant's Exhibit 941, *U.S. v. Moussaoui,* 8, www.rcfp.org/moussaoui/, accessed April 5, 2006.
35. Stephen P. Lambert, *The Sources of Islamic Revolutionary Conduct* (Washington, D.C.: Center for Strategic Intelligence Research, Joint Military Intelligence College, April 2005), 131.
36. FBIS SEP20060327311001, "Indonesia: Ba'asyir Interviewed on Never-Ending 'Fight' against US, Bali Bombing," Jamestown Foundation, in English, September 15, 2005.
37. Harmony document folder AFGP-2002-600083, *Basic Principles of the Jihad War in Tajikistan,* pre-2002.
38. FBIS GMP20021030000045, "Saudi Magazine Publishes 'Important Parts' of Usama bin Ladin's 'Will,'" *Al-Majallah,* London, October 22, 2002.
39. FBIS GMP20030214000152, "Islamist Site Posts Translation of Purported bin Ladin Audio Message," (Internet) *Waaqiah,* February 14, 2003. For a discussion of mental coping mechanisms that al Qaida and the Taliban used to come to terms with the loss of Afghanistan, see David Cook's fascinating article, "Recovery of Radical Islam in the Wake of the Taliban Defeat," *Terrorism and Political Violence* 15, no. 1 (2003): 31–56. Bin Laden's purported "last will," allegedly written during the battle of Tora Bora, elaborates on these catastrophic mistakes. That document nowhere suggests that God will not be victorious, merely that al Qaida and the Taliban have let God down and delayed the ultimate victory. See FBIS GMP20021030000045, "Saudi Magazine Publishes 'Important Parts' of Usama bin Ladin's 'Will.'"
40. Ladan Boroumand and Roya Boroumand, "Terror, Islam, and Democracy," *Journal of Democracy* 13, no. 2 (2002): 9–10. Azzam used an analogous concept, writing

in 1988 that the "[Islamic] movement will represent the spark that ignites the potential of the nation" (quoted in Paz, "Reading Their Lips," 5).

41. Qutb, *Milestones*.
42. FBIS GMP20020108000197, "Al-Sharq al-Awsat Publishes Extracts from Al-Jihad Leader al-Zawahiri's New Book," *Al-Sharq al-Awsat*, London, in Arabic, December 2, 2001; FBIS SAP20011007000086, "AFP Carries Text of Usama bin Ladin's Message Broadcast on Al-Jazeera TV," Hong Kong, AFP, October 7, 2001; see also FBIS GMP20021030000045; FBIS GMP20030122000038, "Commentator Faults US Identification of al-Qa'ida's 'Center of Gravity'; Sees Economy as US's Vulnerable 'Center of Gravity,'" (Internet) *Al-Ansar*, December 19, 2002.
43. Jarret Brachman and William McCants, "Harmony and Disharmony: Exploiting al-Qaida's Organizational Vulnerabilities," February 14, 2006, 2, http://ctc.usma.edu/aq/aq.asp.
44. Robert C. Tucker, "Lenin and Revolution," in *The Lenin Anthology* (New York: W. W. Norton, 1975), xxxix–xl. This section discusses Lenin's *What Is to Be Done?*
45. FBIS GMP20031027000226.
46. Ibid.
47. Ibid.
48. FBIS GMP20021208000059, "Al-Qa'ida Spokesman Abu-Ghayth Confirms Mombassa, Other Operations," (Internet) Jihad Online news network, December 8, 2002.
49. FBIS GMP20021014000148, "Al-Qa'ida Issues Statement under bin Ladin's Name on Afghan War Anniversary," (Internet) *Al-Qal'ah*, October 14, 2002.
50. For a discussion on leaderless resistance and virtual groups/networks, see Peter Chalk, "U.S. Environmental Groups and 'Leaderless Resistance,'" *Jane's Intelligence Review*, July 1, 2001; and, Jessica Stern, "The Protean Enemy," *Foreign Affairs* 82, no. 4 (2003): 27–40.
51. FBIS CEP20050318000153, "Dagestani Mojahedin Vow to Continue Jihad," Kavkaz-Tsentr News Agency, in Russian, March 18, 2005.
52. FBIS GMP20050630514005, "Saudi Writer Says al-Qa'ida in Saudi Arabia Collapsing as Leaders Killed," *Abha al-Watan*, June 30, 2005.
53. We are indebted to Jeffrey B. Cozzens for sharing this idea with us; it is the central idea of his forthcoming doctoral dissertation. For the initial published version of his work, see Jeffrey B. Cozzens, "Approaching al-Qaeda's Warfare: Function, Culture and Grand Strategy," in *Mapping Terrorism Research: State of the Art, Gaps and Future Direction*, ed. Magnus Ranstorp (London: Routledge, 2007), 127–63.
54. Lee Harris provided this neat bracketing of the instrumental school of thought in "Al Qaeda's Fantasy Ideology: War without Clausewitz," *Policy Review*, August–September 2002, 21.
55. Anonymous (Michael Scheuer), *Imperial Hubris: Why the West Is Losing the War on Terror* (Washington, D.C.: Brassey's, 2004), 114.
56. S. P. Huntington, "Al-Qaeda: A Blueprint for International Terrorism in the Twenty-first Century?" *Defence Studies* 4, no. 2 (2004): 229.
57. Bruce Hoffman, "The Leadership Secrets of Osama bin Laden," *Atlantic Monthly*, April 2003, 26. Journalist Peter Bergen also portrayed bin Laden as the CEO of a multinational corporation in *Holy War, Inc.* (New York: Free Press, 2001).
58. Ryan Thornton, "Changing the Game: Assessing al Qaeda's Terrorist Strategy," *Harvard International Review* 27, no. 3 (Fall 2005): 36–37.

59. Brian Michael Jenkins, "Looking for 'High Noon' in a Hundred Years War," at www.rand.org/commentary/082204SDUT.html, accessed September 22, 2007. Jenkins's commentary originally appeared in the *San Diego Union Tribune*, August 22, 2004.
60. Quoted in Anonymous (Michael Scheuer), *Imperial Hubris*, 106.
61. Harris, "Al Qaeda's Fantasy Ideology," 23.
62. Ibid., 26.
63. Ibid., 29–30.
64. Lambert, Sources of Islamic Revolutionary Conduct, 8–17.
65. Wolffsohn, "A German View."
66. Ibid.
67. FBIS GMP20040728000229, "Jihad in Iraq: Hopes and Dangers," Iraq-FBIS Report in English, July 28, 2004.
68. Brynjar Lia and Thomas Hegghammer, "Jihadi Strategic Studies: The Alleged al-Qaeda Policy Study Preceding the Madrid Bombings," *Studies in Conflict and Terrorism* 27, no. 5 (2004): 371.
69. Cozzens, "Approaching al-Qaeda's Warfare," 128.
70. Christopher Coker, *Waging War without Warriors? The Changing Culture of Military Conflict* (Boulder, Colo.: Lynne Rienner, 2002), 9.
71. Cozzens, "Approaching al-Qaeda's Warfare," 137.
72. We do not, however, claim that Cozzens endorses this work. No opprobrium should attach to him for any misunderstanding on our part of his work, or for our extension of his work to areas to which he might not think it applies.
73. Harmony document folder AFGP-2002-600080.
74. See Harmony document folder AFGP-2002-600098, *64 Pages of Historical Overview of the Events in Afghanistan during the Soviet Invasion and the Early Days of Establishing al Qaida*, "Chat from the Top of the World Number 6"; Including *al Qaida's Ties to Egyptian Jihad*, January 1, 1998.
75. Intel Center, *Al-Qaeda's Advice for Mujahideen in Iraq: Lessons Learned in Afghanistan*, vol. 10, April 14, 2003, www.intelcenter.com.
76. "Letters from a Young Martyr," *Atlantic Monthly*, September 2004, 66.
77. FBIS GMP20050201000226.
78. FBIS GMP20050221000155, "Saudi Academic Discusses Background of Jihadist Writer Lewis Atiyatallah," *Al-Quds al-Arabi*, London, February 19, 2005, 19.
79. Jay Tolson, "Cracking al Qaeda's Code," *US News & World Report*, May 17, 2004.
80. FBIS EUP20050307000211, "Spanish Daily Reports on Content of Computer of Madrid Bombers," *La Razon*, March 7, 2005.
81. "Generation Jihad: New Video Includes Saudi Children Advocating Terrorism against the U.S. and Saudi Governments," *Global Issues Report*, August 9, 2005, reporting on a video posted on Tajdid.org.uk, August 8, 2005, entitled "Cubs of the Land of the Two Sanctuaries."
82. Brandon and Thorne, "The Sidewalk Where Terror Breeds."
83. On this point, see also Abou Moussaab Abdelwadoud, GSPC leader, in FBIS GMP20051107711005, "Algerian Salafist Group Leader Interviewed on Peace Referendum, Other Issues," *Al-Hayah*, London, November 7, 2005.
84. FBIS GMP20050901535005.
85. The American researcher was Jessica Stern. See her work *Terror in the Name of God: Why Religious Militants Kill* (New York: HarperCollins, 2003).

86. See, for example, "2003: Bali Bomber Smiles at Guilty Verdict," http://news. bbc.co.uk/onthisday/hi/dates/stories/august/7/newsid_3910000/3910569.stm, accessed September 23, 2007.

87. FBIS GMP20050214000276, "Participant Poses Scenarios for Attacking US Interests, Posts US Army Blood Donation Contest Poster," Jihadist Websites, FBIS Report, February 5, 2005.

88. The first quote is from a Muslim blog. The discussion thread cited is titled "Profiles of Ash Shuhadaa" and can be found under the name of Yahya Senyor al-Jeddawi, a *shaheed* (martyr) killed in Afghanistan in 1985. His eulogy, posted on this site, was written by Sheikh Abdullah Azzam. See http://*ummah*.net/ forum/showthread.php?t=5062, accessed March 7, 2007. The second quote is from the Center for International Issues Research, "Indonesian Militant Recruitment Briefing," December 23, 2004.

89. David Cook, "Women Fighting in Jihad?" *Studies in Conflict and Terrorism* 28 (2005): 378.

90. Nesser, "The Slaying of the Dutch Filmmaker."

91. "Dutch Authorities Report Increase in Islamist Radicalization," *Jane's Intelligence Review*, February 1, 2005.

92. Ontario Court of Justice, *Her Majesty the Queen v. Mohammed Momin Khawaja*, Proceedings, vol. 1, May 3, 2004, 23.

93. Blog entry, December 27, 2003, http://klashinaat.blogspot.com/2003_12_01_ klashinaat_archive.html. The Web site is no longer active.

94. Ontario Court of Justice, 2004, 19; text as written.

95. Aukai Collins, *My Jihad* (Guilford, Conn.: Lyons Press, 2002). See also "An American Fighter's War in Chechnya," www.chechentimes.org/en/people/?id=3024, accessed March 2, 2006; and Seth Hettena, "Islamic Convert Tells Tales of Extremists and the FBI," www.berkeleydailyplanet.com/article.cfm?archiveDate=07-01-02&storyID-13102 as cached by Google on January 7, 2006.

96. Azzam, *Join the Caravan*.

97. FBIS GMP20050214000276.

98. FBIS GMP20030122000038; FBIS SEG20040602000101; Harmony document folder AFGP-2002-600085, *Jihad in Tajikistan, Afghanistan and Other Obstacles Faced in Jihad; Strategy, Tactics, and Operational Concerns; Military and Political*, mid-1990s; Abu 'Ubeid Al-Qurashi, "Special Dispatch Series—No. 344," February 10, 2002, summarizing "Fourth-Generation Wars" in the second issue of AQ's online magazine, *Al-Ansar*. William McCants and Jarret Brachman of the U.S. Military Academy's Combating Terrorism Center described al-Qurashi as "part of a growing subset of Jihadi Theorists we call Jihadi Strategists since their primary intellectual output is secular, analytical studies of the strengths and weaknesses of the Jihadi Movement and the Western governments that oppose them" (*Militant Ideology Atlas*, 9). One example of this influence is Abu Bakr Naji's suggestion in his *Management of Savagery* that all mujahideen should read al-Qurashi's work in *Al-Ansar*. FBIS GMP20030929000003.

99. For more details on the evolution of their thinking on how to do this, see chapter 5.

100. Azzam, *Join the Caravan*.

101. Adel Batterjee, also known as Basil Mohammed, *The Arab Volunteers in Afghanistan* (published under the auspices of the World Assembly of Muslim Yourth [WAMY] and the Committee for Islamic Benevolence, 1991), document 15183, Rohan Gunaratna's International Centre for Political Violence and Terrorism Research database, accessed October 15, 2007.

102. Ibid.
103. Harmony document folder AFGP-2002-600085.
104. Ibid. Also see Harmony document folder AFGP-2002-800560, *Applications to Join the Mujaheedin of Tajikistan Islamic Resistance at Al-Farooq Camp,* 1994, for a series of assessments of specific Tajik recruits.
105. FBIS GMP20011120000057, 5.
106. Jamestown Foundation, *Terrorism Focus 2,* no. 13 (2005), citing a Syrian mujahideen Web site, www.nnuu.org.
107. Al-Zawahiri, Naji, and al-Suri all used "hearts and minds" in the same sense that Americans use it. FBIS EUP20051012374001. See Harmony document folder AFGP-2002-6000080.
108. FBIS GMP20040209000243, "Compilation of Usama bin Ladin Statements 1994–January 2004." This particular quotation is from a *Time* magazine article published January 11, 1999.
109. Harmony document folder AFGP-2002-600053, 1993, 1.
110. GMP20060328336001, "Terrorism: Al-Qa'ida-Affiliated Book Sets Rules for Attacking Economic, Oil Interests," Jihadist Websites, OSC Report in Arabic, March, 28, 2006.
111. FBIS EUP20051012374001.
112. FBIS GMP20060328336001.
113. See Abu Ubayd al-Qurashi, "A Strategic Study of the Pioneer Experience of the Commandos War inside the Cities," in Harmony document folder ISGZ-2005-00000898, *Various Researches on Explosives and Instructions to Educate Resistant Groups on Making Bombs,* 2005.
114. Harmony document folder AFGP-2002-000026.
115. FBIS GMP20011207000085, "Part Six of New Book by Egyptian Islamic Jihad Leader Ayman al-Zawahiri," *Al-Sharq al-Awsat,* London, in Arabic, December 7, 2001, 6–7.
116. Jarret M. Brachman and William F. McCants discussed this incident and the "Shayma effect" in their article "Stealing al-Qaida's Playbook," *Studies in Conflict and Terrorism* 29, no. 4 (2006): 309–21.
117. FBIS GMP20031004000119.
118. FBIS GMP20040623000072, "Al-Qa'ida's al-Zarqawi Threatens to Kill Iraqi Prime Minister Allawi," also part of FBIS Report "Compilation of al-Qai'da Leadership Statements," November 1993–June 2004.
119. FBIS GMP20050601712008, "Part 7 of Serialized Book on al-Zarqawi and al-Qa'ida Published," *Al Quds al-Arabi,* London, in Arabic, May 20, 2005, 17. Other counterproductive operations include Jemaah Islamiyah's Bali nightclub bombings.
120. Maamoun Youssef, "Islamic Web Sites, Known for al-Qaida Support, Criticize Group's Strategy in Jordan bombings," November 14, 2005, http://news.tmcnet.com/news/2005/nov/1204467.htm, Associated Press story, accessed April 10, 2006.
121. Harmony document folder IZ-060316-02, *Instructions to Abu Osamah,* captured in Iraq, also posted at USMA CTC Web site, http://ctc.usma.edu/aq/pdf/IZ-060316-02-Trans.pdf, accessed September 22, 2007.

CHAPTER 3

Intelligence

THE HIDDEN HAND AND IRON FIST

It is understood in war that the lack of knowledge about the enemy is the inevitable beginning of defeat.

ABU UBAYD AL-QURASHI, 2002[1]

The Jordanian Intelligence service has kept its eyes and ears on the knights of Islam and exerted serious efforts to pursue them in all fields of Jihad.

ABU MUSAB AL-ZARQAWI, 2004[2]

Knowing Their Enemies

The bridge between AQAM's view of itself and its perceptions of its enemies is intelligence. Intelligence plays the role of informing the movement's strategic and operational decisions, while counterintelligence and security efforts shape both their internal and external perceptions and operations.[3] Salafi jihadists receive practical schooling in intelligence through their constant interactions with hostile intelligence services, particularly the internal security services in their own countries. At the same time, they also draw heavily on the Qur'an to define the theoretical necessity and morality of intelligence, especially espionage. Notably, AQAM sees intelligence as a form of power in itself, and to some degree engages in a process that might reasonably be called strategic intelligence.

For AQAM's leaders, Western intelligence agencies and their models of intelligence are at once subjects for dread, emulation, and ridicule. In their camps and online publications, the Salafi jihadists teach the history and methods of intelligence tradecraft perfected by countries they despise and against which they have declared war.[4] In other words, jihadist leaders have determined that in order to defeat the Zionist-Crusader enemy, they must know the enemy—to the extent that their religious worldview allows.

For jihadists from the Middle East and North Africa, *intelligence* and *security* are essentially synonymous. The domestic security service, al-Mukhabarat, is both the hidden hand and the iron first of the repressive "apostate" regimes that vigorously hunt them down.[5] Indeed, many of the current AQAM strategists spent time either in prison or in exile as a result of security services' efforts.[6]

Jihadists' ascription of evil intentions, vast power, and grand conspiracies to enemy intelligence organizations—stereotypically the CIA and Mossad—marries their worldview of the degenerate and manipulative West with their own unpleasant history dealing with repressive "apostate" security services. This helps to explain why they are nomadic as they wage holy war across the globe: jihad is seldom possible under the watchful eye of their own countries' intelligence services. For example, Abu Musab al-Suri's compilation of lessons learned on the Syrian jihad recounts the disastrous attempt in the late 1970s and early 1980s to attack head-on the Baathist regime in Damascus. The result was a total defeat inflicted on the coalition of Salafi jihadists and the Muslim Brotherhood by Syrian state security acting in concert with the army, ending in a bloodbath at Hama in 1982.[7] Fifteen years later, Hazim al-Madani pointed to bloody confrontations with the security services as among the mistakes that led the movement to repeated defeats during the past thirty years.[8]

Tenacious Arab counterintelligence services, while lacking the finesse and technical acumen of their Western counterparts, are nonetheless skilled at penetration and provocation. They have repeatedly cracked down on Salafi jihadist activities since the late 1970s, customarily with considerable effectiveness. The result is that "home turf" has become a virtual denied area for group after group. The experience in Egypt has been particularly painful for the jihadists. Aggressive, coordinated counterattacks by Egyptian state security in recent memory—after the 1981 assassination of President Anwar Sadat and following the 1997 brutal assaults on Western tourists—did great damage to the local Salafi jihadist movement and effectively neutered EIJ and the EIG for several years by forcing key members (including Ayman al-Zawahiri) into jail or exile. Although

Cairo has probably overstated the success of its counterintelligence arm against al Qaida, Egyptian state security (like that of Syria and others of the region) has strong cultural advantages as well as determination, and has been an almost unstoppable force opposing AQAM domestically. In short, radical Salafists' fears of al-Mukhabarat appear entirely justified.

The Algerian Jihad

Al Qaida propagandists make few laudatory references to the Algerian jihad of the 1990s, in contrast to other current or recent campaigns such as Afghanistan, Bosnia, Chechnya, Kashmir, and Iraq. This can be attributed in part to the failure of local jihadists, principally the GIA, to destroy the secular state. Algerian security forces defeated the jihadists completely. A GIA splinter-cum-successor group, the Salafist Group for Preaching and Combat (Groupe Salafiste pour la Prédication et le Combat, or GSPC, recently renamed al-Qaida in the Islamic Maghreb), remains an active terrorist organization and has even publicly declared fealty to al Qaida, yet the GSPC is not the threat to the Algerian state that the GIA was in the mid-1990s. AQAM's reluctance to openly embrace and hail Algerian "brothers" can also be traced to the appalling atrocities perpetrated by Algerian jihadists, including widespread massacres of civilians that discredited the GIA by the late 1990s.[9] Instigated by the jihadists, the Algerian civil war claimed as many as 200,000 lives. Much of this violence was brought on by "ignorant and inexperienced" leaders (in the words of Abu-Bakr Naji) who adopted an "unjust rule"—namely, "everyone who is not with us is against us."[10]

Underscoring AQAM's valid reasons for fearing the power of "apostate" regimes are indications that Algerian security services helped discredit the jihad by employing undercover units of army special forces that perpetrated acts of terrorism, including massacring civilians, that were subsequently blamed on the GIA.[11] The Algerian public—the GIA's potential recruiting base—was repulsed and disgusted. So, too, were some of the GIA's own allies. Abu Musab al-Suri was involved in the Algerian campaign for a time, but after 1996 he had to "disassociate [himself] from everyone who deviated from the right path and assailed Muslims as a result of the deceit of the Algerian intelligence."[12]

Algerian intelligence officials have confirmed that the struggle against the GIA was indeed a "dirty war," and they have provided convincing evidence that Algeria's feared Sécurité Militaire helped create the GIA in 1992–93, at the onset of the civil war, with the aim of controlling and discrediting the jihadists.

Several of the GIA's top emirs—those responsible for some of the worst atrocities, including terrorist attacks on Westerners in Algeria and Europe—appear to have been agents provocateurs under government control.[13] Thus, AQAM's fears regarding "apostate" security services were particularly valid in 1990s Algeria.

There is a substantial body of AQAM literature on intelligence from the strategists' perspective, but what does intelligence mean to the movement's foot soldiers? Al-Maqdisi shed some light on this complex question. Writing in *Al-Battar Camp*, he cited examples of "recklessness" through "pre-Islamic" actions by some foot soldiers in the ranks.[14] He complained that these arrogant, negligent young men initially reject advice about operational security, for instance not heeding advice to act in moderation and practice concealment; however, once captured, they undergo a rapid change of heart and mind: "Following their calamity, such people usually become fearful of their own shadow in face of modern technology. They become so terrified of the dreadful capabilities and intelligence of God's enemy that discovered their unhidden weapons and bombs. Meanwhile, God's enemy would laud their security departments and attribute the failure of these men to the cleverness, judiciousness, and power of their intelligence services rather than the foolishness and negligence of these men."[15] Thus, intelligence once again proves its dual nature in a strategist's mind: it seems to be a powerful weapon in the hands of the state, though in reality it merely relies on the foolish mistakes of the jihadists' enemies. If the jihadists could only act with more common sense by employing sensible security practices, they would prove that the power of "apostate" and "infidel" intelligence is ultimately an illusion.

Defining and Validating Intelligence

Those in the Salafi jihadist movement view spying as both a "religious duty and human necessity."[16] The *Al Qaeda Manual* says that "spying on the enemy is permitted and it may even be a duty in the case of war between Moslems and others."[17] The manual even goes so far as to assert that spying is sanctioned only for Islam: "Since Islam is superior to all human conditions and earthly religions, it permits spying for itself but not for others."[18] Ideally, in the new Caliphate there will be no need to spy on Muslims; intelligence efforts will be directed only at enemies.[19]

Divine guidance is never far from the minds of jihadist strategists, and they find ample justification for intelligence in the core works of all Salafist beliefs: the Qur'an and the Sunnah. The *Al Qaeda Manual*'s chapter on espionage revealingly begins with the refrain: "The prophet—Allah bless and keep him—used informants in most of his attacks. . . . In his attacks, the prophet—Allah bless and keep him—would find out the enemy's intention. . . . The prophet—Allah bless and keep him—had local informants in Mecca who told him everything, big and small, that might harm the Muslim's welfare."[20]

Similarly, the EIG manual *Security and Intelligence*, captured in late 2001 at AQ military commander Abu Hafs al-Masri's safe house in Kandahar, offers several examples of supporting evidence from the Qur'an:

1. Intelligence is one type of force that Allah has ordered us to prepare. He said, "Prepare for them as much force as you can to intimidate Allah's enemies and yours." One of the requirements of preparing force is gathering information about the enemies' political, military, and cultural situations.
2. Intelligence and gathering information bridge security gaps . . . similar to what was mentioned in the story of the hoopoe with Prophet Solomon. . . .[21]
3. Intelligence aims at hurting the enemy and foiling their plans. Allah said, "Any step they take to upset the infidels or to hurt the enemy will be rewarded by Allah via granting them a righteous deed." Hurting the enemy can be done by destroying his economy, establishments and so forth.
4. Intelligence protects the state and its institutions from the enemy by being alert and cautious with the help of vanguards and surveillance. Allah says, "The infidels wish to see you neglect your arms and belongings in order to deal a collective massive blow to you."[22]

Most of the examples of the Prophet's use of intelligence are tactical in nature. All the same, it is clear that through his extensive reliance on spies and informants the Prophet Muhammad left a timeless and apparently divinely sanctioned legacy that still informs the higher-level intelligence functions of Salafi jihadists. The Prophet's own intelligence history drives today's fighters to desire effective operational security and to know as much about the enemy as possible before acting.

Though their terminology differs, AQAM's understanding of the necessity of strategic intelligence is similar to Western views. Intelligence in the global jihad should provide a broad awareness of the world and specifically targeted countries, counter enemy intentions, ensure that offensive actions strike the enemy where they are vulnerable, and fill an information void that might otherwise leave the movement open to attack.

Al Qaida's security chief, Sayf al-Adl, a former officer of the Egyptian Army, offered a practical definition of intelligence and where it comes from: "Information is available everywhere. Your normal talk contains information. If a piece of information has a value it becomes what is called intelligence. A good intelligence person is someone who realizes the importance of an ordinary piece of information and turns it into intelligence, such as the 'license plates of embassy vehicles.' The word refers to information picked up by an informant and delivered to an intelligence agency."[23]

Echoing Western discussions on the merits and advantages of various types of intelligence, the *Al Qaeda Manual* states that the information has two general sources:

1. Public Source: Using this public source openly and without resorting to illegal means, it is possible to gather at least 80% of information about the enemy. The percentage varies depending on the government's policy on freedom of the press and publication. . . .
2. Secret Sources: It is possible, through these secret and dangerous methods, to obtain the 20% of information that is considered secret.[24]

Abu Fath al-Pastuni used a similar typology in his book *Gerilya*, published in Indonesia in 2004: "Broadly speaking, there are two sources of data and information—open sources and closed sources. Open sources are free sources of news and data such as television, the Internet, books, magazines, dailies, journals, and working papers. Closed sources are sources of information obtained covertly or secretly. This information comes mainly from agents infiltrated into an enemy."[25]

Numerous captured and open source documents refer to the specific need for aggressive infiltration and penetration of opponents and adversaries as part of a larger intelligence effort. Abu Bakr Naji, for instance, stressed the importance of broad and redundant infiltration: "It is necessary to infiltrate police forces, armies, and various political parties, newspapers, Islamic groups, oil companies (working as laborers or engineers), private security firms, and sensitive civic institutions, and so forth. Indeed, we started this activity decades ago, but now we need to do more in light of recent developments. We also need to infiltrate the same place with more than one member, who do not know each other, to carry out different roles or even the same role, if this role requires more than one person."[26]

It is difficult to gauge the extent to which AQAM infiltrates agents into its enemy's camp, as the evidence itself is anecdotal and the scope of this problem is inadequately understood. Nevertheless, it is clear that AQAM aims to infiltrate; moreover, it has done so successfully not only in numerous Arab and Muslim entities but also in the U.S. military. Most notable, perhaps, is the case of Ali Mohammed, a former Egyptian Army officer who immigrated to the United States, joined the U.S. Army in 1986 as a permanent resident alien, and eventually became a supply sergeant assigned to the Army's John F. Kennedy Special Warfare Center and School at Fort Bragg. While serving there, he reportedly took leave to fight in the jihad against the Soviets in Afghanistan. After an honorable discharge from the Army, he is said to have become an FBI informant at the same time that he was giving military training to Islamic radicals in the New York area, some of whom were later convicted for their involvement in the 1993 bombing of the World Trade Center and other plots.[27] Mohammed's military skills contributed significantly to Afghan training camp curricula, and he is probably the officer referred to in a captured document on the early history of al Qaida. "The major dangerous training in the Arabian training in Afghanistan came from the Egyptian officer 'Hanzalah' who carries the American citizenship and worked in the American Army for a period of his professional life and precedent by Egyptian jihad to train his skills in Afghanistan. He trained numbers of the most important military leadership for that organization and they trained all human resources of Jihad organization operating in Egypt. Al Qaeda gained the same training benefits from 'Hanzalah' because of the organizational merging with Egyptian jihad as we explained earlier."[28]

In addition, there is solid evidence that AQAM thinks in terms of offensive counterintelligence (agent operations or provocations to disrupt and diminish the effectiveness of the enemy's intelligence) as well as defensive. The case of Munib Zahiragic is instructive in this regard. A Bosnian Muslim, Zahiragic worked for the Bosnian Foreign Ministry in the early 1990s and made the acquaintance in Kuwait of Enaam Arnaout, an al Qaida activist and financier who had been a close associate of bin Laden since the later years of the Afghan jihad. Arnaout, in turn, ran the Illinois-based Benevolence International Foundation, among other al Qaida fronts, which supported the movement's Afghan and Bosnian jihads. Probably under Arnaout's direction, Zahiragic joined the Bosnian secret service in 1995, and during the next five years passed large amounts of classified information to al Qaida via Arnaout. When he was arrested in 2002 on espionage charges, Zahiragic had at his residence about one hundred classified Bosnian secret service documents, including information about Sarajevo's intelligence relations with Western governments. While the extent of Zahiragic's activities remains unknown, it is clear that al Qaida gained access to large quantities of secret materials through him. It is likely that al Qaida used this information to protect mujahideen in Bosnia wanted by local and Western authorities. The regular appearance through 2005 of highly classified intelligence reports (e.g., agent and personnel information and details on the Bosnian secret service's links to American intelligence) in Sarajevo media outlets close to Salafi jihadism—most notably *Saff*, the magazine of the Active Islamic Youth, a Bosnian AQAM front—is evidence that AQAM sympathizers continued to penetrate the Bosnian secret service.[29]

Intelligence as a Necessary Source of Power

In 2005, interviewers asked Abu Bakr Ba'asyir about the conditions required for Islam to be strong. He responded, "If there is a state, the infidel country must be visited and spied upon."[30] This observation reflects a widely held view that, whether the purpose is offensive or defensive, intelligence should be an intrinsic element of Islamic power. According to some strategic thinkers within AQAM, this centrality of intelligence to operations and planning is problematic due to the movement's deficient intelligence capabilities.[31]

The captured EIG manual *Security and Intelligence* is particularly instructive in this regard. The manual's unidentified author was candid about the weakness of "Islamic" intelligence vis-à-vis the West; however, he took pride in the Prophet Muhammad's robust intelligence system, which allowed for the rapid expansion of Islam in the seventh and eighth centuries CE and "was used on a wide scale, especially by the Mogul, during the Crusades, and the Ottoman Caliphate."[32] The loss of this alleged pan-Islamic intelligence apparatus with the end of the Caliphate in 1924 constituted a crippling blow from which Muslims have yet to recover: "Our intelligence system did not see the light after the collapse of the Islamic Caliphate. It is still controlled by sources and cowards who are from our people, speak our language, and claim that they are Muslims although Islam has nothing to do with them."[33] The current situation is even more humiliating because "the politics, the economy, the military and the rest of vital fields are under the control of the world intelligence community. Muslims do not have any role in these fields except subordinating, yielding, and imitating."[34] On this point especially the manual's author was not alone in attributing much of what goes on in the world to the "hidden hand" of the powerful intelligence services that wield the weapon of information to keep down Muslims.

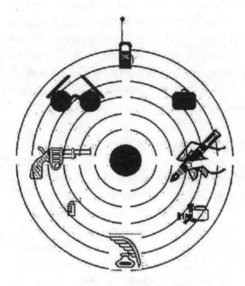

Graphic from EIG manual *Security and Intelligence. Source*: Harmony document folder AFGP-2002-002857.

The manual's author likewise recognized that modern science and technology play a role in creating this power gap: "The international community is using nowadays modern means in dealing with its friends as well as its enemies in order to have the upper hand and know how the world revolves around it. Intelligence systems played an important role in achieving these functions."[35] Specifically, the author observed Islamic weakness in the field of technical intelligence, such as "listening, photographing, recording, early warning, and satellites."[36] Regardless, jihadists must eliminate this disparity in power: "[Allah] ordered us to challenge this evil and its masters by material force and . . . by the force of faith and this religion."[37] The solution is an Islamic-based intelligence system to rival the West's: "If the Muslim nation wants sovereignty, leadership, independence, and prominence, it must have a special and distinguished intelligence system. This system must be capable of lifting the nation from its fall and weakness to look around at the world around it."[38]

Before his 2004 death in a battle with Saudi police, the emir of Saudi al Qaida, Abd-al-Aziz al-Muqrin, expressed a similar view, writing: "It is extremely important to establish an Islamic intelligence agency to be responsible for recruiting individuals, protecting the organization from penetration, and devising security plans for individuals, leaders, and installations."[39] Abu-Bakr Naji, author of a 2005 Center for Islamic Studies and Research (CISR) book outlining a phased strategy for the global jihad (paraphrased below), noted that the future Islamic state will require an intelligence system: "The mujahideen will take control and manage the anarchy resulting from the previous phase. During this period, they will preserve the security of the area under their control [which includes, among other things] establish[ing] an intelligence system . . . and improv[ing] the administrative abilities in preparation for the establishment of the Islamic State."[40]

The Abu Sayyaf Group (ASG) in the Philippines also agrees. A 2004 document entitled *Mini Manual of the Urban Mujahideen* says:

> The creation of a Muslim intelligence service with an organized Jihad structure is a basic need for us. The urban Mujahid has to have essential information about the plans and movements of the *Taghut* [anyone who ascribes to himself any of the rights of Allah, such as legislation] enemy, where they are, and how they move, the resources of the ribaa [interest] banking network, the means of communication, and the secret moves the Taghut enemy makes. The trustworthy information passed along to the urban Mujahideen represents a well-aimed blow at the Taghut government.[41]

Views of Enemy Intelligence

AQAM's strategists agree on the urgent need for an Islamic intelligence service. What to do about the intelligence power currently in the hands of the hated "infidels" in the West and in "apostate" Muslim countries is another matter entirely. Al Qaida strategists, including bin Laden and al-Zawahiri, have expressed strong views on counterintelligence concerns. Veterans of the Afghan jihad of the 1980s learned security and counterintelligence fundamentals in a hard school, waging a shadowy struggle against Soviet intelligence that cost the lives of many mujahideen. Soviet penetration of their camps and units, including the establishment of fake or pseudo-jihadist groups with missions to confuse, disrupt, and kill, was particularly effective. The acute awareness of enemy intelligence efforts persisted in al Qaida's Afghan training camps in the late 1990s.[42] A pre-9/11 document captured in Afghanistan contains a prioritized al Qaida "enemies list" that includes "1. Enemy's Intelligence (USA, Saudi Arabia, Egypt, Pakistan, the Jews)."[43]

There can be no doubt that AQAM views American intelligence as a powerful enemy. U.S. intelligence lacks the cultural awareness and sheer ruthlessness of Arab services but can compensate with technical acumen and vast resources. Nonetheless, AQAM thinks it is important to keep its followers from being intimidated into inaction by the power of its enemies. Bin Laden, for instance, lamented: "The infidels, the Russians and the Americans, have so much impacted the minds of Muslims, making them believe that they [the infidels] are indefatigable super powers, that they have all kinds of gadgets and intelligence and stuff of that type. Most of that is inflated and far from true. If people were to believe in those exaggerations they would stop moving."[44]

Such concerns have produced a genre of AQAM literature that, in essence, holds American intelligence up to ridicule. One prominent example is Muhammad Khalil al-Hakaymah's book *The Myth of Delusion: Exposing the American Intelligence* (August 2006), which displays an extensive knowledge of the critiques of American intelligence, ranging from the scholarly to the utterly delusional.[45] The introduction to this lengthy work states, "We will act in accordance with the saying 'from the words of your mouth I condemn you' and will use the published reports, news and research, which expose the extent of the failure of the American intelligence services inside and outside the United States."[46] The book consists largely of recitations of American intelligence failures, scandals, spy flaps, malfeasance, and alleged anti-Islamic plotting. Even this book, however, has running throughout it a subtle tendency to overplay American intelligence capabilities. It notes, for example, that "the number of people working at the CIA is estimated at 250 thousand employees and spies," and reports that "some sources say that most activities of the [Echelon signals intelligence system] have been directed to the Internet since the early nineties to the extent that the system eavesdrops on 90% of the communications through the international network."[47]

Al-Hakaymah is but the most recent and verbose contributor to this body of jihadist literature. Abu Hafs al-Mauritani, writing from Afghanistan after 9/11 but prior to Operation Enduring Freedom, stated that the attacks confirmed

> the huge gap in the American and international intelligence and security agencies. The prevalent impression that was there regarding the CIA, FBI, Mossad, and its European equivalents that are "fighting terrorism" is that they hear and see every movement of the enemies and even their friends. And they even know the shoe and shirt sizes of the people they surveil. . . . These intelligence apparatuses have tens of millions of informers in addition to the most cutting edge technology, such as spy satellites and global listening stations. Each one of these of intelligence apparatuses has a budget bigger than the budgets of several developing countries together. . . . Who would've believed that these intelligence apparatuses who made themselves into that monster that scares the hearts of the people [would] have such huge security gaps that can allow such a destructive act.[48]

Other AQAM sources also highlight the ineffectiveness of the West's impressive technology against God's holy warriors. According to Abu Ayman al-Hilali, the 9/11 attack "was a blow to the credibility and competence of the famed security and intelligence agencies and their legendary status in the U.S. and global imagination. They were revealed as weak and ineffective against the mujahideen. Moreover, they had miscalculated. The minds that stood behind their equipment and computers had not been able to calculate anything."[49]

In February 2002, al Qaida strategist Abu Ubayd al-Qurashi pointed to what he viewed as the failure of the vaunted U.S. signals intelligence system's technology: "No form of surveillance can provide early warning or permit rapid decision making. Even the Echelon satellite surveillance system, which cost billions of dollars . . . did not manage to stop the nineteen mujahideen wielding knives."[50] Interestingly, al-Qurashi also argued that American intelligence is handicapped in its efforts to understand the Muslim world and cannot compensate with close relationships with "apostate" regimes: "By resorting to the Arab intelligence services, with a mentality that befits the Bolshevik museums, America's eyes will suffer from a new permanent disability: blindness."[51]

Intelligence and Knowing the Enemy

AQAM strategists possess a clearly defined worldview shaped by their Salafi jihadist beliefs and their own understanding of intelligence. As is the case with many other functions within their global movement, they acknowledge intelligence as a good and necessary practice but routinely leave the exact details to be dealt with at lower levels. Though this may be a reasonable and efficient approach for tactical intelligence, it probably comes at the expense of strategic- and operational-level understanding. Ineffective and disjointed operations are a frequent result.

Abu Fath al-Pastuni envisioned a direct link between intelligence and strategy, suggesting that "the data should be analyzed to serve as useful information to determine a strategy when it is needed."[52] His vision of the substantive scope of strategic intelligence is indeed very wide: "A strategy is a way of achieving a general objective. In the military world, this means a way of achieving the objective of a war or a comprehensive military victory. A strategy is the result of an analysis of all direct or indirect factors such as the past and current situation and a future situation. This primarily concerns the best understanding of oneself and one's enemy."[53]

As al-Pastuni suggested, knowledge of the enemy should have a direct impact on military planning and should be tied to the exercise of command and control. Similarly, in a passage from the *Al-Qaeda Manual* reminiscent of Sun Tzu, a quotation from Gen. Mahmoud Sheet Khattab cautions: "The nation that wants to achieve victory over its enemy must know that enemy very well. . . . Those who fight an enemy that they do not know do not win because a successful military plan must be built on clear and trustworthy information. The commander who fights an enemy and does not know his strength (number and materiel) is blind and destined to fail and fall."[54]

Of course, none of this proves the existence of a formal role for intelligence information in AQAM's strategic planning.[55] Though *Security and Intelligence* and al-Pastuni both discuss the importance of carefully categorizing and then analyzing disparate data, there are no diagrams of the classic "intelligence cycle" showing finished intelligence being delivered to AQAM policy makers who then issue new requirements, thereby starting the process all over again. Nonetheless, material dating to the 1990s suggests that some senior members were specifically trying to create at least rudimentary formal processes to take into account information about the outside world. Thus, senior camp trainer Abu Hudaifa, writing in 1998 or after, called for a centralization of information in a "huge database of actual data." "The movement that endeavors to know its status quo, follows up on its developments and events, knows how to analyze these events, and evaluates them via relying on a strong database for arriving at practical conclusions will be a strong movement. Such organization will be standing on a solid ground that enables it to establish a strategy capable of meeting its aspirations and achieving its goals and mottos."[56] Hudaifa recommended establishing a "strategic research" initiative: "Subsequently, the leadership of the movement should be updated [with] these huge amounts of real data that will enable it to manage [the] struggle cleverly. This is what states endeavor to do by establishing strategic research centers to replenish this aspect and to carry on the appropriate strategies for each crisis that faces the state."[57]

Another undated document (classified "Very Secret" by al Qaida) champions a plan for a command organization that would include a special group devoted to "studies and research" that sounds like an attempt to establish all-source analysis:

> It is important to have studies and research that comes out regularly, whether normally or following [an] emergency situation from the interior or the exterior or on special occasions, which is distributed to the cadre and the headquarters for them to read. . . . And in this section many experienced and knowledgeable people work. These papers will have special studies whether from the outside or the inside or something that was written recently or a translation, or the collection of military information or managerial . . . etc. And it is very important to inform the commanders and the responsible people at a special level about the events and its development from the interior and the exterior, and it is important to have combined work for the whole organization which completes the work.[58]

Hidira al-Argentini (the Argentinian) wrote an undated "Secret" study found in Abu Hafs's document cache entitled "Terrorist Groups' Operations and Plans of the U.S. to Defeat Them" that exemplifies the type of topical research conducted and disseminated throughout a camp. Of particular interest is the section that poses the question "How does the United States respond to terrorism?" Al-Argentini went straight to a primary source on U.S. policy, the *Public Report of the Vice President's Task Force on Combating Terrorism*, written in 1986 under the aegis of then Vice

President George H. W. Bush, and quoted in his own report the U.S. stance on terrorism and the various "levels of anti-terrorism operations."

During the 1990s, members of AQAM could also acquire knowledge of the outside world through the book and video collections in camp libraries. According to Abu Jandal, a former bodyguard for Osama bin Laden, "the libraries of the al Qaida organization's military training camps contained many books and the best in the military field, especially American books."[59]

> We studied many American books in the strategic and military fields. One of which was the report that the former U.S. secretary of state Henry Kissinger presented in the 1970s following the 1973 war and the discussion that he held with Saudi King Faysal Bin-Abd-al-Aziz. . . . One of the U.S. books, which we studied, was a book by U.S. President Roosevelt entitled: *1999, Year of Oil without War*. In this book, Roosevelt explained how the United States would control the outside world. The most important element in studying this book is to know the U.S. viewpoint about us and what they want from us. The al Qaida organization depended on what the Americans themselves say and on what they publish in order to invite condemnation against them and convince the al Qaida organization members of the correctness of al Qaida aims to impede these U.S. plots and prevent their implementation.[60]

Reading enemy literature and watching videos not only provides direct knowledge about their enemy, it also helps AQAM strategists discover how their enemy perceives them. In turn, this allows AQAM to use the "Crusaders'" own words—through carefully selected literature choices—as a propaganda weapon and to further indoctrinate the cadre to the al Qaida worldview.[61]

The types of formal research organizations that Abu Hudaifa envisioned populating databases and issuing written reports have apparently not come to fruition. This is unsurprising, given the present status of AQAM as a broad theological and intellectual movement rather than a unitary military organization. Nevertheless, AQAM thinkers continue to be interested in understanding their enemy and vigorously use open source materials, many of which are easily obtained via the Internet. Their "end products" are reminiscent of—yet more sophisticated than—those written by Hidira al-Argentini. Abu Ubayd al-Qurashi, for instance, was clearly familiar with Western military and strategic literature. In 2002, he published an online article about Americans' understanding of Clausewitz's concept of the "center of gravity." Footnoting Peter Paret and Michael Howard's definitive English translation of *On War,* and showing an awareness of the work of Col. Harry Summers of the U.S. Army, Qurashi looked at the American experience in Vietnam, Operation Desert Storm, and Kosovo through a decidedly Clausewitzian lens. He concluded by elaborating what he thought the United States had identified as al Qaida's center of gravity in the present war. His analysis demonstrates an impressive use of source materials, including American military manuals, the U.S. Army War College's Strategic Studies Institute, CNN, the *Washington Times,* and other Western open sources.[62]

Finally, there remains the important question of whether AQAM strategists are wearing cultural, religious, or other blinders that interfere with their ability to produce or consume objective intelligence. Such blinders are common everywhere, and one leading scholar argues that they are inevitable in totalitarian regimes, which al Qaida aspires to be, with grave consequences for intelligence effectiveness.[63] There can be no doubt that AQAM's tendencies toward conspiratorial thinking are a hindrance. Are the elite AQAM strategists capable of looking outside the Salafi jihadist worldview to understand the world around them? What happens when they encounter information that does not conform to their outlook? (Chapter 4 discusses this subject as well.)

Several sources hint that there may indeed be such obstacles and that the more thoughtful members of AQAM recognize this. The author of "Jihad in Iraq: Hopes and Dangers" referred to a hadith about the Roman Empire that illustrates "that enmity among us should not prevent us from recognizing the characteristics of the enemy."[64] Abu-Bakr Naji echoed this point in *The Management of Savagery* when he called for the mujahideen to understand the views of the infidel enemy and then outlined the "rules of the political game" that the "mujahid youth" need to learn. First is that "the aim which motivates the enemies is a material aim. Thus, the doctrine of conflict which the people of non-belief and apostasy possess is a material, worldly doctrine in most of its structure."[65]

One measure of the sophistication of Abu Bakr Naji's analysis is his caution against a common analytic pitfall: mirror imaging. In language any good Western intelligence service would endorse, he warned jihadists undertaking this "skillful understanding" and "mapping of interests" not to project their own motivations on the enemy. "A person might deeply understand the politics of the two groups," he wrote, "and so that his study will be removed from the rigid notion that the enemy acts only in accordance with religious motives. He will find that the motive of religion among many of the factions of the enemy is secondary or evanescent."[66]

Despite Naji's warnings, ideological and cultural misperceptions occur on every level within the movement. A telling example is the conclusion drawn in one al Qaida–affiliated Web site's chat room that a flier promoting an ROTC blood drive on a U.S. university campus proved the huge undisclosed losses inflicted on the U.S. Army and hence an urgent need for blood.[67] Even one of their most-forward-looking military thinkers sees only what he wants to see: Qurashi attributes American military strength primarily to a long history of "fraud and deception."[68] Therefore it might reasonably be hypothesized that AQAM does not "know its enemies" in the classic sense. All but the most intelligent and fastest-learning Salafi jihadists betray stereotyped views of the West that undermine critical analysis and assessment of strategy.

One Vision of a Jihadist Intelligence Service

Excerpt from *The First 24 Hours after the Establishment of the Islamic State*, by Omar Bakri Muhammad (Al-Muhajiroun Publications, no date)

The Department of Internal Security

Its duty is to supervise all security matters; it includes intelligence services, emergency services and military intelligence. The present security service will be scrapped, for its word involves spying against the *Ummah* and this is forbidden for Allah (SWT) says: "And do not spy on each other."

This department will be formed of three units independent of each other and headed by the director general of the department.

The first Unit will collect information about the enemies, which is known as military intelligence. This unit will be forbidden from spying against any members of the army, for the words of Allah (SWT) "do not spy" is general in its meaning.

Evidence about the permissibility of spying against the enemy is represented in the Messenger of Allah's (SWT) initiative when he sent Abdullah ibn Jahsh in an expedition to spy on Quraish in the heart of Makkah.

The second unit will monitor the activities of foreign residents of the Islamic State, and the same evidence applies here; spying against the enemies is allowed whether they were in our country or in theirs.

The third unit will be the police. . . . It is forbidden to arrest any citizen for questioning except by the police, this is to prevent giving the same mandatory powers to several authorities as is the case in the Arab countries today. . . . This will not be allowed in the Khilafah state; only the police will have the power to [arrest people] and with an official warrant. . . .

There will be coordination between the overseas intelligence unit, the home intelligence unit and the police unit. It will be preferable if they had high and equal salaries to prevent any corruption and misconduct, and to discourage the individuals within the three units from competing with each other over salaries and to make them concentrate on their jobs. . . . The two intelligence services will have to work with the utmost secrecy, they will not have special uniforms, they will be allowed to buy information and gather intelligence in countries at war with the state by any legal means. Information will not be obtained by using women, drugs, alcohol, etc. However, it will be allowed to buy such information from people who happen to go to such places if necessary. New techniques and methods in acquiring information about the enemy military and political moves will have to be adopted.

Conclusion

The Salafi jihadist strategists see intelligence as a form of power in its own right. In the Western field of "intelligence studies," some scholars study intelligence in its role as a means of obtaining new information that can be harnessed to decision making, usually in the international context. Other scholars focus on intelligence as a tool governments use to surveil and repress domestic populations.[69] The Salafi jihadists have adopted both approaches. They believe that intelligence—specifically in the form of the internal security services—is perhaps the strongest tool that the "apostate" regimes have with which to suppress the jihadists. Furthermore, they seek to use these same counterintelligence approaches to maintain the security and purity of their own movement. At the same time, they perceive the utility of "knowing the enemy." In pursuing this goal, they try to draw on Western ideas about the organization and operation of foreign intelligence services and the place of these services in military planning processes. At best, these models are an imperfect fit for the reality of the inchoate global Salafi jihadist movement. AQAM is a movement, not a bureaucracy, so while the strategists would prefer to have a bureaucratized but "Islamic" intelligence process resembling Western intelligence services, circumstances prevent this. Thanks to the loss of sanctuaries, AQAM's intelligence function has become diffuse to the point where high-level intelligence and assessment are now carried out largely by motivated individuals self-publishing on the Internet. Indeed, it may no longer be accurate to speak of AQAM having a systematic intelligence function, at least at the strategic level.

Moreover, the jihadists, perhaps to a greater degree than most intelligence analysts, have difficulty removing their ideological blinders and objectively assessing the outside world. Whatever their capabilities in tactical intelligence and counterintelligence, coupled with the occasional act indicating a genuine strategic understanding, AQAM's would-be intelligence officers remain hobbled by operational realities, enemy pressure, and a tenacious worldview that enables jihad yet, in the final analysis, also undermines their ability to conduct Western-style strategic intelligence and assessment.

Notes

1. FBIS GMP20020613000138, "Article Says al-Qa'ida War Tactics Based on Old Chinese Military Books," (Internet) *Alneda*, June 13, 2002.
2. FBIS GMP20040430000022, "Jordan: Al-Zarqawi Denies Jordanian Intelligence Story on Chemical Bomb," Jordan-FBIS Report, April 29, 2004.
3. There are numerous captured documents and Internet articles published by AQ on these subjects. Even the most theoretical of the AQ manuals on intelligence usually include discussions of how intelligence is performed at the tactical level, including recruiting agents, surveillance, and encoding communications. See Harmony document folders AFGP-2002-006274, *Small Notebook Contains a Complete Intelligence Manual*, no date; AFGP-2002-003656, *Part of a Training Manual that Teaches Intelligence-Gathering, Surveillance, and Special Operations Execution*, no date; NMEC-2004-641848, *A Page from a Training Document on Intelligence Gathering and Espionage*, no date; AFGP-2002-003686, *Instruction Manual Related to Intelligence Gathering Operations*, no date, captured in Kabul; and 2RAD-2004-600812, *Training Manual on all Aspects of Intelligence Gathering and Security*, no date, captured in Fallujah in November 2004. The provenance and theological approach of the last document are unclear. It may be a product of Iraqi nationalist insurgents.
4. One jihadist discussion of intelligence even quotes Allen Dulles, the late director of central intelligence, on the importance of intelligence gathering. See Harmony document folder NMEC-2006-633117, *Part of an Article Discussing the History of Intelligence Gathering by Using Spies and Military Campaigns*, no date. Much of the intelligence and security curriculum previously taught in Afghan training camps such as Al-Farouq has since been provided by online articles authored by head of AQ security Sayf al-Adl, in *Al-Battar Camp* and *Sawt al-Jihad* (2004).

These articles almost match verbatim the training documents captured in Afghanistan since late 2001.

5. Ed Blanche, in "Arab Intelligence Services in the Crosshairs," *Middle East*, June 2005, noted that "for decades, intelligence and security services in the Arab world have been untouchable, answerable to no-one but the political leaderships" (8). Blanche quoted Palestinian analyst Daoud Kattab, who confirmed that "the intelligence services are the main power brokers in most of the Arab world, irrespective of whether the country in question is a monarchy or a republic."

6. FBIS GMP20040430000022; see al-Zawahiri's *Knights under the Prophet's Banner*, 2. The security crackdowns had the positive outcome for al-Zawahiri of driving him to Afghanistan, which was a "gift on a gold platter" in the form of a secure base for jihad.

7. See Harmony document folder AFGP-2002-600080, available in an unclassified English translation at http://ctc.usma.edu/aq/pdf/AFGP-2002-600080-Trans.pdf, accessed September 22, 2007. This document was captured in Abu Hafs/Mohammed Atef's house in Kandahar in 2001 and had at one time been posted on the Internet. See also Harmony document folder NGIC-2002-00675, *Remarks on the Jihad Experience in Syria*, no date.

8. See www.lahdah.com/vb/showthread.php?tht=22636 or www.muslm.net/vb/archive/index.php/T-62772.html, last accessed September 23, 2007. We are grateful to Laila Sabara for her translation of these Web sites.

9. The best general work in English is Luis Martinez, *The Algerian Civil War 1990–1998* (New York: Columbia University Press, 2000).

10. Naji, *Management of Savagery*, 26.

11. Such use of "pseudoterrorists" is hardly an unknown practice in counterinsurgency and was plausibly described in detail by a veteran of Algerian special forces, Habib Souaïda, in *La sale guerre: Le témoignage d'un ancient officier des forces spéciales de l'armée algérienne* (Paris: Découverte, 2001). For a positive but cautious discussion of other such operations in counterinsurgency contexts, see Lawrence E. Cline, *Pseudo Operations and Counterinsurgency: Lessons from Other Countries* (Carlisle: U.S. Army War College, Strategic Studies Institute, 2005), which observes that "pseudo forces can thrive in environments in which guerrilla forces have problems in their communications and in which centralized control of the guerrilla groups has been weakened," v. Available online at www.strategicstudiesinstitute.army.mil/pdffiles/PUB607.pdf, accessed October 15, 2007.

12. FBIS GMP20050201000226.

13. The most precise evidence was provided by Mohammed Samraoui, a former Sécurité Militaire lieutenant colonel, who testified in French court about the "hidden hand" behind the GIA; see his book for details: *Chronique des années de sang—Algérie: comment les services secrets ont manipulé les groups islamistes* (Paris: Denoël, 2003).

14. FBIS GMP20040823000252, "Jihadist Writer Urges Muslims to Find Balance between Normal, Concealed Actions," Jihadist Websites, FBIS Report in Arabic, August 14, 2002. This is an article by Abu-Muhammad al-Maqdisi entitled "Caution and Concealment, between Excessiveness and Negligence," *Al-Battar Camp* issue 16, issued by the Military Committee of Jihadists in the Arabian Peninsula.

15. FBIS GMP20040823000252.

16. In late 2001, Manchester, England, police captured a document that has become known as the *Al-Qaeda Manual*. Translations are available at www.usdoj.gov/ag/manualpart1_1.pdf, accessed September 23, 2007. The document is useful for its reflection of many of the themes also found in captured documents.
17. Ibid.
18. Ibid.
19. Sheikh Omar Bakri Muhammed, *The First 24 Hours after the Establishment of the Islamic State* (Al-Muhajiroun Publications, no date).
20. *Al-Qaeda Manual*, no date.
21. The hoopoe is an Old World bird said to have been used as a messenger by King Solomon.
22. Harmony document folder AFGP-2002-002857, *The Egyptian Islamic Group, Al-Gama al-Islamia, Prepared and Published This Manual as a First Step in Building an Islamic Intelligence Organization, Able to Compete with Western and Israeli Intelligence Agencies*, pre–Operation Enduring Freedom.
23. FBIS GMP20041018000218, "Al-Qa'ida's Sayf al-Adl Defines 'Intelligence.'" Al-Adl was clearly focused on teaching tactical-level intelligence in the article for *Al-Battar Camp* in October 2004, although he did discuss the more operational and strategic levels of intelligence by outlining the types of intelligence (military, state security, and external). This document is substantially the same as Harmony document folder AFGP-2002-600172.
24. Secret sources are said to include recruited agents, surveillance (recording, monitoring, photography), interrogation, and documents.
25. FBIS SEG20040602000101. A similar discussion is in Harmony document folder AFGP-2002-600351, *Document Prepared by Hidira al-Argentini, which Outlines al-Qaeda Views on United States Definition and Reaction to Terrorist Organizations*, no date.
26. FBIS GMP20050810371012, "Al-Qa'ida Book on 'Managing Savagery' Describes Stages for Creation of Islamic Nation; Urges Terrorism, Violence."
27. Benjamin Weiser and James Risen, "A Soldier's Shadowy Trail in U.S. and in the Mideast," *New York Times*, December 1, 1998, 1.
28. Harmony document folder AFGP-2002-600098.
29. This problem, including the Zahiragic-Arnaout case, is elaborated in detail in John Schindler's *Unholy Terror: Bosnia and the Global Jihad* (St. Paul, Minn.: Zenith Press, 2007), particularly in chapters 9 and 10.
30. Atran, "The Emir."
31. Naji, *Management of Savagery*, 11–12, 18; Omar Bakri Muhammad, *The First 24 Hours after the Establishment of the Islamic State*; Abu-Hajar 'Abd-al-'Aziz al-Muqrin's Battar Camp pieces at FBIS GMP20040223000176, "Terrorism: Al-Battar Camp on Guerilla Warfare Leadership, Forces"; and Harmony document folder 500MI-2005-RP-MLA00011.
32. Egyptian Islamic Group manual, Harmony document folder AFGP-2002-002857.
33. Ibid.
34. Ibid.
35. Ibid.
36. Ibid.
37. Ibid.
38. Ibid.
39. FBIS GMP20040223000176.

40. FBIS GMP20050308000220, "Al-Qa'ida Book on 'Managing Savagery' Describes Stages for Creation of Islamic Nation; Urges Terrorism, Violence," Jihadists Websites, FBIS Report in Arabic, March 8, 2005.

41. Harmony document folder 500MI-2005-RP-MLA00011, 2004. Compare this quotation with the following passage from Carlos Marighella's *Mini-Manual of the Urban Guerrilla* as rendered in English at www.marxists.org, accessed October 18, 2006: "The creation of an intelligence service with an organized structure is a basic need for us. The urban guerrilla has to have vital information about the plans and movements of the enemy; where they are, how they move, the resources of their banking network, their means of communication, and the secret activities they carry out. The reliable information passed on to the guerrilla represents a well-aimed blow at the dictatorship."

42. Vasiliy Mitrokhin discussed the Soviets' use of "false bands" to kill the real mujahideen and provoke clashes between mujahideen groups in "The KGB in Afghanistan," Cold War International History Project, Working Paper no. 40, Washington, D.C., February 2002, 117, 140. Available at www.wilsoncenter.org/topics/pubs/ACFAE9.pdf, accessed September 23, 2007.

43. Harmony document folder AFGP-2002-600002, *Site Security, Internal & External, the Enemy*, pre-9/11. The top three enemies are rounded out by (2) "The deviators (from the faith)" and (3) "The surrounding environment (opposition, tribes, agents, criminals)."

44. Batterjee, *The Arab Volunteers.*

45. West Point's Combating Terrorism Center has made Hakaymah's book available in translation at http://ctc.usma.edu/secure/Hakaymah--the%Myth%of%Delusion--UNCLASS.pdf, accessed June 6, 2007. See also Brian Fishman, "Al Qaida's Spymaster Analyzes the U.S. Intelligence Community," November 6, 2006, www.ctc.usma.edu/MythofDelusion.pdf, accessed September 22, 2007.

46. FBIS GMP20061012281002.

47. Ibid.

48. Harmony document folder AFGP-2002-801121, *Legal and Realistic Outlook on the Motivations behind the Attacks in the USA*, September–October 2001.

49. FBIS GMP20031027000226.

50. Wikipedia.com, citing popular wisdom available to any Salafi jihadist with an Internet connection, explains: "ECHELON is thought to be the largest signals intelligence and analysis network for intercepting electronic communications in history. Run by the UKUSA Community, ECHELON can capture radio and satellite communications, telephone calls, faxes and emails nearly anywhere in the world and includes computer automated analysis and sorting of intercepts. ECHELON is estimated to intercept up to 3 billion communications every day."

51. FBIS GMP20020702000138, "*Al-Ansar* Writer Views Reasons for US Intelligence 'Failure' against Mujahidin," (Internet) *Al-Ansar*, June 26, 2002.

52. FBIS SEG20040602000101.

53. Ibid. *Security and Intelligence* makes a similar argument. See also Harmony document folder AFGP-2002-002857, no date. This is information related to a potential adversary's war-making capability that the U.S. military would label PMESII (political, military, economic, social, infrastructure, and information); see JFCOM online glossary at www.jfcom.mil/, accessed October 9, 2007.

54. *Al-Qaeda Manual*, no date.

55. See chapter 6 for a discussion of whether AQAM engages in a strategic planning process at all. In the past, AQAM has often sent members on fact-finding mis-

sions or requested reports from operators in the field. Examples include situation reports sent to bin Laden et al. regarding Somalia. See Harmony document folders AFGP-2002-600103, *Operational Report Dated December 1993 Prepared by Abu Hafs*; AFGP-2002-800639, *Terrorist Attacks . . . Somalia*; and AFGP-2002-600053. Military/security chief Al-Adl was sent to East Africa in the early 1990s to gather information: "Brother Sayf al-Adl was sent by sea via Mombassa to try to reach them to once again evaluate the situation, because the information available to us about the region and especially about the tribes is not sufficient" (Harmony document folder AFGP-2002-600103).

56. Harmony document folder AFGP-2002-003251. The identity of Hudaifa is unknown, but he is certainly someone who, from the tone of his letter, gave direct and unvarnished advice to bin Laden. His letter includes a discussion of the mistakes made in Somalia.

57. Ibid.

58. Harmony document folder AFGP-2002-000112, *Blue Print to Setup Command and Sections of al-Qaida*, no date. This document was recovered in Kabul and is also known as "Al Qaida Staff Count Public Appointments," available at http://ctc. usma.edu/aq/pdf/AFGP-2002-000112-Trans.pdf, accessed September 22, 2007.

59. FBIS GMP20050323000113, "Former bin Ladin 'Bodyguard' Discusses al-Qa'ida Training Methods, 'Libraries,'" *Al-Quds al-Arabi*, London, March 23, 2005, 19.

60. Ibid. A search for the book by "President Roosevelt" yielded no results; it is possible that Abu Jandal was referring to a book by Kermit Roosevelt Jr. (Teddy Roosevelt's grandson and a CIA officer) titled *Arabs, Oil and History*, first published in 1949.

61. FBIS GMP20050323000113, 19.

62. FBIS GMP20030122000038, 10–16.

63. On closed worldviews habitually ignoring solid intelligence, see Christopher Andrew and Vasili Mitrokhin, *The Sword and the Shield* (New York: Basic Books, 1999); and David Kahn, *Hitler's Spies: German Military Intelligence in World War II* (New York: Macmillan, 1978), which impressively detail the analytical shortcomings of the Soviet and Nazi espionage systems, respectively.

64. FBIS GMP20040728000229. The hadith mentions "four good characteristics" of the Romans that showed that "the Hour will come when the Romans will be in the majority."

65. Naji, *Management of Savagery*, 38, 84.

66. Ibid., 39.

67. FBIS GMP20050214000276. "Notice, my fraternal mujahid, have you ever seen in your entire life someone who holds a contest for blood donation? My God, this is strange. The question is: Do you know why the blood donation ad is published in the form of "a challenge"? Do you know why it is not published in the form of a typical public notice, for instance, that calls on Americans to donate blood? The answer is: The number of wounded Americans in various US Army divisions is huge, praise be to God."

68. FBIS GMP20021126000154. Past success is attributed to U.S. use of the media and psychological warfare.

69. Len Scott and Peter Jackson, "The Study of Intelligence in Theory and Practice," *Intelligence and National Security* 19, no. 2 (2004): 143.

CHAPTER 4

AQAM's Perception of Its Enemies

We have seen in the last decade the decline of the American government and the weakness of the American soldier. America is prepared to wage easy wars but not prepared to fight long and bitter wars. This was proven in Beirut when the Marines fled after two explosions. It also proves they can run in less than 24 hours. This was repeated in Somalia. We are ready for all occasions.

OSAMA BIN LADEN, 1998[1]

The Roots of AQAM's Perception

Even a cursory examination of AQAM's beliefs illuminates a core, unchallenged assumption that the world is sharply divided along religious lines.[2] It consists of *dar al-Islam* (the house of Islam), on the one hand, and, on the other, *dar al-harb* (the house of war), five billion implacably hostile people who seek to oppress Muslims and stamp out Islam. The "Zionist-Crusader" enemy, of which the United States is the single largest component, looms large on the *dar al-harb* side. That the Qur'an describes Jews and Christians as "people of the book" scarcely moderates this harsh assessment of the "infidels." A confidant of Abu Musab al-Zarqawi explained: "Wherever you look, you find one truth. With deep-rooted hatred in their soul, infidels are oppressing Muslims ruthlessly in various fields and countries. This is a Koranic fact."[3] Al-Maqdisi preaches a similar line: "The hostility of the Jews, Christians and other polytheists against us, the Muslims, is an undeniable fact. They are against our religion and God told us this fact in the Holy Qur'an."[4]

In this Manichean analysis, the world is fundamentally riven along religious lines, and has been in this condition since the time of Muhammed. Sayf al-Din al-Ansari expressed this view in 2002 when he wrote:

> The clash continues because of the deep-seated hostility between the two camps: "for the Unbelievers are unto you open enemies" [Qur'an 4:101]. This hostility is not a random state of affairs that results from personal considerations or temporary stands that depend on earthly calculations of profit and loss. It is an attitude toward Muslims that is firmly established in the souls of the infidels. It is automatically countered by hostility from Muslims toward the infidels: "Thou wilt not find any people who believe in Allah and the Last Day, loving those who resist Allah and His Messenger" [Qur'an 58:22]. . . . The hostility between the two camps and the unchanging relationship between truth and falsehood are the main variables in the struggle. When we state that this is the nature of the relation, all we are doing is presenting reality as it is and as God created it—without rosy dreams and delusions."[5]

The enemies of Islam, with the Zionists and Crusaders at the forefront, purportedly have been oppressing and slaughtering Muslims for centuries. The Internet conveniently provides the medium for a cottage industry among Muslims (most of them not Salafi jihadists) of disseminating graphic horror stories and sometimes photographs of "infidel"—primarily Christian and Jewish—atrocities.[6] In the realm of broad Salafi jihadist rhetoric, however, bin Laden's words in 1996 on this topic are typical.

> You are not aware of the injustice, repression, and aggression that have befallen Muslims through the alliance of the Jews, Christians and their agents, so much so that Muslims' blood has become the cheapest blood and their money and their wealth are plundered by the enemies. Your blood has been spilled in Palestine and Iraq. The image of that dreadful massacre in Qana, Lebanon, is still vivid in one's mind, and so are the massacres in Tajikistan, Burma, Kashmir, Assam [India], the Philippines, Fatani [Thailand], Ogaden, Somalia, Eritrea, Chechnya, and Bosnia-Herzegovina where hair-raising and revolting massacres were committed before the eyes of the entire world clearly in accordance with a conspiracy by the United States and its allies.[7]

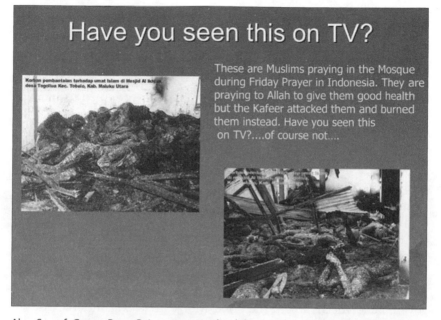

Abu Sayyaf Group PowerPoint propaganda slide. *Source*: Harmony document folder 500MI-2005-RP-MLA00013.

In a similar vein, al-Maqdisi wrote in a book published after the coalition invaded Afghanistan: "Remember what the crusaders did when they occupied Al-Aqsa Mosque in Jerusalem [late eleventh century] or what they did in the Inquisition Courts when they restored Spain [fifteenth–sixteenth centuries]. In modern history, I do not think that there is an intelligent or stupid man who can forget the crusaders' conspiracies and massacres in Lebanon, Bosnia, the Philippines, Indonesia in the Kings Islands, Kosovo, the Balkans [late twentieth century]."[8] Note the easy sense in which—for al-Maqdisi—Pope Urban II, Ferdinand and Isabella of Spain, Ariel Sharon, Slobodan Milosevic, Bill Clinton, and (presumably) George Bush, separated by centuries and different faiths, are identical by the only standard that matters: their rejection of Islam and the violence that inexorably flows from that fact.[9]

AQAM's Understanding of International Politics and the International System

Though, in the minds of the jihadists, the dividing line between Muslims and all others is by far the most salient fact of international politics, many Salafi jihadist thinkers see additional nuances in the international system. Hence Abu Bakr Naji invoked Lord Palmerston when he wrote, "The politicians of the West summarize [have] a slogan which says, 'There is no eternal enmity in politics and no eternal friendship; rather, there are eternal interests.'"[10] With this statement Naji enunciated the founding axiom of the so-called realist school of international relations theory. Hans Morgenthau first systematically codified realism in his 1948 *Politics among Nations*. For years, realism virtually defined the field of international relations until eventually other scholars began to propose other useful models.[11] Even today, however, political realism and the companion term *national interest* remain deeply embedded not only in academic discourse but also in popular culture and in the minds of government officials around the world. Morgenthau explained the essence of his theory thus:

> The main signpost that helps political realism to find its way through the landscape of international politics is the concept of interest defined in terms of power. This concept provides the link between reason trying to understand international politics and the facts to be understood. It sets politics as an autonomous sphere of action and understanding apart from other spheres, such as economics (understood in terms of interest defined as wealth),[12] ethics, aesthetics, or religion. . . . We assume that statesmen think and act in terms of interest defined as power, and the evidence of history bears that assumption out. That assumption allows us to retrace and anticipate, as it were, the steps a statesman . . . has taken or will take on the political scene. . . . Thinking in terms of interest defined as power, we think as he does, and as disinterested observers we understand his thoughts and actions perhaps better than he . . . does himself.[13]

Naji is not the only thinker in AQAM whose analysis of the international system parallels Morgenthau's. Maysarah al-Gharib, a member of the legal council of Jama'at al-Tawhid wa-al-Jihad and a confidant of al-Zarqawi, also subscribes to this idea: "Force, not goodwill or noble feelings, is the foundation that governs relations among states. International politics is the policy of force. The language it uses is the language of force. Force may sometimes be cloaked in beautiful colors and sugary words called diplomacy. Under the cloak, however, it is force that steers diplomacy. Force is a key element to win or prevent war and impose will on others."[14]

In the 1990s, a similar view held sway in the EIG, which even quoted the Qur'an to the effect that God himself endorses political realism. "This is the only language the world community is using—the language of power—(this age worships power) whether this power is material or moral. We have been ordered to prepare the necessary force to intimidate the enemies of Allah and the infidels 'Prepare for them as much force as you can to intimidate Allah's enemies and yours' [Qur'anic verse]."[15]

The understanding that the currency of international relations is power and "interest" has important implications for Naji: "Therefore the difference of interest among them is a cause for the bloodiest wars. Therefore, the difference of that should not make us forget the reality that the shared enmity toward Islam represents a common ground of action for the different communities of unbelief and apostasy. Nevertheless, we can also say that their ideological alliance against Islam is a fragile alliance and limited by a ceiling of material interests that each faction among them possesses."[16] Put another way, among the infidels' permanent interests is enmity toward Islam. However, the infidels have many other conflicting interests that a politically adept AQAM movement should be able to exploit.

In January 2004, Nabil Sahraoui, commander of Algeria's Salafist Group for Preaching and Combat (GSPC), expressed a comparable sentiment. Obviously, the desire to keep Muslims down is among America's motives, he argued, but so too are purely economic and strategic interests that happen to come at the expense of Muslims, yet are not defined in religious terms:

> The United States does not know any laws and does not respect anything. All its actions are to serve its own interests and goals. It wants to fight against any Muslim group that aspires to establish an Islamic state. It wants to control the important strategic points in the world (Iraq, the Arab Maghreb, the Horn of Africa, the Arabian Peninsula, and other places). It wants to protect its economic interests, such as the oilfields that it owns in southern Algeria. It wants to support the Jews in their efforts to establish their big goal of "Greater Israel."[17]

The anonymous author of "Jihad in Iraq: Hopes and Dangers" (2003) likewise did not see the infidels as monolithic and believed that Muslims should be ready to take "advantage of the disagreements of the forces of atheism among themselves."[18] In fact, "disagreement among infidels might result in mutual interests between some of them and Muslims. This prompts the infidels to occasionally support Muslims. However, we should not rely on this at all."[19] Notably, this anonymous author is not the only member of AQAM to emphasize the divisions among the Christians and other infidels while still recognizing the unifying pull exerted by their purported hatred for Islam. In 2004, Maysarah al-Gharib opined: "An observer of history discovers outstanding disputes among atheists themselves that ignite destructive conflicts, including the 1939–1945 World War II that claimed the lives of 50 million people worldwide and World War I from 1914–1918 in which 10 million people were killed. The Almighty's dictum: 'Thou wouldst think they were united, but their hearts are divided' [Qur'anic verse] and 'We have put enmity and hatred among them till the day of resurrection' [Qur'anic verse]."[20]

An important implication is that some AQAM strategists believe that they can have interests in common with their infidel or apostate opponents—at least on a temporary basis. This suggests that diplomatic engagement with them, if only in the form of tacit bargaining in the midst of the present war, is at least theoretically possible. The Prophet Muhammed opened the door for such a possibility by his diplomatic maneuvers with his enemies, the Quraysh. The resulting cessation of hostilities, known as the Treaty of Hudaybiyah, lasted ten years.[21] To the jihadists, however, a temporary accommodation or a pause in hostilities is not a compromise on principles, goals, or means; it is merely a pause that each side presumably believes to be in its own interest. In a 1999 book on the Kashmiri jihad, Esa al-Hindi stated that "under such intricate political power struggles it may even be sometimes necessary to conclude a temporary peace treaty (*Dar-ul-Aman*) with other nations as a stratagem of war. Such as was signed at Hudaybiyah by the Prophet and later by many other far-seeing revolutionary military leaders of old. We are not speaking of compromise—far from it. Compromise does not exist where it implies an association of partners with the True Oneness."[22]

The idea that political realism opens the way for counter-coalition efforts appears in an early-to-mid-1990s document entitled "Basic Principles of the Jihad in Tajikistan."[23] The author quoted Lord Palmerston's line and explained that it is important for a movement to know who its friends and enemies are; however, the two categories should not be viewed as immutable.

Most of the parties we deal with search for their interest and move wherever these interests will be achieved. Therefore, the mentioned political classification will be continuously changing, whether by moving up or down inside one list or moving from one list into another; that is to say from friendship to hostility and vice versa. [Among] the duties of the political activity is increasing the list of friends and decreasing the list of enemies. On the other hand, moving some enemies to neutrality is considered a big success. As we previously mentioned, persuasion and threat have a vast use in the field of politics. We must be skillful in negotiations and using the bullet at the appropriate time and place.[24]

Political realists tend to be highly skeptical of the value of international law, noting that the means of enforcing it are lacking and thus commitments under international law amount to little more than nonbinding pledges. The anonymous author of "Jihad in Iraq: Hopes and Dangers" perceived this clearly. International law consists of "laws that the major powers respect only when their interests are helped. . . . No country is forced to heed its pledges and agreements unless it is in need for another country, group, alliance, or international organization. This means that a powerful country does not need anyone. No one can force it to abide by its pledges and treaties."[25] The author then used that premise as a foundation for a strategy to split the U.S.-led coalition in Iraq.

One implication of the skepticism about international law is skepticism about, even disdain for, the United Nations. Here, too, AQAM thinkers hew to the realist line. Maysarah al-Gharib thinks that, "to maintain power, conquerors set down the foundations of world policy in harmony with their interests. An example is the establishment of the League of Nations in 1920, and then the United Nations in 1945 to empower the conquerors to adopt the resolutions they wish in the name of the entire world while they exclusively maintain the so-called veto right."[26]

From innumerable members of AQAM the vitriol pours forth, presenting the UN as a "tool" or a "cover" for the Crusaders.[27] "The United Nations is nothing but a tool to domesticate Muslims and train them to submit gradually to the goals of the Zionist and crusader project. The modern age we live in confirms this truth to us. Suffice it to say that imperialism grew strong only through the treachery of international institutions," said Sayf al-Din al-Ansari.[28] Abu Ubayd al-Qurashi variously referred to the UN as the "executive branch" of U.S. policy and as "a tool to domesticate Muslims and gradually tame them to submit to the goals of the Zionist and Crusade designs."[29] An anonymous member of al Qaida wrote in the early 1990s that the UN is a "cover" for the Crusader nations and that "United Nations forces are a purely Crusader army."[30]

AQAM on U.S. Values and Society

While AQAM thinkers hate the United States and the West for their opposition to Islam, some see an even more fundamental problem, namely, the secularism that dominates the West. Qutb wrote that the West suffers from a "hideous schizophrenia," by which he meant that it separates religion from government, thereby leading to disastrous results for both as well as for the people.[31] Ever since the era of Qutb, Salafi jihadists have seen weakness, decay, and moral poverty when they looked at the West generally and the United States particularly. Qutb addressed this question in *Milestones*: "The leadership of mankind by Western man is now on the decline, not because Western culture has become poor materially or because its economic and military power has become weak. The period of the Western system has come to an end primarily because it is deprived of those life-giving values which enabled it to be the leader of mankind."[32]

Bin Laden confirmed Qutb's mid-twentieth-century diagnosis of schizophrenia in the West: "You [the United States] are the nation who, rather than ruling by the Law of Allah, chooses to implement your own inferior rules and regulations, thus following your own vain whims and desires. You run a society contrary to the nature of mankind by separating religion from your policies."[33] Al-Zawahiri said in March 2006 that the problem with the West is that it is fundamentally secular. "The injustices against the Prophet, God's peace and blessings be upon him, were not caused by freedom of opinion but because of replacing holy things with unholy things in this deteriorating civilization. The noblest Prophet, God's peace and blessings be upon him, and Jesus Christ, God's peace and blessings be upon him, are no longer holy, while Semitism, the Nazi Holocaust, and homosexuality have become holy things. A law was issued in France punishing any person who casts doubt on the Nazi Holocaust against the Jews at a time when Muslim females are not allowed to cover their heads at schools."[34]

The jihadists imagine for themselves a future Sunni Caliphate in which all Muslims are equal and race and ethnicity have no role. Meanwhile, they see the United States as embodying precisely the opposite values. Qurashi referred to "the Disunited States of America" as "a mixture of nationalities, ethnic groups, and races united only by the 'American dream,' or, to put it more correctly, worship of the dollar, which they openly call 'the Almighty Dollar.'"[35] Similarly, bin Laden sees an immoral America thoroughly penetrated by wicked Jews:

> We ask you [America] next to stop your unfair acts, lies, immorality and debauchery. We regret to tell you that you are the worst civilization in the history of mankind. . . . [The American] people believe that even if they commit adultery, theft, and other wicked acts, as long as they go and confess, everything will be okay. You are the nation who allows *ribaa* [interest on money], even though all the religions, including Christianity, have forbidden partaking in *ribaa*.[36] Yet you build your economy and investments on *ribaa*. As a result of this, the Jews controlled your economy and then your media and now control all aspects of your life, making you their servants and achieving their aims at your expense, which is what [Benjamin] Franklin warned you against.[37]

A few observers in AQAM even believe that the United States is willing to destroy its own freedoms in an effort to preserve American lives. This view has primarily been associated with the CISR, which published an article in August 2003 claiming that "the economy, which is the source of American strength, depends on the following pillars: Advanced technology; Freedom; Security."[38] The article continues with the assertion that "the United States has begun unwillingly to abandon its principles. It gave a free hand to espionage and violated its commitment to maintain individual rights. It restricted the freedoms of investors and account holders with many regulations as a precaution against terrorism. Its economy has lost security and capital has fled. Other capital stopped flowing into the country. The shares of American companies and corporations declined in world stock exchanges. Companies reduced their research and development investments. The three pillars of the American economy are quickly collapsing."[39]

Numerous strategists draw direct parallels between the United States and the Soviet Union. Many believe that similar societal weaknesses existed in the USSR and tangibly contributed to the downfall of that superpower.[40] One AQAM analyst has even argued that liberalism is intrinsically weaker than communism.[41] Many of them also believe that disintegration—the fate of the Soviet Union—will also be the fate of the United States. Since at least 2000, for example, bin Laden has insisted that the United States will sooner or later break into its component states.[42]

Yusuf al-Ayiri portrayed an America riven with disputes, including seces-
sionist tendencies, in 2003:

> Within the United States there are extremely serious political prob-
> lems—the conflict between hawks and doves, the conflict between the
> two parties, the veritable state of emergency that has been in effect since
> the September attacks, the martial law that has overridden U.S. law, the
> new laws coming from the White House, the conflict between the State
> Department and the Defense Department over who will control U.S.
> foreign policy, numerous burning political questions that affect the people
> and the government, the weakness or collapse of the U.S. economy. All of
> this will have an effect on the world. Yet another political problem in the
> United States is the state of New York's renewed demand to secede from
> the United States. This is not a new demand, but a very old one. And New
> York is not the only state that wants to secede—more than seven other
> states are making the same demand. Peter Vallone, Jr., a member of the
> New York City Council, justifies the state's demand to secede: "It's a very
> simple issue. The city pays $3.5 billion in taxes to the state of New York
> and it doesn't get any services for that money." Vallone adds, "We want our
> money back. In the past, the idea of secession was a romantic dream. Now,
> it's the city's only life preserver." As we noted, this is not a new demand.
> The novelist Norman Mailer requested independence for the city in 1969
> during his campaign to be elected mayor. The idea goes back to the 19th
> century, when the [southern states seceded] to defend slavery.[43]

Abu Bakr Naji does not speak to the question of secessionism, but
while discussing America and the Soviet Union, he pointedly noted:

> This overwhelming [military] power is also assisted by the cohesion of the
> society in the central country and the cohesion of that society's institu-
> tions and sectors. The overwhelming military power (weapons, technology,
> fighters) has no value without the cohesion of society and the cohesion of
> (society's) institutions and sectors. But this overwhelming military power
> may become a curse to this great superior power if the cohesion of society
> collapses.
>   Several elements that cause the collapse of this entity are summarized
> in the statement "elements of cultural/civilizational annihilation, such
> as the corruption of religion, moral collapse, social iniquities, opulence,
> selfishness, giving priority to (worldly) pleasures, the love of the world over
> all values, etc."[44]

Naji argued that when "the opulence and (worldly) pleasures which
those societies thirst for" are threatened, "competition for these things
begins" and "social iniquities [probably meaning "inequities"] rise to the

surface . . . which ignites political opposition and disunity among the (various) sectors of society."[45]

The Illusion of American Strength

AQAM thinkers also believe that the United States has deluded the rest of the world into believing that America is omnipotent: economically overwhelming, politically powerful, and able to fight and win a war anywhere on the globe.[46] The United States has done this, they believe, to make it inexpensive to control the world; in effect, every other power on earth is so cowed that the United States seldom has to flex its muscles at all. As early as 1993, al Qaida's Salih 'Abd-al-Wahid wrote to Abu Hafs that the U.S. intervention in Somalia represented, among other things, an "attempt to convince the world of the American superiority and terrorize the movements that attempt to oppose the American interests in the region."[47] Ten years later, the author of "Jihad in Iraq: Hopes and Dangers" wrote: "The more the power of the antagonist that is based on delusion increases, the more its domination over others increases at the lowest cost, and without the need, in most cases, to use force. Consequently, we often see that the United States flexes its muscles in an exaggerated manner in an attempt to strengthen this reality—delusion in the soul of mankind—individuals and nations."[48]

He went on to describe American power as a "reality-delusion":

> It combines both: reality in the sense that the United States is the most powerful nation in the world at present. It has the potential to be a super power for reasons particular to the U.S., or for reasons related to the backward state of Muslim nations. At the same time, it is an illusion since a large portion of its power is the result of the conviction of others in their inability to challenge [the United States]. It is true that there is no other power on earth as powerful as the United States. However, it is possible for other nations to enhance their power in a relative sense, and at the same time destroy an important and major part of the U.S. power at a relatively simple cost.

There are many ways, the author argued, to attack America's illusion of invulnerability and omnipotence, and to increase the relative power of other actors on the international stage. He likened the U.S.-led "new world order" to a spiderweb. "Although it is largely intertwined, the spiderweb is the weakest. A slight wind is enough to dismantle this web.

We believe that political relations between some countries that have been strong for decades require only one sentence uttered by an intoxicated official to destroy everything."[49] The U.S. economy is similarly fragile, he claimed: "Stock markets, for instance, are established on two illusions, fear and greed, if we believe in relative facts. This is delusion that accommodates reality sometimes, but more often disagrees with it. The prices of the stock markets accommodate the actual economic situation. In many cases, stock markets collapse as a result of fear. The blessed September attacks were a stark example of the truth of the theory of illusion."[50]

Abu Bakr Naji followed a very similar line of argumentation, concluding that America's power is, in fact, quite limited:

> There is no doubt that the power which God gave to the two superpowers [America and Russia] was overwhelming in the estimation of humans. However, in reality and after careful reflection using pure, human reason, [one comes to understand that this power] is not able to impose its authority from the country of the center—from America, for example, or Russia—upon lands in Egypt and Yemen, for example, unless these [latter] countries submit to those powers entirely of their own accord. It is correct that this power is overwhelming and that it seeks help from the power of local regimes controlled by proxies who rule the Islamic world. Yet all of that is not enough [to completely control the satellite states]. Therefore, the two superpowers must resort to using a deceptive media halo which portrays these powers as non-coercive and world-encompassing, able to reach into every earth and heaven as if they possess the power of the Creator.[51]

Naji even suggested that the United States has begun to believe its own propaganda and thus that its existence is in peril.

> The interesting thing that happened is that these two superpowers believed, for a time, their media deception. . . . According to the media deception, it is an all-encompassing, overwhelming power and people are subservient to it not only through fear, but also through love because it spreads freedom, justice, equality among humanity, and various other slogans.

When a state submits—whatever the extent of its ability—to the illusion of the deceptive power and behaves on this basis, that is when its downfall begins. It is just as Yale historian Paul Kennedy says: "If America expands the use of its military power and strategically extends more than necessary, this will lead to its downfall."[52]

Bin Laden, like Naji, finds similarities between the two former Cold War superpowers. Based on his personal experience fighting in

Afghanistan, the Soviet Union of the 1980s projected the same illusion of power as the United States does today, and needed only to overreach and suffer a strategic defeat for this fallacy to be exposed. Intelligence and media manipulation can no longer hide America's weakness: "The infidels, the Russians and the Americans, have so much impacted the minds of Muslims, making them believe that they [the infidels] are indefatigable super powers, that they have all kinds of gadgets and intelligence and stuff of that type. Most of that is inflated and far from true."[53]

America's Center of Gravity Is Its Economy

Salafi jihadist strategists, especially those with knowledge of foreign military literature, naturally seek to define the source of America's strength—its "center of gravity." Al-Qurashi discussed Clausewitz and, specifically, the idea of the center of gravity in a December 2002 article in which he concluded that America has failed to correctly identify al Qaida's center of gravity; however, "God has graciously enabled the mujahideen to understand the enemy's essence and nature, and indeed his center of gravity. A conviction has formed among the mujahideen that American public opinion is not the center of gravity of America." Instead, America's center of gravity is its economy.[54] Other observers use a different metaphor but nevertheless focus on the U.S. economy. Abu Ayman al-Hilali, for example, wrote in September 2002 that "the enemy continues to bleed on all levels, especially economically, which is his strong point and backbone."[55] The CISR similarly wrote in 2003 that "the backbone" of the United States "is its economic strength."[56]

"Jihad in Iraq: Hopes and Dangers" is one of many Salafi jihadist documents that nowhere uses the term *center of gravity* but implicitly argues that the American economy plays that role. This particular document argues that the best way to drive the United States from Iraq is to ensure that the full burden of the war there falls on the United States alone, pursuant to which the other members of the coalition should be stripped away. While American casualties were certainly a component of the author's calculation, the amount of space devoted to economics in the text clearly indicates that he saw the economic costs of the war to America as the decisive factor. There is only a relatively cursory mention of the impact of American casualties on U.S. government decisions about the war.[57]

Similarly, "Akram Hujazi," a self-described Jordanian scholar, wrote in a January 2007 article posted on a jihadist Web site:

> The Islamic nation entered, through al Qaida's battle with America, a new
> level [of conflict] differing from previous levels [of conflict] that Muslims
> have fought against their enemies. This level [of conflict] is based primarily
> on economic warfare, reflecting the difference of the enemy in this fierce
> war. Usually, war is based on military power, and the victory belongs to
> the most powerful militarily and he who prevails on the battlefield. As for
> our war with America, it differs fundamentally in that it depends, at the
> most basic level, on defeating [America] economically.[58]

American Military Weakness and Cowardice

Another important American vulnerability, according to AQAM, is the weakness of its military. AQAM observers see an American military inspired by mercenary motives. Its members do not fundamentally believe in their mission and are alienated from each other and from their leadership. Ayman al-Zawahiri touched on these themes in a message in late 2003, but other jihadists in less exalted positions share the perception.[59] Among them is "Barbarossa," who posted his views on a jihadist Web site in 2005. Barbarossa saw at least latent tendencies toward greed and selfishness within the U.S. military and advocated sowing chaos and division among its members through grievances relating to racism, greed for war booty, jealousy of superiors, and partisan politics.[60] He may have been echoing bin Laden, who said in 2003 that American soldiers "are completely convinced of the injustice and lying of their government."[61]

In case the American soldiers needed further convincing of the futility of their war, al Qaida released a video on the fifth anniversary of the September 11 attacks that featured the American jihadist Adam Gadahn (now known as Azzam al-Amriki) "inviting Americans to Islam." Gadahn included a "special invitation to all of you fighting Bush's Crusader pipedream in Afghanistan, Iraq, and wherever else W has sent you to die": "You are considered by Bush and his bunch of warmongers as nothing more than expendable cannon fodder and a means to an end. . . . So, instead of killing yourself for Bush or killing yourself out of despair, depression, guilt, or remorse why not surrender to the truth, escape from the unbelieving army and join the winning side."[62]

Al-Qurashi invoked Sun Tzu to make his argument to U.S. soldiers:

Sun Tzu . . . said: "When a commander looks at his soldiers the way the father looks at his sons, then the soldiers would die for their commander." Now if we compared this with U.S. commanders, who give order to their soldiers from a long distance across the oceans, then we can understand the soldiers' lack of trust in their commanders. What makes things even worse is the U.S. Command's denial of losses within its army ranks, which affects the morale of the U.S. soldiers. For these soldiers understand that they are making sacrifices that no one hears about, which shows that their commanders attach no value to their lives.[63]

Three months later, in September 2002, he wrote that American troops were fighting only for "a fist full of dollars."[64]

A far more important component of American military weakness, according to AQAM analyses, is cowardice. Salafi jihadists offer a variety of explanations, yet most in the movement agree with the anonymous member of the Pakistani group Harkat-al-Mujahideen who told Harvard's Jessica Stern that "non-Muslims love their life too much, they can't fight and they are cowards."[65] A letter from a Tunisian jihadist residing in Canada expressed much the same view: "My brothers, every time we pronounce the word Jihad, the enemies become frightened. They love life and safeguard it like we safeguard life after death. So let us raise the horror in their hearts."[66] Similarly, bin Laden described Americans as "afraid of death" and "like little mice."[67]

Though Soviet soldiers earned a degree of grudging respect from the jihadists (at least in retrospect), AQAM fighters often observe that American soldiers are no match for the Soviet soldiers they faced during the Afghan jihad. Abu Bakr Naji's comment is typical: the "viciousness of the Russian soldier is double that of the American." American soldiers have grown soft since the "colonial era," he explained. "They reached a state of effeminacy which made them unable to sustain battles for a long period of time and they compensate for this with a deceptive media halo."[68]

Whatever the reason for it, there is general consensus that such cowardice exists. Bin Laden's view is that American troops "are too cowardly and too fearful to meet the young people of Islam face to face" and ultimately are no serious threat on the battlefield; in fact, the U.S. Army is a "paper tiger."[69] Operation Enduring Freedom left Sayf al-Adl with the impression that "the American soldier is not fit for combat," and that "the American forces do not have a single fighter who can advance and occupy the land."[70] Indeed, "the American soldier is not fit for combat. This is the truth that the leaders of the Pentagon know, as much as we and everyone who was engaged with them know. The Hollywood promotions will not succeed in the real battlefield."[71] Abu Musab al-Zarqawi said in 2004, "As you know, [Americans] are the most cowardly of God's creatures. They are also an easy prey."[72] In 2006 he still believed that "the lack of will to fight is widely spread among the armies of the Crusaders."[73]

In AQAM's view, America tries in several ways to compensate for its soldiers' lack of ardor. Al-Qurashi said that "if not for technological superiority and advanced logistical tools, the United States would not have endured on this earth."[74] This technological edge manifests itself in at least two important ways. The first is by depending on a "huge media machine," a point bin Laden highlighted in 2003.[75] (See chapter 7 for a discussion of media and information operations.) More to the point, however, bin Laden claimed that the Americans "also depend on massive air strikes so as to conceal their most prominent point of weakness, which is the fear, cowardliness, and the absence of combat spirit among U.S. soldiers."[76] Sayf al-Adl agreed: "American commanders tend to use the air forces and missile bombardment to vacate the ground from any resistance, paving the way for the advance of the American phonies."[77]

In the end, AQAM believes that its technology will not help the United States to victory. Al-Zarqawi found that it was still easy for the mujahideen to "reap [American] heads" and, in fact, "advanced technology or the intelligent lethal weapons have failed to defend and protect these idiots."[78] The CISR concurred.

> Regarding the American army, the mujahideen have tested it in many fields. The mujahideen gained experience in fighting the biggest power in the world then, the army of the Soviet Union. Whoever was engaged in the two wars can confirm that there is no comparison between the two armies. The United States' superiority is in its air power only, and air power, as everyone knows, cannot decide a war. Advancing in enemy territory is impossible without ground forces. Although the U.S. ground forces are strong technologically and in air support, their strength is inconsistent with the power of the United States and its international reputation. In all its history, the United States has not waged a successful ground war and has not depended on ground forces in battles in a large way. Its greatest strength was air power.[79]

Maysarah al-Gharib sees America's preference to fight as part of a coalition as further evidence of the U.S. military's weakness and cowardice. Observing that the United States brought thirty countries to Operation Desert Storm and twenty coalition partners to Somalia in 1992, he concluded that "the United States wanted the soldiers of weak allies to be in the forefront so that they sustain[ed] casualties while U.S. soldiers remained safe."[80] Al-Zarqawi similarly offered that American soldiers try to hide behind "the black men and the cheap soldiers from the Third World."[81]

AQAM observers claim that the cowardice of American soldiers is matched by a lack of backbone among American military and political leaders. When an enemy bites back, American leaders are quick to order a withdrawal. This was the lesson bin Laden drew from the Khobar Towers bombing, for example, which "prompt[ed] them [the Americans] to move their bases from the cities to the desert."[82] In December 2003, al-Zawahiri held out hope for an American withdrawal from Iraq, citing the precedents of Vietnam, Beirut, and Mogadishu.[83] By mid-2005, al-Zawahiri was still expecting Iraq to have the same outcome as Vietnam when he wrote to al-Zarqawi: "The aftermath of the collapse of American power in Vietnam— and how they ran and left their agents—is noteworthy. Because of that, we must be ready starting now, before events overtake us, and before we are surprised by the conspiracies of the Americans and the United Nations and their plans to fill the void behind them."[84] Vietnam is frequently offered as a precedent showing the fundamental weakness of America and its leadership.[85] The withdrawal from Beirut in the 1980s is mentioned frequently as well. Indeed, bin Laden has cited the incident in hopeful terms since at least 1996.[86] "America is prepared to wage easy wars but not prepared to fight long and bitter wars," he said in January 1999. "This was proven in Beirut when the Marines fled after two explosions."[87]

AQAM's worldview finds particular vindication in the "battle of Mogadishu," where, in the words of Abu Ubayd al-Qurashi, "a single Somali tribe humiliated America and compelled it to remove its forces from Somalia."[88] The CISR described the incident in dramatic terms: "When the valiant soldiers of Islam came to them with the rod of Moses and the mujahideen poured their fire on them, the Americans withdrew from Somalia in an unexpected haste."[89] Bin Laden concurred: "In one explosion [in Somalia, 1993] one hundred Americans were killed, then 18 more were killed in fighting. One day our men shot down an American helicopter. The pilot got out. We caught him, tied his legs and dragged him through the streets. After that 28,000 U.S. soldiers fled Somalia. The Americans are cowards."[90]

On at least one occasion the enemy drew lessons about America's unwillingness to stick to a cause from an event most Americans scarcely remember. On December 29, 1992, two bombs exploded in Aden, killing two people, neither of them Americans. Bin Laden recalled this incident and publicly referred to it in 1996 when he ridiculed the secretary of defense for a lack of courage in directing the withdrawal of U.S. forces from Aden immediately afterward.[91] Later in the year, bin Laden gave a reporter a fulsome account of his understanding of the incident:

> With regard to Yemen, I do not want to add anything significant. However, the press said that the Americans left Yemen in less than 24 hours and that those who hit the airport and tried to blow up a U.S. bus at Aden airport did so because U.S. forces had entered Yemen by force and were heading for Aden. [UN Secretary General] Boutros-Ghali contacted the Yemeni president and told him that there was a U.S. plan to send forces to restore security in Somalia, and we hope that you will give it [the United States] a base, because we want to use Aden airport as a rear base. The Yemeni Government was surprised by the aircraft, and some young men carried out an action against them, so the U.S. forces had to leave in less than 24 hours.[92]

A decade later, the writers at the Center for Islamic Studies and Research and Abu Ubayd al-Qurashi still remembered the event and used it to support their claims of American military cowardice.[93]

So deeply engrained is the view of American weakness in Salafi jihadists' minds that some members of the movement see it even as they are being defeated. The author of bin Laden's purported last will, written during the battle of Tora Bora, seemed oblivious to the contradiction when he wrote "we saw the coward Crusaders and the humiliated Jews remain steadfast in the fighting while the soldiers of our nation lifted a white flag and surrendered to the enemies like women."[94]

Jihadist Coping Mechanisms

David Cook observed that one way jihadists reconciled themselves to losing Afghanistan was by drawing an analogy between the Byzantine Empire and the United States.[95] Early Muslims fought against the Byzantine Christians but sometimes also fought alongside them, much as Muslims fought alongside the Americans against the Soviet menace in the 1980s. The Muslims also refused to hand over fellow Muslims to the Byzantine Christians, much as Mullah Omar refused to hand over Osama bin Laden to the Americans after September 11. In the end, however, the Byzantine Empire was weak and the Muslims defeated it in 1453. The analogy is clear to jihadists: despite America's initial and temporary victory in Afghanistan, the Muslims will eventually triumph over yet another hollow force.

Cook also noted the extensive use of dreams reported as factual events to "disconfirm" what was truly happening in Afghanistan.[96] A dream reported on a jihadist Internet site shortly after the fall of Kandahar suggested that the Taliban did the coalition a favor by ceding the field: "An old lady from a well-known area in Kandahar, Charsoo, saw a dream before the evacuation of the Taliban from Kandahar in which there was a clear indication to give respite to the disbelievers. The old lady saw a rush of beautiful men and women in the streets. . . . Their foreheads were shining and the old lady got the feeling that these men, women and children were those who were martyred due to the American bombing. These *shuhada* were indicating to the Taliban to leave the city, and they were reciting . . . [the Qur'anic verse] 'So give the unbelievers some respite.'"[97]

There were also reports of God intervening in the skies—causing American aircraft to collide or striking them with lightning—and on the ground. One jihadist told Al-Jazirah: "The truth is that we have started to believe that it is not even us who have attacked those Americans, so all of this is a miracle by Allah, for the mujahideen who are defending Afghanistan. . . . All of the brothers here became really confused as to how they killed such great numbers of Americans even though we did not do much in the battle."[98]

In short, AQAM views about American weakness and cowardice are nonfalsifiable, or at best falsifiable only over an exceptionally long period. If objective facts (as we understand them) do not support the jihadists' worldview, the jihadists adduce alternate facts, or they interpret a defeat as a withdrawal in good order or as providing a "respite" to the enemy, as God requires. One implication is that AQAM will portray any American withdrawal from Iraq, Afghanistan, or any future battlefield in the war on terrorism as a defeat for the United States, and this will be widely believed throughout the movement. Al-Zawahiri actually claimed such credit in January 2006 when he said that the Americans in Iraq "are now begging to leave and negotiating with the mujahideen. Bush the liar was forced to announce in late November that he would withdraw his troops from Iraq. However, being addicted to lying, he justified his withdrawal by saying that the Iraqi troops have reached a good level and that he will not announce a timetable for withdrawal."[99]

"Apostate" Regimes: Corrupt Lackeys

Today's Salafi jihadists are obedient students of Sayyid Qutb, who taught that the rulers of Muslim countries are apostates and, having knowingly turned their backs on God and "true Islam," are in some ways even more loathsome than "infidels."[100] Al-Maqdisi said that they "prevent Muslims from doing their religious duties."[101] Yusuf al-Ayiri claimed that "these governments promised to follow U.S. instructions to westernize the community in its entirety, to transform Islam, westernize it, and split it off from its essence. These governments pledged, promised, and swore that if any voice of truth and good counsel should sound, they would stifle it."[102] The story of Abu Raghal, famous as the first Muslim traitor, is known to every Muslim. The members of AQAM repeatedly invoke his name in referring to the leaders of the "apostate" governments.[103]

Furthermore, the "apostate" rulers are themselves enslaved, controlled by the Americans and the Israelis (or in some cases the French or British), and are thus not in full control of their own governments and countries.[104] Al-Zawahiri wrote in 2001 that "the masters in Washington and Tel Aviv are using the [apostate] regimes to protect their interest and to fight the battle against the Muslims on their behalf." Abu Bakr Naji considers that the United States is fighting a "war by proxy" against Islam through the local regimes.[105]

AQAM members believe that the "apostate" regimes are wreaking havoc on Islam. Not only are these nations repressive police states (see chapter 3), they also spread pernicious alien values. Saudi Arabia, for example, "is controlled by an oppressive family that destroys everything, cause[s] a lot of harm to the people, spread[s] the Western culture and values under the names of civilization, democracy, and freedom, and the aim is to reshape our minds so that we can accept the Western way of life. Moreover, they want to change our educational curriculum to reshape the history to make our students read Western history."[106]

The "apostate" regimes are also criticized for being deeply corrupt. One AQAM observer complained about "high level princes" and their sons "supervising theft and corruption."[107] Ayman al-Zawahiri is particularly assertive on this question. After a ferry sank in early 2006 while crossing the Red Sea, he said the tragedy "reveals the rampant corruption in our country under the agent governments, which were imposed by the United States. . . . The approach of these governments is based on fighting Islam, torture, illicit profiteering, bribes, and paying no heed to lives and sanctities."[108] Along similar lines, al-Zawahiri said that the Pakistani Army "is a bribed one, whose concern is to fill its pockets with money and [which does] not care if the interests of Muslims in Pakistan go to hell after that."[109]

Salafi jihadists consign every "Muslim" country to this lamentable category. In 2003, for example, bin Laden listed Jordan, Morocco, Nigeria, Pakistan, Saudi Arabia, and Yemen as among the countries "enslaved" by the United States.[110] The CISR voiced similarly sweeping conclusions when it said of Afghanistan:

> The United States occupied that country and installed an Afghan agent, Hamid Karzai. As everyone can see, this agent has been more eager to promote the interests of the United States than the United States itself. . . . The Karzai system is the system officially in use in all the Muslim countries. . . . There is no difference between the Karzai of Yemen, the Karzai of Pakistan, the Karzai of Jordan, the Karzai of Qatar, the Karzai of Kuwait, the Karzai of Egypt, and the long list of Karzai traitors ruling the Muslim countries.[111]

Yusuf al-Ayiri typically portrayed the government of Kazakhstan as groveling before the infidel. "President Nazarbayev of Kazakhstan was against taking part in the war [Operation Enduring Freedom] but during his visit with the Pope he pledged his readiness to cooperate with the United States. . . . He said, 'Words are not enough to support the United States in its war against terror. We will prove this with actions. We are ready to offer anything the United States wants.'"[112]

Mocking the "Apostate" Regimes

A Web site broadly sympathetic to the jihadists has published a satirical list of the pillars of *"Istislaam,"* which the site translates as "humiliative [*sic*] surrender," a religion practiced by the "rulers of the Muslims' lands." The pillars are:

1. To testify that there is no god but the American president, and that his ambassador is the messenger of this god
2. To establish the obligatory obedience while facing the White House (more than five times a day)
3. To give *Jizyah* (tax) to the American government . . .
4. Fasting eternity [probably "eternally"] with one's tongue from saying anything negative regarding the American government (even if just one word) . . .
5. Pilgrimage to the White House, for whoever is capable or incapable of doing so . . . [ellipses as published][113]

Ultimately, however, the "apostate" governments are thought to be intrinsically weak. Al-Qurashi believes that they "cannot keep their tyrannical regimes going for a single minute without U.S. help."[114] The author of "Jihad in Iraq: Hopes and Dangers" agreed, discussing the "weakness of Arab regimes and their structure. When you learn how oppressive and tyrannical the Iraqi regime was, you will realize the fragility of the other regimes that are not similar to the injustice of Iraq's tyrant or any other material or human power on earth."[115]

The militaries of the "apostate" regimes are commensurately weak, despite outward appearances. The CISR concluded that in the case of Saudi Arabia, at least, this is because the U.S. military controls the local forces, even choosing which weapons the country can buy. The United States maintains such tight control over them that, for example, it can steer a Saudi missile after it has been launched, thereby eliminating any possibility of attacking Israel.[116] The CISR bitterly observed in 2003: "The small state of Israel, which has a population of no more than six million people, has an army of more than one million soldiers, and all men able to carry arms are in the reserves. However, in Saudi Arabia, the army is the smallest and weakest in terms of armament, men, equipment, and preparedness to defend our religion and honor."[117]

Conclusion

AQAM bases its perceptions of its enemy on a bedrock of religious beliefs that begin and end with the insurmountable divide between *dar al-Islam* and *dar al-harb*. First among the enemies across this divide is the foremost "Crusader" nation, the United States, though there is still plenty of venom reserved for the "Zionist" power Israel and the "apostate" regimes throughout the Middle East. Hostility to Islam does not imply intrinsic strength, however. Western societies are intrinsically weak and decadent, and thus are in no position to support the various elements of their national power. Indeed, the power of the West, particularly the United States, is ultimately illusory, based on a delusion the West not only believes but has managed to promulgate throughout the world. The Western economies—their strategic center of gravity—and militaries are weak and vulnerable. In particular, the American military is a paper tiger, made up of cowards and led by military and political leaders who lack resolve. Most of those fighting the global jihad think that the United States has overstretched itself and needs only to face an implacable foe to meet its inevitable destiny of humiliation and defeat. The jihadists view the "apostate regimes" as also intrinsically weak, corrupt, and even feckless. These states are propped up primarily by their Western patrons, though, as we saw in chapter 3, the jihadists do have a great deal of respect for their intelligence and security services. This is a fundamentally optimistic (some might say delusional) worldview that offers many fruitful avenues of approach for the dedicated jihadist.

Notes

1. FBIS GMP20040209000243, "Compilation of Usama bin Ladin Statements 1994—January 2004," in English, February 9, 2004, 103. This quote is from an American Broadcasting Company (ABC) interview with bin Laden recorded in 1998 and rereleased September 18, 2001.
2. See, for instance, Momin Khawaja: "u know the way the world is split into two camps . . . one of *Iman* and anotha of *Kufr* (and that's the non-believers) (Ontario Court of Justice, 19; text as written).
3. FBIS GMP20041014000206.
4. Harmony document folder ISGM-2005-001834, *Book Titled "The Position of the Scholar Mujahidin in the Event of the Islamic Emirate of Afghanistan,"* 2002–5.
5. FBIS GMP20031027000226.
6. For two examples that do come out of the Salafi jihadist milieu, see Harmony document folder 500MI-2005-RP-MLA00013; and Center for International Issues

Research, "Indonesian Militant Recruitment Briefing," 2004, for one from Jemaah Islamiyah.

7. FBIS GMP20040209000243, from "Bin Ladin Declares Jihad on Americans," *Al-Islah*, London, September 2, 1996.

8. Harmony document folder ISGM-2005-001834. See also bin Laden making a similar sweeping argument in FBIS GMP20040209000243, "Sunday Times Obtains Film of bin Ladin Vowing Revenge on UK, US, Others," *Sunday Times*, London, May 19, 2002.

9. Note that Salafi jihadists do not appear to view "infidel" status as a genetic failing. See, for example, the interview with Abu Bakar Ba'asyir and the questions about "essentialism" and Jewish children being raised as Muslims at www.sitemaker. umich.edu/satran/files/atranba_asyirinterview020905.pdf, accessed September 23, 2007.

10. Naji, *Management of Savagery*, 38.

11. Notably, see Graham Allison and Philip Zelikow, *Essence of Decision*, 2nd ed. (New York: Longman, 1999), a book-length exposition of Allison's article that appeared in 1969 in *American Political Science Review*, "Conceptual Models and the Cuban Missile Crisis."

12. Later scholars of "international political economy" would differ with Morgenthau on this point. So, too, would Marxists.

13. Hans J. Morgenthau, *Politics among Nations*, 3rd ed. (New York: Alfred A. Knopf, 1960), 5.

14. FBIS GMP20041014000206.

15. Harmony document folder AFGP-2002-002857.

16. Naji, *Management of Savagery*, 38.

17. FBIS GMP20040109000138.

18. FBIS GMP20040728000229.

19. Ibid.

20. FBIS GMP20041014000206.

21. Mary Habeck noted that "the jihadis generally believe that cease-fires are possible under very circumscribed conditions, most especially that they do not allow unbelievers to have possession of Islamic land and that they have a definite time limit. Qutb wrote that a truce could be declared without a specific period, but that 'if treachery is *feared* on the part' of the unbelievers, it could be brought to an end" (*Knowing the Enemy*, 130). Bin Laden offered a truce to Europe in April 2004 and to the United States in January 2006—both contingent upon the withdrawal of all forces from the Middle East.

22. Esa al-Hindi, *The Army of Madinah in Kashmir* (Birmingham, U.K.: Maktabah al Ansar Publications, 1999), 111. British authorities arrested al-Hindi (real name Dhiren Barot) in 2004 and convicted him in 2006 for his role in planning terrorist operations in the United States and United Kingdom. Mary Jordan "Al-Qaeda Figure Gets Life for Plots Targeting U.S., Britain," *Washington Post*, November 8, 2006, 16.

23. Harmony document folder AFGP-2002-600083, pre-2002. This document was found in the house of Abu Hafs/Mohammed Atef, the onetime al Qaida military leader. It lays out a distinctly Maoist strategy for a three-phase guerrilla war. Its author remains anonymous, but the document bears a striking resemblance to a four-part series of articles on guerrilla warfare that appeared in *Al-Battar Camp* in early 2004 that were attributed to al-Muqrin. This may suggest that al-Muqrin

had a hand in writing the Tajikistan document or that the separate authors of the two documents both drew on the same exposition of Maoist thought.

24. Harmony document folder AFGP-2002-600083.

25. FBIS GMP20040728000229.

26. FBIS GMP20041014000206.

27. Naji, *Management of Savagery*, 6.

28. FBIS GMP20031027000226.

29. FBIS GMP20020918000157, "Al-Ansar Writer Views Goals, Religious Grounds of September Attacks" (Internet), Jehad.net, September 18, 2002.

30. Harmony document folder AFGP-2002-600053.

31. Berman, "The Philosopher of Islamic Terror."

32. Qutb, *Milestones*.

33. FBIS GMP20040209000243, "Islamist Site Publishes bin Ladin's 'Letter to the American People,'" (Internet) *Waaqiah*, October 26, 2002.

34. FBIS GMP20060305535004, "Jihadist Website Posts al-Zawahiri's Speech on HAMAS, Prophet Cartoons, Others," (Internet) Jihadist Websites—OSC Report, March 5, 2006.

35. FBIS GMP20030122000038, 10–16.

36. Bin Laden was probably referring to Exodus 22:25, Deuteronomy 23:20, and Psalms 15:1–5. The first says, "If you lend money to my people, to the poor among you, you shall not deal with them as a creditor, you shall not exact interest from them."

37. FBIS GMP20040209000243, from bin Ladin's "Letter to the American People." A common urban legend in the Middle East, not merely among Salafi jihadists, is that Benjamin Franklin urged the drafters of the U.S. Constitution to exclude Jews from the new United States, warning that if they did not do so, the Jews would control the country within two hundred years. For appearances of this story in nonjihadist media, see, for example, FBIS GMP20021209000064, "Egyptian 'Horseman' Series Criticized at Home; Search for Arab Backers," Cairo, FBIS Report in Arabic, December 9, 2002; FBIS GMP20021029000010, "Article Citing 'Protocols of Elders of Zion' on Jewish Plan for World Domination," Al-Jazirah Riyadh, Internet version in Arabic, September 6, 2002; FBIS GMP20020701000225, "Cairo Columnist Sees Americans 'Enslaved' by Jews as Benjamin Franklin Predicted," *Al-Wafd*, Cairo, in Arabic, July 1, 2002, 14; FTS19980712000441, "Al-Thawrah: US Foreign Policy Dominated by 'Zionist Jews,'" *Al-Thawrah*, Baghdad, in Arabic, July 6, 1998; and FBIS GMP20011107000100, "Saudi Paper Says US Must Look for Terrorism inside It, Blames Zionism," Jedda Ukaz, Internet version in Arabic, November 7, 2001. One source alleges that the father of 9/11 hijacker Mohammed Atta believed the story: GMP20020906000121, "Al-Jazirah Airs 'Part One' of Program on al-Qa'ida Link to 11 Sep Attacks," Doha al-Jazirah satellite channel television, in Arabic, 1905 GMT, September 5, 2002.

38. FBIS GMP20031004000119, "Islamic Research Center Publishes Book on 12 May Riyadh Operation," August 1, 2003.

39. Ibid.

40. See, for example, Naji's *Management of Savagery*, 8–9, where Naji attributed a similar argument to Abdullah Azzam. See also Abu Ubayd al-Qurashi in FBIS GMP20020814000145, "Al-Ansar Writer Views Futility of US Tactics against Islamic 'Mujahidin,'" August 10, 2002.

41. See Hazim al-Madani, ICPVTR-13453 in the database of Rohan Gunaratna's International Centre for Political Violence and Terrorism Research, www.pvtr. org/coreprojects_pathfinder.htm, accessed October 15, 2007.

42. FBIS GMP20040209000243, "Usama bin Ladin Denounces US-Sponsored 'World Order,'" Islamabad, Pakistan, January 9, 2000; see also FBIS GMP20040209000243, "Usama bin Ladin Would Make Life 'Miserable' for United States if Taleban Allows," Islamabad, Pakistan, May 17, 2001. In 2002 or 2003, the Pashto Islamic Freedom Movement picked up this theme, as seen in Harmony document folder AFGP-2004-002509, *Islamic Freedom Movement Propaganda Letter*, 2002–3.

43. FBIS GMP20030929000003, "Future of Iraq, Arabian Peninsula after the Fall of Baghdad," August 1, 2003.

44. Naji, *Management of Savagery*, 7. The authors inserted the words in brackets; the translator the ones in parentheses.

45. Naji, *Management of Savagery*, 7.

46. Abu Ubayd al-Qurashi made an incomplete form of this argument in FBIS GMP20021126000154. Others have fleshed it out.

47. Harmony document folder AFGP-2002-600111, *Report Dated 11/28/1993 from Saleh Abdul Wahid to Abu Hafs re a Meeting with Shaykh 'Abdullah Sahl and Shaykh Hasan Tahir and Their Discussion about Hitting American Forces in Somalia*, November 28, 1993.

48. FBIS GMP20040728000229.

49. Ibid.

50. Ibid.

51. Naji, *Management of Savagery*, 7.

52. Ibid.

53. Batterjee, *The Arab Volunteers*.

54. FBIS GMP20030122000038, 10–16.

55. FBIS GMP20031027000226.

56. FBIS GMP20031004000119.

57. FBIS GMP20040728000229. The article contains a lengthy discussion of the U.S. economy, touching on such issues as the national debt, the growth rate, the unemployment rate, and the cost of the war. In the course of this discussion, the author cites the views of such people as Treasury Secretary John Snow, former "under secretary of defense for financial affairs" Dov Zakheim, and former presidential candidate Howard Dean.

58. Center for International Issues Research, "A Study of al-Qaeda's Interests in China Appears on an MRI Website," *Global Issues Report*, March 26, 2007. Hujazi's original article was titled "China under the Microscope of the Salafi Jihadist" and raised the possibility that the jihadists might have to fight China in the future, in part because China will soon become the world's greatest economic power and will take control of the world's oil supplies. For a similar argument about the fundamentally economic nature of the war with the United States, see SITE Institute, "Al-Qaeda's Battle Is an Economic Battle and Not Military," October 27, 2005, which discusses a paper of the same title written in 2005 by a Saudi jihadist.

59. FBIS GMP20040209000243, "Al-Arabiyah Broadcasts Excerpts of Previously Aired bin Ladin Tape," Dubai al-Arabiyah television, December 20, 2003.

60. FBIS GMP20050628381001. "Barbarossa" was the nom de guerre of the first emir of the jihadists in Bosnia in 1992, Abu Abdel Aziz, a noted Saudi mujaheed, but this is probably not the same person.

61. FBIS GMP20040209000243, "Usama bin Ladin's Message to Iraq, Urges Muslims to Overthrow Regimes," Doha al-Jazirah satellite channel television, February 11, 2003.

62. FBIS GMP20060902635004, "Jihadist Site Posts Video of 'Azzam the American' Inviting Americans to Islam," September 2, 2006.

63. FBIS GMP20020613000138, "Article Says al-Qa'ida War Tactics Based on Old Chinese Military Books," June 13, 2002.

64. FBIS GMP20021001000100, *"Al-Ansar* Writer Views, Compares al-Qa'ida and Elements of Power," September 22, 2002.

65. Stern, *Terror in the Name of God,* 123.

66. Harmony document folder AFGP-2002-800073, *Letter/Notes, Including Letter from UBL and one from a Canadian Arab; Schematic Diagram of a Possible Korean Missile-Carrying Vehicle, Interrogation Notes, Passport of Saudi National,* December 2, 1999.

67. FBIS GMP20040209000243, "Pakistan Interviews Usama bin Ladin," Islamabad, Pakistan, March 18, 1997.

68. Naji, *Management of Savagery,* 6–9, 41, 61.

69. FBIS GMP20040209000243, "Time Magazine Interview with bin Ladin," January 11, 1999; FBIS GMP20040209000243, "Muslim Leader Warns of a New Assault on US Forces," London, *Independent,* March 22, 1997.

70. IntelCenter, "Al-Qaeda's Advice for Mujahideen in Iraq: Lessons Learned in Afghanistan," v1.0, April 14, 2003. The original document dates from March 2003. In the Shadow of the Lances series, The Fifth Chapter, Islamic Research and Studies Center.

71. Ibid.

72. FBIS GMP20040615000107, "Text of al-Zarqawi's Letter to bin Ladin on Future of Mujahidin in Iraq," June 15, 2004.

73. FBIS GMP20060425398001, "Al-Zarqawi Addresses Islamic Nation in First Statement since Formation of the Mujahidin Shura Council," Jihadist Websites, OSC Report, April 25, 2006.

74. FBIS GMP20031027000226.

75. FBIS GMP20040209000243.

76. Ibid.

77. IntelCenter, "Al-Qaeda's Advice."

78. FBIS GMP20040623000072, "Al-Qa'ida's al-Zarqawi Threatens to Kill Iraqi Prime Minister," Jihadist Websites, FBIS Report in Arabic, June 23, 2004.

79. FBIS GMP20031004000119.

80. FBIS GMP20041014000206.

81. FBIS GMP20040723000200.

82. FBIS GMP20030214000152, "Islamist Site Posts Translation of Purported bin Ladin Audio Message," February 14, 2003.

83. FBIS GMP20040723000200.

84. FBIS EUP20051012374001, "Report: Complete Text of al-Zawahiri 9 July 2005 Letter to al-Zarqawi," October 11, 2005.

85. These include the Pashto Islamic Freedom Movement; see Harmony document folder AFGP-2004-002509, *Islamic Freedom Movement Propaganda Letter,* 2002–3; the anonymous author of "Jihad in Iraq: Hopes and Dangers," FBIS GMP20040728000229; Salih Abd-al-Wahid writing in 1993 to Abu Hafs, see Harmony document folder AFGP-2002-600111, *Report Dated 11/28/1993 from Saleh Abdul Wahid to Abu Hafs re a Meeting with Shaykh 'Abdullah Sahl and*

Shaykh Hasan Tahir and Their Discussion about Hitting American Forces in Somalia, 1993.

86. FBIS GMP20040209000243, "Bin Ladin Declares Jihad on Americans," *al-Islah,* London, September 2, 1996.

87. FBIS GMP20040209000243, "CBS Releases Interview with bin Ladin," CBS *This Morning,* January 13, 1999. Al-Zawahiri also mentioned the precedent in December 2003. See FBIS GMP20040723000200.

88. "Special Dispatch Series—no. 344," February 10, 2002, summarizing "Fourth-Generation Wars" by Abu Ubayd al-Qurashi in the second issue of AQ online magazine *Al-Ansar.* Al-Qurashi also addressed this topic in FBIS GMP20031027000226. See also Harmony document folder AFGP-2004-002509, 2002–3; and al-Zawahiri in FBIS GMP20031219000224, "Al-Jazirah Airs al-Zawahiri Recording on 2nd Anniversary of 'Tora Bora Battle.'"

89. FBIS GMP20031004000119.

90. FBIS GMP20040209000243.

91. Ibid.

92. Ibid.

93. FBIS GMP20031004000119; see also FBIS GMP20031027000226.

94. FBIS GMP20040209000243.

95. Cook, "Recovery of Radical Islam," 45–47. This equation of the United States with Byzantium has been in AQAM thought at least since 1993–94. See Harmony document folder AFGP-2002-600053.

96. Cook, "Recovery of Radical Islam," 40. Taking dreams seriously is not only the province of the uneducated. Sayf al-Adl, a former Egyptian army colonel, wrote in his captured "diary" that "four months before the [September 11] raid on America I saw several dreams and there were specifically three that were both strategic and forward thinking."

97. Ibid., 41.

98. Ibid., 43.

99. FBIS GMP20060106532004, "Al-Jazirah Net Carries Full Text of al-Qa'ida's al-Zawahiri Speech."

100. Harmony document folder SFOR-2003-A00842, *Arabic Article that Defends the May 2003 Bombings in Riyadh,* May 25, 2003. This document, captured in Bosnia, explains that "the leaders of Saudi Arabia are unbelievers based on the following: a. The government appoints idolaters in various government agencies. b. The government gives the unbelievers high powers in the state, and the unbelievers have established their own state within a Muslim country that is against Muslims. c. The government mocks God and the verses of the Koran." Harmony document folder 500MI-2005-RP-MLA00011 provides the comparable perspective of the Abu Sayyaf Group of the Philippines.

101. Harmony document folder ISGM-2005-001834, *Book Titled "The Position of the Scholar Mujahidin in the Event of the Islamic Emirate in Afghanistan,"* 2002–5.

102. FBIS GMP20030929000003, "Future of Iraq, Arabian Peninsula after the Fall of Baghdad."

103. See, for instance, "Communiqué from 'al-Qaeda's Jihad Committee in Mesopotamia' (Abu Musab al-Zarqawi)," *Global Terror Alert,* November 7, 2005; FBIS GMP20030313000103, "Bin Ladin's Statement Calls for Revolt against Saudis, Death to Americans, Jews," March 1, 2003. See also Harmony document folder ISGZ-2004-00044592, *The 27th Edition of the Voice of the Jihad's Biannual Magazine, October 2003.*

104. See Harmony document folder ISGZ-2003-602390-HT-NVTC, *Military Science: The Targets within the Cities by Abu-Hajir'Abd-al-'Aziz al-Muqrin*, no date. See also FBIS GMP20041001000122, "Al-Zawahiri Urges Defense of Palestine, Forming 'Resistance' Command," Al-Jazirah, October 1, 2004.

105. Al-Zawahiri, 2001, part 11, in Sageman, *Understanding Terror Networks*, 22; Naji, *Management of Savagery*, 10.

106. See ICPVTR-13449, Hazim al-Madani, "Jihad as We See It and Want It," www.al-qaedun.com in the database of Rohan Gunaratna's International Centre for Political Violence and Terrorism Research, www.pvtr.org/coreprojects_pathfinder.htm, accessed October 15, 2007.

107. Harmony document folder AFGP-2002-002883, *Abu Massab al-Soory's Computer Disks, PGP Program, Information about Taliban, and Computer Program*, no date.

108. FBIS GMP20060305535004, "Jihadist Website Posts al-Zawahiri's Speech on HAMAS, Prophet Cartoons, Others," March 5, 2006.

109. FBIS GMP20060106532004. See also bin Laden in FBIS GMP20041029000220, "Bin Ladin Addresses American People on Causes, Outcome of 11 September Attacks," Doha al-Jazirah, October 29, 2004, in which he compares the corrupt "apostate" regimes to the Bush family.

110. FBIS GMP20040209000243. See also bin Laden in FBIS GMP20030214000152, "Islamist Site Posts Translation of Purported bin Ladin Audio Message," February 14, 2003.

111. FBIS GMP20031004000119.

112. FBIS GMP20030929000003.

113. Shakyh Husayn ibn Mahmood, "Reviving the Creed of Tawheed: The Religion of Humiliative Surrender (*Istislaam*)," www.streetdawah.com/articles/Current%20afrais/The%20religion%20of%20Istislaam.pdf, accessed January 10, 2007. The Web site reproduces Qutb's *Milestones* and the works of al-Wahab. It also extols the virtues of Abdullah Azzam and describes the evils of democracy. *Istislaam* is better translated as "surrender."

114. FBIS GMP20031027000226.

115. FBIS GMP20040728000229. Al-Zawahiri tangentially addressed this point in FBIS GMP20020108000197, "Al-Sharq al-Awsat Publishes Extracts from al-Jihad Leader al-Zawahiri's New Book," December 2, 2001.

116. FBIS GMP20031004000119.

117. Ibid.

CHAPTER 5

Strategic Adaptation in the Global Salafi Jihadist Movement

Fighting the enemies must be based on solid grounds, not on illusions that vanish at the first collision.

ABU UBAYD AL-QURASHI, 2002[1]

AQAM's Changing Strategy

Chapter 2 explained that the Salafi jihadists hold a variety of opinions about their individual places in the jihad. The foot soldiers believe their obligation to God stops at fighting and that combat against virtually any sanctioned target will suffice; for them, jihad is at most a matter of tactics. The strategists believe that God expects them to do their best to bring about victory; they consider higher-level questions that include those of strategy and grand strategy.

Though their understanding of the faith is essentially immutable, it is clear that the strategists' military ideas have evolved. History, their own experience, and the writings of others have taught them a number of important strategic lessons. Significantly, they have begun recording such lessons in their own writings and (with rather less success) have tried to embody them in their operations.

The first strategic lesson is that it is important to have a strategy. Strategy has not always played a significant role in jihadists' thinking. Sayyid Qutb, for instance, initially paid scant attention to it. Fifteen years later in the early 1980s, the era of Anwar Sadat's assassination, Mohammed Abd al-Salam

Faraj, the head of the Cairo branch of the Tanzim al-Jihad, was thinking about the theological justifications for jihad and about the various "rules of engagement" (to use a Western term) for jihad, but strategy was still largely absent from his analysis. Indeed, Sadat's assassins seem to have believed that all they had to do was assassinate the Egyptian president and God would miraculously amplify their act and destroy the entire Egyptian government.[2] Of course, that did not happen; the Egyptian regime not only survived, but also launched a crushing counterattack on the revolutionaries.

Writing years later about this period in Egyptian history, Ayman al-Zawahiri, who had been a minor player in Faraj's group and later became a leader of the EIJ, admitted that "good planning and preparations have been missing in many of the acts of violence, beginning with the Technical Military College's incident [in 1975] and up to the events in Asyut.[3] Shortcomings in planning were evident . . . the fundamentalist movement must rid itself of the haphazardness and rashness that continue to dominate many of its actions."[4]

Despite al-Zawahiri's best intentions, the EIJ and the EIG (another spinoff from Faraj's organization) still had trouble following a strategy. Sayf al-Adl, a colonel in the Egyptian special forces during the 1980s as well as a secret jihadist, recalled afterward: "The brothers at the Al-Jihad movement [EIJ] and the Islamic Group [EIG] lacked practical experience that could enable them to achieve the desired change. In my opinion and the opinion of some brothers, this was due to over-enthusiasm that resulted in hasty action or recklessness at times. Moreover, they lacked the necessary expertise, a short-term and long-term plan in advance, and a vision to employ the nation's human resources at the highest level."[5]

Egypt was not the only place where lack of strategy was a shortcoming. During the late 1970s and early 1980s, the opposition in Syria—which consisted of an uneasy alliance of Salafi jihadists (al-Tali'a al-Muqatila, or the Fighting Vanguard) and members of the Muslim Brotherhood—had similar shortcomings. They were ultimately crushed at Hamah. One observer of this debacle, Abu Musab al-Suri, operated from the perspective that "it is crucial to have a strategic plan for jihad revolutionary insurgency."[6] In 1989, he wrote a brutally frank assessment of this experience in which he argued that the problem was not the absence of strategy per se, but rather the absence of sound strategy: "When the original mujahideen set out to lay the path to military jihad [in Syria] they lacked a strategic vision that took into account the existing conditions on the ground and the expectations for the future, they did not take into consideration the conditions inside the country, its topography, demography, its ethnic and religious composition, political affiliations, the nature of the regime; they did not compare their strengths to those of the regime, they did not determine who is friend and who is foe."[7]

In the early 1990s, the jihadists went to Somalia. It was clear then to the author of the remarkable set of captured documents now known as the "Five Letters to the Africa Corps" that al Qaida had "not enter[ed] the Somali arena with a clear vision, specifically a strategic vision, either militarily or politically." Fortunately, from this person's point of view, the United States made the same mistake and "did not enter the Somali arena with a clear vision of the objectives of its presence." He thought that this mutual lack of strategy allowed the few and poorly armed mujahideen to operate on roughly equal terms with the one surviving superpower.[8]

Over the years, critiques by people such as al-Suri and the anonymous author of the "Five Letters" have rooted themselves in the minds of many of AQAM's thinkers. Abu Ubayd al-Qurashi, for example, whose writings on military aspects of the jihad were prominent in 2002 and 2003 before he disappeared from public view, is among the new generation of AQAM thinkers who understand that strategy is an absolute prerequisite for accomplishing anything. In a critique that might have been aimed at Faraj, al-Qurashi urged jihadists not to lock themselves in the past, but to pursue pragmatic, modern means of bringing about revolutionary change.

> In the decades that preceded the fall of the Islamic Caliphate many Islamic slogans were raised. They all sought to revive the Islamic Caliphate and, along with it, the lost Islamic glory. Some of these slogans may have been suitable for that period, of time, but they are unrealistic today. Having ignored focusing on the concept of preparing a comprehensive and actual power, including the military, political, economic, and social aspects, these visions now seem shallow. In addition, they have fail[ed] to endorse an agenda, neither in terms of time nor location, which represent the key to any strategy. Therefore, confusion and haphazardness were the natural outcome of these efforts.[9]

Similarly, in his 2005 book, *The Management of Savagery*, Abu Bakr Naji attributed the EIG's "defeat"—the group renounced violence in 1997 after determining that its long-standing efforts to instigate an insurgency against the Egyptian government would not succeed—to the fact that "its leadership lacked a clear concept for a military strategy."[10]

Today, insightful discussions of strategy are common in the Salafi jihadist world. "Jihad in Iraq: Hopes and Dangers," for instance, is a carefully structured exegesis of a possible path to victory in Iraq. It appears to have informed the Madrid train bombers, but, as might be expected in a movement with little command structure and control, the perpetrators of this act did not act precisely in accordance with the document's prescriptions. The frequency with which copies of al-Suri's work are captured on the battlefield also indicates that terrorist operators have at least considered applying his concepts. A telling piece of evidence of the inroads made by strategic (if not deep) thought is the flow chart, reproduced below, that a jihadist recently posted at a militant jihadist Web site. The chart illustrates his vision of how to defeat the Americans and the Maliki government in Iraq.

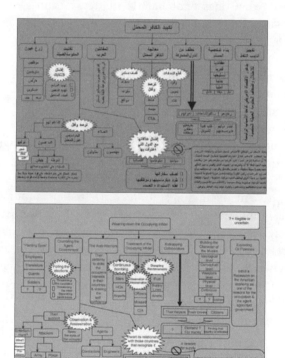

One jihadist's vision of how to defeat the Americans and the Maliki government in Iraq (original and translation). *Source*: Center for International Issues Research, "Militant Islamic Website Posts Insurgent Strategy for Iraq," Global Issues Reports, November 22, 2006. Translated by Thomas Holaday and Laila Sabara.

Aside from the inculcation of strategy itself, four changes in strategy within the Salafi jihadist movement are particularly significant: (1) the development of the global jihadist movement out of what had been largely a conglomeration of disconnected local jihads;[11] (2) al Qaida's choice to neutralize the United States rather than try to immediately overthrow local regimes;[12] (3) al Qaida's increasing emphasis on attacking the American economy (see chapter 6); and (4) the increasing emphasis on the use of *dawah* (proselytizing or, in American terms, information) alongside kinetic jihad (see chapter 7).

There is reason to believe that additional strategic changes are under way within the movement. After many years of following the philosophy of the al Qaida charter—which maintains that theirs is a "path of fighting jihad" that does "not handle matters of aid"—some jihadists such as Ayman al-Zawahiri and Abu Bakr Naji are starting to argue for an approach that pays closer attention to the needs of the people in order to attract adherents to the jihadists' banner.[13]

The movement has also become more aware of weaknesses in its structure that hinder its effectiveness. The core of the concern is that uncoordinated and ill-considered actions are at best unhelpful and at worst counterproductive. This has led to two sets of prescriptions. On the one hand, some jihadists argue that the movement must strengthen its discipline and tighten its command and control. For instance, in late 2006 an online jihadist media organization warned the members of its forum against "negative media manifestations" and "media outbursts" by overly enthusiastic individuals that could undercut the movement's efforts.[14] Similarly, Sayf al-Ansari wrote in a document posted on the Internet in 2002: "A feeling of individual responsibility regarding the issue of jihad should not give rise to a kind of improvised behavior that translates jihad into a kind of spontaneous activity and makes the issue an undisciplined current in which everyone weaves on his own loom. A feeling of responsibility does not mean embodying jihad in scattered individual actions. The feeling needs to be deepened by striving for well-planned action emanating from a position of collective activity."[15] And in 2005 Abu Bakr Naji called for an immediate end to "both arbitrary and traditional methods of management." On the other hand, Abu Musab al-Suri recently argued that the movement must do precisely the opposite: loosen its command and control but ensure the promulgation of a common doctrine—what American military officers might call "a commander's intent"—so that large numbers of jihadists can operate in parallel without the kind of command and control infrastructure that Western militaries and "apostate" security services are so good at dismantling.[16]

Sources of Learning

Given that AQAM does innovate strategically, it is unfortunate that few scholars have written about innovation in terrorist groups at anything other than the tactical level.[17] Martha Crenshaw, one of the few who has grappled with innovation in terrorists' strategy, observed that many analysts argue that terrorism is not innovative. Instead, in the words of Bruce Hoffman, it is "politically radical, but operationally conservative."[18] Crenshaw took issue with this line and argued that innovation does occur in terrorist organizations at the strategic, tactical, and organizational levels, though it is most common at the tactical level.[19]

Whatever Western scholars may think, AQAM's intellectual leadership stresses the importance of lesson learning to warfare and repeatedly emphasizes thinking about war and the enemy. AQAM's writers extol the virtues of the scholar warrior (there may be some degree of self-congratulation at work). Examples abound. The March 2006 issue of the online magazine *Vanguards of Khorasan* featured an article by Mansur al-Shami arguing that fighting and scholarly pursuits go hand in hand.[20] Abu Hudaifa, writing to Osama bin Laden sometime between 1998 and 2001, opined, "In the world of tactics and strategies, which are man-made, there are no confirmed unchangeable principles or absolute facts. Everything is subject to negotiations except (the infallible sharia)."[21] A document from the Abu Sayyaf Group in the Philippines lists military reading and learning among its ten requirements for mujahideen: "10. Introduction to the great Muslim personalities of the recent past and present. Additional from [Islamic texts and histories], the urban mujahid must constantly train and read military strategy, tactics and various knowledge on how to improve his fighting ability."[22]

Islamic history is rife with battles worthy of analysis from a jihadist perspective.[23] Until recently, however, Islamic literature has been short on significant strategic writings to guide today's thinking, probably in large part because most jihadists believed that strategy should be left to God.[24] Most Salafi jihadist leaders today hold the pragmatic view that they should learn from whatever sources seem useful. Two sources are particularly important for learning and for improving their military performance: (1) non-Islamic writings, including military and political theory and history; and (2) their own experience and the experience of related Islamic movements during the past few decades. Underlying the use of both of these sources is the sense that history is important and has much to teach the present generation. Jihadists believe that God expects them to learn from the past. Abu Musab al-Suri, among the most influential AQAM military thinkers between at least 1989 and his capture in 2005, wrote in a widely read assessment of the failed Syrian "jihad" (1970s to early 1980s): "History is full of trials, scientific experiments, and human experiences that evolved over time, wars and revolutions are not different—that is why the Koran and the teachings of the Prophet urge us to seek education and learn from previous examples."[25] A former confidant of Abu Musab al-Zarqawi agreed in 2004:

> It is interesting to draw lessons from the events that happened to infidels and sinful people. It is similarly interesting to tell the stories of believers that show their obedience, ethics, tolerance, hardships, or jihad. These tales reinforce the heart and prompt a person to compare himself to the proponents of good guidance, knowledge, and good deeds—things that an estranged Muslim needs nowadays. . . . [Moreover,] by studying history, we know the reasons why nations rise or fall. We learn about the nature of people and countries. We learn from the mistakes of our ancestors to avoid these mistakes and continue from where our ancestors left, not from where they started. This is attributed to the fact that history repeats itself. In other words, certain consequences happen as a result of certain events. The sharia anticipates events of history since these events are God's will on earth that will never change. . . . Thus, you find that military history is a prerequisite course for students in military colleges. In such a course, various battles are studied, including the reasons why a certain party triumphed and another was defeated. For that reason, history professors are major participants in the process of drawing up the strategies of nations or outlining their national security.[26]

Learning from Experience

The jihadists are clearly open to outside intellectual influences, but they also learn from their own experience. This happens in two ways. First, a Darwinian process weeds out the groups (and freelance individuals) within the broader movement that are ineffective in the environment in which they choose to operate and that do not improve their performance quickly enough.[27] Al-Suri's list of defeated jihads attests to this fact (see text box titled "Jihadist Failures"). The "apostate" security services have destroyed many Salafi jihadist organizations, often helped by strategic errors made by the organizations themselves. "Through our own fault events took the opposite direction to the one we intended," one jihadist commented with regard to the jihad in Syria.[28] On at least one occasion the EIG decided to give up violence because it was failing to achieve its objectives.[29] Thus, the only groups operating at any given time are those too new to have been destroyed and those with a proven ability to adapt and learn.

Abu Bakr Naji noted that "understanding the abilities of the enemy and the time of his defeat only comes to us by plunging into active war with him."[30] Naji is right: of all the movement's sources of learning, actual experiences have been the most valuable and influential. Certainly, AQAM has struggled with the same disinclination to self-criticism that exists in most traditional militaries, incompetence, and the natural human tendency to cling to preconceived notions. However, the record indicates that Abu Hudaifa was being too negative when he wrote to Osama bin Laden sometime between 1998 and 2001 that "criticism was considered until recently some sort of discouragement, frightening, and inspiring failure."[31] In fact, AQAM's intellectual leadership has engaged in serious self-criticism since at least 1989. For instance, Ayman al-Zawahiri noted that after Sadat took power in Egypt, "a new phase of growth began for the Islamic movement. But this time there was no repetition of the past; rather the Islamic movement built on it, benefiting from previous experiences, lessons, and events."[32] Since then, the jihad movement has claimed several victories, each in itself a learning opportunity. In the "Five Letters to the Africa Corps," an anonymous al Qaida leader writing to an operator in Somalia, probably in 1993–94, urged the latter to keep a careful record of what had happened so as to enable future learning.

[Somalia] is a splendid victory and a unique experience that deserves recording, evaluation, derivation of lessons, and determination of courses of future action in light of its results. . . . The Muslim victory in Somalia over America has profound implications ideologically, politically, and psychologically that will require lengthy studies. You have the duty to record notes about these implications and keep them until it is time to study them in depth. . . . We intend to enter this experience in the future, God willing, but our circumstances here demand certain changes. It is important that we review the results of the experience before we undertake it.[33]

The author of that document even demonstrated the rare quality of look-ing for the small failures concealed by a bigger success. "What are the advan-tages and faults revealed by the Somali campaign in the ranks of the Africa Corps?" he asked. "The success or failure of future campaigns will depend on the precise answer to this question and how it is exploited in practice."[34]

The movement has striven to learn from defeat. From AQAM's point of view, there have been numerous catastrophic defeats and only one unambiguous victory, the defeat and destruction of the Soviet Union.[35] The author of the "Five Letters" believed that while "a defeat can lead to additional defeats because it destroys morale and creates despair . . . it can lead to great victories if the causes are analyzed and the lessons learned are used in a future successful action."[36] Abu Hudaifa noted that "leadership shouldn't squelch debate. Some of the advantages of the jihad movement after the setbacks it suffered in some countries is [sic] that the door for self-criticism in a loud voice regarding its presented ideas, strate-gies, and mechanisms was wide open. . . . We support this trend in public thinking and discussing ideas in the open and in a healthy environment away from any psychological pressure practiced by some groups on their Movement."[37] In fact, Abu Hudaifa attributed the strategic reorientation of the early to mid-1990s when al Qaida started to focus on the United States rather than on the local regimes in Islamic countries to that process of self-criticism and learning.[38]

Jihadist Failures

In his last book, *The Call to Global Islamic Resistance*, Abu Musab al-Suri wrote: "From the end of 1996 until the end of 1997, I spent long hours contemplating and conversing with some of the cream of the jihadist elite from the Afghan Arab cadres and the jihadist organizations resident in London. We evaluated the reasons for the repeated armed jihadist failures in the modern era." These failures included:

- Morocco (1963)[39]
- Syria (1965)
- Egypt (1965)
- Turkey (1970)
- Syria (1975–82)
- Algeria (1976)

- Egypt (1981)
- Libya (1989)
- Algeria (1990–96)
- Libya (1994–96)

as well as "limited experiences" in Tunisia, Jordan, Yemen, and Lebanon.

The defeat in Afghanistan in late 2001 occasioned a round of self-critical analysis. Abu Musab al-Suri, among the most insightful al Qaida military thinkers, was so inspired by those events that he wrote a monumental book, *The Call to Global Islamic Resistance*, that was published on the Internet in 2005 not long before his capture. He described the genesis of his book in the following terms:

In the aftermath of the September 2001 events and the downfall of the Islamic Emirate in Afghanistan in December 2001, I made a decision to go into total solitude, sever . . . relations with the outside world, devote my time to following and examining events via the media, and occupy myself with reading and writing to analyze the tremendous changes all over the world, reassess our previous jihadist experiences and modus operandi, modernize them, and find out means to confront our enemy in a post-September world and in the wake of the occupation of Afghanistan and Iraq. During this period of time . . . [I focused on filling] another significant Muslim gap—reflecting on our former experiences, drawing out lessons, and focusing on the nature of upcoming confrontations and battles.[40]

AQAM strategists repeatedly go to the well of experience. In a work from the summer of 2006 arguing for reorienting AQAM's approach, Egyptian jihadist leader Muhammad Khalil al-Hakaymah wrote that he was putting forth a proposal "founded on personal experience, study, comparison, and the debate with the expert leaders of the Mujahideen and their cadres. Most of these topics are not religiously related issues, but they are opinions founded on lessons learned from experiments with the issues of the views of war and plots."[41]

Learning from Non-Muslim Military Literature

AQAM's military thought, while often muddled and certainly not monolithic, is firmly situated within global military thought, particularly with regard to revolutionary warfare. A 120-page book entitled *Winds of Revolution* found in a house in Afghanistan and associated with Osama bin Laden makes this clear. The book's contents include:

Chapter 2. The War of the Flea (a reference to Robert Taber's book of the same name): the organization of revolutionary forces, Che Guevara's thinking on guerrilla warfare[42]

Chapter 3. Revolutionary Warfare in Cuba

Chapter 4. Revolutionary Warfare in China: the long war, the strength of the people against regular armies, the sayings of Mao Tse-Tung, studies from the Chinese

Chapter 5. Resistance against the French in Indochina: colonial war and the experience of the French, strategy and tactics of Van Nguyen Giap, how the Vietnamese won in Indochina

Chapter 6. The American Experience in Vietnam

Chapter 7. Studies in the Armed Uprising in Ireland: unrest in Ireland and the role of the "Black and Tans" in it

Chapter 8. Popular Uprisings in North Africa: Morocco, Tunisia, and Algeria

Chapter 9. Guerrilla Warfare in Cyprus: General Grivas and guerrilla warfare in Cyprus, political terrorism operations, strategic errors of Britain

Chapter 10. Disappointment in the Guerrilla Wars of the Philippines, Malaysia, and Greece: why the Communists failed in Greece

Chapter 11. Guerrilla War in Cities and the Country: the art of war from the view of Sun-Tzu, initial strategy and tactics of guerilla war

Chapter 12. Future Guerrilla wars in the Third World and America's New Policies: Al Qaida's anticipated revolutionary operations against the United States.[43]

The jihadists' use of foreign military ideas has two important implications for adaptation: first, it is evidence of an intellectual openness that bodes well for adaptation; second, it is possible—in some cases, at least—to pinpoint when particular non-Muslim (particularly Western) ideas entered the jihadist debate. Arguably, this is adaptation—at least at the purely intellectual level—in action. References to foreign works sometimes begin to appear in jihadist writings at a particular time because the works have just been published in the West. Jihadists' references to *asymmetric warfare,* a term that emerged in the late 1990s, are one example. In other cases, it appears that jihadists may have belatedly "discovered" certain long-extant foreign writings; Carlos Marighella's *Mini-Manual of the Urban Guerrilla* may be one example. More broadly, the mid-1990s saw a sharp increase in the salience of non-Muslim military thought in jihadist writings, and the post-9/11 period has seen an explosion of references to foreign works.

Sayyid Qutb set the precedent in *Milestones* for the use of non-Muslim military literature. He made a distinction between learning from non-Muslims about philosophical or theological subjects, on the one hand, and physical sciences and similar fields, on the other. The latter he described as not being "related to the basic concepts of a Muslim about life, the universe, man, the purpose of his creating."[44] Therefore, "a Muslim can go to a Muslim or a non-Muslim to learn abstract sciences such as chemistry, physics, biology . . . military arts and similar sciences and arts."[45] Forty years later, Abu Bakr Naji wrote in a section of *The Management of Savagery* entitled "Using the Time-Testing Principles of Military Combat": "Wisdom is the goal of the believer, and even if we generally follow in the footsteps of the Prophet . . . and his Companions . . . we only accept that our policies in any jihadi action are sharia policies, unless the sharia permits us to use the plans and military principles of non-Muslims in which there is no sin."[46]

Non-Muslim sources serve several distinct functions in Salafi jihadist literature. Some writings appear to influence the content of jihadist thought directly or to be otherwise intricately woven into their thinking. These, among others, include to varying degrees Mao and other leftist writers, Clausewitz, Sun Tzu, and modern Western strategists concerned with "fourth generation warfare" and similar issues. AQAM does not, however, wholly accept any one work or author. Rather, it integrates these works into its existing ideological, political, and theological doctrines.

Given the commonalities between Marxist-Leninist thought and Salafi jihadist thought (see chapter 2), it is not surprising that there is particularly wide acceptance in the movement of communist or leftist texts or analyses of them, albeit with corrections for any portions the jihadists view as incompatible with Islam. Among the most important perspectives jihadists share with leftist writers on revolutionary war is the deeply political nature of the struggle and thus the importance of being one with the people. To a substantial degree, one can understand the efforts of AQAM's strategists as a continuing effort to find the formula for rallying the support of the masses. Abu Ubayd al-Qurashi noted that "based on what (Clausewitz) the famous plotter has declared centuries ago, Mao Tse Tong has mentioned in his book about the revolutionary war, the basic relation between war and politics; a relation which render[s] military operations relevant to the political leadership. In this regard, Mao declared, 'war can never be separated from politics.' He added, 'politics is a war itself, but without shedding any blood.' Thus, Mao further says that all the operations executed by the revolutionary army especially the military ones . . . should be an implementation of political aims."[47]

In the late 1980s, Abu Musab al-Suri realized the importance of this as well. "No matter how big or capable the vanguard organization is," he wrote,

> the war it wages is waged on behalf of the masses, those masses are its source of information, supplies, personnel, and refuge. A gang warfare theorist once said (The masses are the sea in which the vanguard organization should swim like a fish). All revolutionary wars that were able to mobilize the masses on their behalf were successful; such as Algiers, China, and Vietnam, however the revolutionary wars that failed to achieve that and were isolated from their masses ended up in defeat, like Malaysia, Philippines, and Greece. (Refer to the translated book: The war of those deemed weak)[48] [as written]

Mao

Of the communist and leftist thinkers who wrote about war, Mao Tse-Tung has had the greatest influence on AQAM's thought. Its theorists approvingly cite his ideas about the importance of the masses, stages of insurgency, and the political end of consolidation of forces and eventually statehood and sovereignty. These citations range from formally footnoted references and mentions of the thoughts of "a Chinese expert" to uncredited appropriations of his ideas.

With the goal of reestablishing the Caliphate at the forefront of its strategic thinking, AQAM learns from Mao's *On Guerrilla Warfare*, a text that repeatedly asserts the importance of the masses and popular support for the insurgency: "Because guerrilla warfare basically derives from the masses and is supported by them, it can neither exist nor flourish if it separates itself from their sympathies and co-operation."[49] Mao's fish analogy—"the guerrilla must move amongst the people as a fish swims in the sea"—appears repeatedly in jihadist literature in writings from

Southeast Asia to Saudi Arabia.[50] The mujahideen have taken this message to heart. Abu Fath al-Pastuni, for example, the author of *Gerilya*, Jemaah Islamiya's guerrilla warfare handbook, argued: "Guerrilla war is a people's war. . . . Guerrillas are likened to the fish while people are to the water. If the fish is separated from water, it will automatically die."[51]

Abu Ubayd al-Qurashi used Mao's fish analogy when describing U.S. counterinsurgency strategy: "In U.S. opinion, targeting civilians is a measure intended to achieve military advantage over the mujahideen. It aims to minimize the logistical support that the people normally provide the mujahideen. If the early theoreticians of guerrilla warfare believed that a revolutionary war required guerrillas to deploy and live among the population 'like fish in water,' the U.S. strategy is based on drying up the water, the population, so that the fish, the fighters, would perish."[52]

The jihadists have also been deeply impressed by Mao's construct of the three stages of guerrilla warfare, and references to it are legion. The work of the late Abu-Hajar Abd-al-Aziz al-Muqrin, at one time the head of al Qaida in Saudi Arabia, is typical in its Maoist roots. The first several issues of *Al-Battar Camp*, an online al Qaida military magazine, featured a series of articles on guerrilla warfare under his name. These nowhere mention Mao by name, but they describe at some length Mao's three stages.

> The first stage: Strategic defense. The mujahideen seek to defend Islam, Muslims and their sacred religious honor.
> The second stage: . . . The stage of relative strategic balance or the so-called "thousand-wound policy." The mujahideen form "semi-regular forces that gradually become regular forces with modern formations."
> The third stage: Decisive military strike—"the final attack."
> It is the duty of any emerging movement or group that wishes to launch a successful guerrilla war to pay attention to the affairs of the public and the people, fulfill their rights and needs, and share with them their sorrow and joy.[53]

Sometimes Maoist military thought slips unobtrusively into jihadist writings. For example, a sixty-six-page study of the war in Afghanistan as of mid-2006 written by Hossam Abdul Raouf, a member of al Qaida's Committee of Information and Strategy, states that the mujahideen in Afghanistan "have now gained the upper hand and gained initiative, shifting from the stage of guerrilla warfare and hit-and-run, to the stage of direct confrontation, facing each other with big numbers, which could sometimes reach more than hundreds of mujahideen participating in one operation."[54] Other AQAM thinkers have written similar documents. Abu Fath al-Pastuni, writing for an Indonesian audience in 2004, presented an outline of the theory of guerrilla warfare clearly influenced by Mao.[55] A thirteen-page document captured in 2004 at an unspecified location in Iraq is entitled "The Holy War: Guerrillas War."[56] The document contains only one explicit reference to Mao, but again it describes the three phases of guerrilla warfare.

At the tactical level, some AQAM writers also use Mao's dictum about how to harrass the enemy. A document captured in Afghanistan explains: "Mao-tse-tung's principles are: when the enemy advances, we retreat—When the enemy stops, we disrupt—When the enemy gets tired, we attack—When the enemy retreats, we chase."[57]

Other Guerrilla and Leftist Writers

The experiences of other leftist revolutionary groups and the writings of communist and leftist intellectuals—particularly those who wrote on guerrilla warfare—have also found a place in AQAM literature. Abu Ubayd al-Qurashi wrote an incisive analysis of the experience of leftist Tupamaro urban guerrillas in Uruguay in the 1960s and early 1970s crediting the guerrillas for their tactical prowess and good organizational skills.[58] Nonetheless, he attributed their defeat primarily to their own mistakes, not the brutal actions of the Uruguayan government. Al-Qurashi believed that the thuggery of the Tupamaros destroyed the reputation of the rebels and proved that there was no difference between them and their foes. In short, the Tupamaros alienated themselves from the people, which left them exposed to the security forces.

Carlos Marighella, a Brazilian rebel of the 1970s best known for his work on urban guerrilla warfare, has influenced parts of the Salafi jihadist movement. For example, the Abu Sayyaf Group (ASG) of the Philippines adopted his *Mini-Manual of the Urban Guerrilla*, a pamphlet about strategy and tactics with tips for insurgency; the *Mini-Manual of the Urban Mujahideen* merely changed its title and otherwise Islamicized Marighella's vocabulary.[59]

Robert Taber's *The War of the Flea* discusses protracted insurgencies and reiterates many of Mao's tenets. "The guerrilla fights the war of the flea," Taber explained. "The flea bites, hops, and bites again, nimbly avoiding the foot that would crush him. He does not seek to kill his enemy at a blow, but to bleed him and feed on him, to plague and bedevil him, to keep him from resting and to destroy his nerve and his morale."[60] AQAM's thinkers refer repeatedly to this work, incorporating the flea analogy to describe insurgency. Al-Muqrin noted that "nonconventional war is called guerrilla warfare or 'a flea-dog war.' The fleas bite the dog and fly away. The dog scratches its skin raw. The fleas return and bite the dog repeatedly until the dog loses consciousness and dies."[61] Abu Musab al-Suri's lessons-learned document from the jihad in Syria mentions Taber's thoughts on the importance of a protracted war: "The mujahideen should utilize successive and strategic military operations that exhaust the regime and its institutions, they should play 'The dog and the fleas game.'"[62] An article by Abu Ubayd al-Qurashi recovered in Baghdad also refers to Taber.[63]

Clausewitz

Carl von Clausewitz's analysis of warfare has transcended generations of military technology and strategic goals, so it is not surprising to see his ideas, although seldom cited explicitly, suffusing jihadist writings. The elites of al Qaida and the broader movement believe they are pursuing political goals that are simultaneously religious goals: the unification of the *ummah* and the restoration of a nation-state, the Caliphate. Many of them are aware of Clausewitz's assertion that "war is merely the continuation of policy by other means."[64] One mujahid, for instance, paraphrased Clausewitz's statements about the connections between war and politics: "We talked earlier about war and politics. However, both have one objective, with different techniques of achieving the target."[65] According to al-Suri, losing sight of this goal was the downfall of previous jihads, such as the revolt in Syria in the late 1970s. "With the exception of some mujahideen leaders, and some members, most of the people who waged this revolutionary war were low on religious instruction and lacked political awareness . . . they did not comprehend that this war was a means to a political end. Their ignorance made them incapable of developing a comprehensive strategic plan."[66]

Clausewitz's influence emerges in other ways as well. In an article entitled "A Lesson in War," al-Qurashi, the movement's most prolific and direct user of Clausewitz's work, examined the concept of the "center of gravity," which he considers Clausewitz's most important contribution to strategic thought. It provides a clear line of comparison between the United States and the mujahideen. Al-Qurashi's analysis gives the advantage to the mujahideen because "the enemy cannot ascertain the center of gravity let alone aim a mortal blow at it," whereas "it is clearly apparent that the American economy is America's center of gravity. This is what the Sheikh Osama bin Laden has said quite explicitly."[67]

One cannot overestimate the importance of religion and faith to AQAM's strategic thought, so it is not surprising that its thinkers appreciate strategic texts that leave space for their beliefs to play a role in informing strategy. In particular, while AQAM literature does not cite the importance of Clausewitz's "fog of war," this notion parallels AQAM's conception of God's presence on the battlefield. Clausewitz's statement that warfare is interactive, and thus there can be no prescriptive plan for victory because there are too many unknowns, is similar to the mujahideen's "insha'Allah" attitude that God determines the outcome of the battle. While they would argue that God essentially determines each event, the reality for the soldiers is the same.

Sun Tzu
AQAM puts a lot of effort into understanding its enemy (see chapters 3 and 4). Of course, all jihadists contributing to that endeavor are operating in accordance with Sun Tzu's famous dictum to "know thy enemy." Some members of the Salafi jihadist elite consciously draw on Sun Tzu's work, however. The words of an anonymous poster to a jihadist Web site are typical: "Philosophy states: know your enemy and know your abilities. This is the only way that you can minimize your casualties during the time of war."[68]

Fourth-Generation Warfare and Asymmetric Warfare
To a lesser degree, military thinkers in AQAM draw on a variety of other sources as they consider military problems. A body of literature surrounding fourth-generation warfare and asymmetric warfare appeals to al-Qurashi in particular. For example, in early 2002 he analyzed two seminal articles, one by William Lind and colleagues, the other by Thomas Hammes, that appeared in the *Marine Corps Gazette* fifteen years ago and started the debate in the United States over fourth-generation warfare. Not surprisingly, al-Qurashi concluded that al Qaida has a distinct advantage in the application of fourth-generation warfare.[69] In a separate article al-Qurashi defined al Qaida's asymmetric approach: "The asymmetric strategy that al-Qa'ida is pursuing entails the use of means and methods that the defender cannot use, recognize, or avoid."[70]

Al-Qurashi referred to the works of former senior American intelligence official Ray Cline and the late defense analyst Trevor Dupuy to argue that the mujahideen are strategically on a par with or stronger than the enemy forces, regardless of military might, because they have a psychological and theological advantage.[71] The movement has internalized this factor as a perceived strength, and thus implements a strategy that includes insurgency and guerrilla warfare while relying extensively on soft power. Though he did not mention al-Qurashi, Dupuy, or Cline by name, bin Laden in essence reiterated al-Qurashi's point that the "the difference between us and our adversaries in terms of military strength, manpower and equipment is very huge. But, for the grace of God, the difference is also very huge in terms of psychological resources, faith, certainty, and reliance on the Almighty God."[72]

The underlying concept of asymmetric warfare, though rarely the term itself, is an integral part of the fabric of AQAM debate. Yusuf al-Ayiri used the term and commented, "However great [American] military power may be, God is more powerful. There are also military methods that can paralyze or hinder this terrifying military machine."[73] Abu Hafs al-Mauritani touched on the issue shortly after the 9/11 attacks: "If we added to American losses [on September 11] the losses that reached America's allies we can imagine the volume and extent of these losses that the 'small enemies' can cause to 'the big.'"[74] Bin Laden has crowed that the September 11 attacks did a million dollars' worth of damage for every dollar spent.[75]

Conclusion

AQAM's operations are not ruled by strategy, but they are influenced by evolving strategic thought. Most visibly, analysts and practitioners within the movement write, often critically, about what they have observed and offer suggestions for improvement. These writings add to the existing body of jihadist literature circulating around the globe, influencing the thinking of present-day and future jihadist leaders and thinkers.

There may be an additional, Darwinian, mechanism at work. AQAM comprises numerous individual groups (laying aside for a moment the numerous relatively independent sympathetic individuals). Some of these groups successfully and appropriately adapt their ideas and behaviors in the face of real-world events; these groups tend to survive. The other groups remain rigid in their approach or else adapt in ways that turn out to be inappropriate; these groups tend not to survive. The GIA in Algeria is an example of the latter. It changed its behavior over time, but in an unhelpful way by becoming more and more violent and thus destroying its basis of support in the population. Taken as an aggregate, the movement not only endures but also adapts, conforms to the changing circumstances around it, and generally becomes more dangerous over time.

In short, the United States and its partners and allies face an intelligent, adaptive enemy. We must respect this enemy for his abilities, though not his values, and we must be at least as adaptive as he is. This requires constant study of the enemy's thinking. The alternative is catastrophe.

Notes

Mary Kathryn Keegin made important contributions to this chapter.

1. FBIS GMP20021001000100.
2. Jansen, *The Neglected Duty*, 190 (also 15–16), referring to section 65 of Faraj's document.
3. In 1975, members of the Islamic Liberation Party in Egypt (who later became known as the Technical Military Academy group) planned a coup d'état that would involve obtaining weapons from a military academy, assassinating Sadat and other government officials, and taking over the radio and TV building. The plan went awry and the security services arrested everyone involved. See Mustapha Kamel al-Sayyid, "The Other Face of the Islamist Movement," Carnegie Endowment for International Peace, Working Paper no. 33, January 2003, available at http://www.carnegieendowment.org/files/wp33.pdf, accessed September 23, 2007. A violent uprising that occurred in Asyut two days after Sadat's assassination was also crushed by the Egyptian security service.
4. FBIS GMP20020108000197, al-Zawahiri, 2001.
5. FBIS GMP20050606371001, "Detained al-Qaida Leader Sayf al-Adl Chronicles al-Zarqawi's Rise in Organization," Jihadist Web sites, May 21, 2005.
6. Harmony document folder AFGP-2002-600080, *Al-Qaeda Captured Document (Part 2) Discusses Lessons Learned from Jihad in Syria*, 1989, http://ctc.usma.edu/aq/pdf/AFGP-2002-600080-Trans.pdf.
7. Ibid.
8. AFGP-2002-600053, 12.
9. FBIS GMP20021001000100.
10. Naji, *Management of Savagery*, 83. In 2006, a new "Egyptian Islamic Group" emerged and announced its alliance with al Qaida.
11. See Sageman, *Understanding Terror Networks*, 3; and Gilles Kepel *Jihad: The Trail of Political Islam* (Cambridge: Harvard University Press, 2002), 146–47.
12. Sageman, *Understanding Terror Networks*, 18, discussed the reversal of Faraj's influence: "the priority was now the 'far enemy' over the 'near enemy.'" See also Lawrence Wright, *The Looming Tower: Al-Qaeda and the Road to 9/11* (New York: Alfred A. Knopf, 2006), 169–75. This change was crystallized in bin Laden's

1998 fatwa, "Jihad against Jews and the Crusaders," http://www.fas.org/irp/world/para/docs/980223-fatwa.htm, accessed September 23, 2007.

13. Harmony document folder AFGP-2002-000080. The popularity among the strategists of Mao's writings on guerrilla warfare (see below) suggests that there may be further movement in this direction. See also the discussion of disaster relief in chapter 6.

14. Center for International Issues Research, "Insurgent Media Organization Attempts to Impose Discipline on Militant Forum Participants," *Global Issues Report*, November 17, 2006.

15. FBIS GMP20020307000167, "Fighting in Jihad against Unbelievers Seen as Individual Duty of Every Muslim," February 27, 2002.

16. See chapter 6; see also Brynjar Lia, "The al-Qaida Strategist Abu Mus'ab al-Suri: A Profile," Norwegian Defence Research Establishment, March 15, 2006, at www.mil.no/multimedia/archive/00076/_The_Al-Qaida-strate_76568a.pdf, accessed November 29, 2006.

17. A 2005 study by the RAND Corporation titled *Aptitude for Destruction* is typical of the work done on innovation and learning in terrorist groups. The work discusses organizational learning but harnesses its sophisticated analysis to entirely tactical problems. Learning, as defined in this work, boils down to using a new weapon or a new tactic: a "terrorist group's learning capabilities define the options they have available to defeat security measures and counter the actions of security forces." See Brian A. Jackson et al., *Aptitude for Destruction*, vol. 1: *Organizational Learning in Terrorist Groups and Its Implications for Combating Terrorism* (Santa Monica, Calif.: RAND, 2005), xiv.

18. See in particular Martha Crenshaw, "Innovation: Decision Points in the Trajectory of Terrorism," paper prepared for the conference on "Trajectories of Terrorist Violence in Europe," March 9–11, 2001, Harvard University; Bruce Hoffman as quoted in Crenshaw, 2.

19. Ibid., 3–6. Many more Western scholars study innovation or adaptation in militaries than study these processes in terrorist groups, despite the fundamental unity of the two topics. (Both militaries and terrorist groups apply violence for political ends, after all.)

20. FBIS GMP20060316336002, "Al-Qa'ida-Affiliated Al-Sahab Publishes Fifth Issue of The Vanguards of Khorasan," Jihadist Web sites, OSC Report in Arabic, March 16, 2006.

21. Harmony document folder AFGP-2002-003251.

22. Harmony document folder 500MI-2005-RP-MLA00011. This English-language document plagiarizes Carlos Marighella's *Mini-Manual of the Urban Guerrilla*, merely substituting Islamic terminology for communist terminology.

23. For Salafi jihadists, whose theological foundation is based on the actions and words of the Prophet Muhammed and the rightly guided caliphs, several touchstone battles in early Islamic military history are relevant today, particularly given their association with the expansion of Islam. The battles of Badr (AD 624), Uhud (AD 626), Khandak (AD 628), and Yarmuk (AD 636) are prominent in AQAM discussions of strategy, rules of engagement, tactics, and the providence of God in the face of numerically and technologically superior enemies. For more information, see FBIS GMP20031211000267, "Orator of the Peninsula: Compilation of Essays in Tribute to Saudi 'Martyr' Yusuf al-Ayiri," August 1, 2003.

24. The belief that strategy should be left to God is implicit in the lack of discussion of strategy in jihadists' writings. See also Jansen, *Neglected Duty*.

25. AFGP-2002-600080, 8. This book went through a sort of peer review by Abdullah Azzam and Shaykh Abd-al-Qadir ibn Abd-al-Aziz, an ideologue of the EIJ in its heyday. FBIS GMP20050413336001, "Terrorism: Biography of Abu-Mus'ab al-Suri Chronicles Work, Travels," Jihadist Websites, FBIS Report in Arabic, April 13, 2005.

26. FBIS GMP20041014000206.

27. The global Salafi jihadist movement is in some ways analogous to the human body. In the body, cells die in great numbers and are replaced in comparable numbers. Likewise, in the Salafi jihadist movement individual organizations routinely cease to exist when they are decisively defeated by their own incompetence or the actions of the security services, but new organizations spring up to replace them. This is why the extensive literature about the death of terrorist groups is of only partial relevance to defeating the global Salafi jihadist movement.

28. Sheikh Abu Baseer al-Tartusi, quoted in Stephen Ulph, "Jihadi After Action Report: Syria," Combating Terrorism Center, U.S. Military Academy, West Point, N.Y., no date, www.ctc.usma.edu/aar/CTC-JAAR-Syria.pdf, accessed November 29, 2006.

29. See FBIS GMP20020108000197.

30. Naji, *Management of Savagery*, 9.

31. Harmony document folder AFGP-2002-003251.

32. FBIS GMP20020108000197.

33. Harmony document folder AFGP-2002-600053, 12.

34. Ibid., 13.

35. Naji, *Management of Savagery*, 8–9.

36. Harmony document folder AFGP-2002-600053, 13.

37. Harmony document folder AFGP-2002-003251.

38. Ibid.

39. Al-Suri is incorrect in his dating of the defeat of the Moroccan group Harakat al-Shabiba. It actually took place in 1969. See David Cook, "Paradigmatic Jihadi Movements," Combating Terrorism Center, U.S. Military Academy, 2006, 5, http://ctc.usma.edu/brachman/CTC-Pardigmatic_Jihadi_Movements-10_06.pdf, accessed January 11, 2007.

40. FBIS GMP20050201000226.

41. SITE Institute, *"A New Strategic Method in the Resistance of the Occupier* Prepared by Muhammad Khalil al-Hukaymah," September 29, 2006, www.siteinstitute.org.

42. Al-Qurashi mentioned Guevara in a much shorter but similarly broad review of guerrilla and revolutionary warfare; unfortunately, no translated copy is available. See Harmony document folders NMEC-2006-627615, *An Article about Revolutionary Wars Written by Abu-'Ubayd al-Qarshi*, no date; and NMEC-2006-621703, *Revolutionary and Guerrilla Wars by 'Ubayd al-Qurashi in His Series of Articles on Military Jihad*, no date, for two separately acquired copies.

43. Harmony document folder AFGP-2002-601078, *Winds of Revolution: Studies of Guerrilla Wars and Advocating Their Implementation*, no date.

44. Ibid.

45. Qutb, *Milestones*, 75. Qutb did of course encourage Muslim societies to develop in order to produce these types of scientific works and experts.

46. Naji, *Management of Savagery*, 28.

47. Abu Ubayd al-Qurashi, "A Strategic Study of the Pioneer Experience of the Commandos War inside the Cities," in Harmony document folder ISGZ-2005-

00000898, *Various Researches on Explosives and Instructions to Educate Resistant Groups on Making Bombs*, 2005.

48. "The war of those deemed weak" is probably a reference to Robert Taber's book *The War of the Flea*.

49. Mao Tse-Tung, *On Guerrilla Warfare*, trans. Samuel B. Griffiths (Chicago: University of Illinois Press, 1961).

50. Ibid.

51. FBIS SEG20040602000101, "Indonesia: 'Gerilya' Text of Indonesia Language Book on Guerrilla Warfare," Indonesia, FBIS Report, June 2, 2004; FBIS SEG20040602000101; and FBIS SEP20031214000010, "Singapore Daily Reports Sales of JI Book on Terror Tactics in Indonesia," *Sunday Times*, Singapore, December 14, 2003.

52. FBIS GMP20020805000114, *"Al-Ansar* Writer Reviews US Military 'Barbarity,' 'War Crimes' against Civilians," *Al-Ansar*, July 24, 2002. Other Salafi Jihadist writers have used the fish analogy too, including Abu Musab al-Suri; see Harmony document folder AFGP-2002-600080; the previously mentioned Harmony document folder ISGZ-2004-M1000074-0178, *Memorandum about the War of Struggle or the Guerilla Warfare*, no date; and a 2006 letter from a senior al Qaida leader called Atiyah to Abu Musab al-Zarqawi, http://ctc.usma.edu/publications/pdf/CTC-AtiyahLetter.pdf, accessed September 23, 2007.

53. These articles are translated in FBIS GMP20040120000262, "Terrorism: Al-Qa'ida-Affiliated Magazine Begins Series on Warfare," January 20, 2004; FBIS GMP20040121000214, "Terrorism: Al-Qa'ida-Affiliated Magazine Analyzes Guerrilla Warfare," January 15, 2004; FBIS GMP20040209000260, "Terrorism: Al-Battar Camp on 'Thousand-Wound' Policy of Guerrilla Warfare," February 2, 2004; and FBIS GMP20040209000260, "Terrorism: Al-Battar Camp on Guerilla Warfare Leadership, Forces," February 1, 2004. At least three untranslated documents referring to Mao were captured in a safe house in Riyadh associated with al-Muqrin. In November 2006, Muhammad Khalil al-Hakaymah's Web site posted an article by a "Dr. Abduh" describing a distinctly Maoist three-stage construct for guerrilla warfare. Perhaps overoptimistically, Dr. Abduh said the jihadists were in the second stage. See FBIS GMP20061115281001, "Jihadist Forum Participant Posts 3 Stage Guerilla Strategy," OSC Report in Arabic, November 15, 2006.

54. SITE Institute, "The Crusaders Admit: Our Troops Are Being Defeated in Afghanistan; an Analytical Study of the Crusader Forces Occupying Afghanistan," October 9, 2006, www.siteinstitute.org.

55. FBIS SEG20040602000101.

56. Captured documents appear to contain expositions of Mao's thoughts, but they have not been translated. See, for instance, Harmony document folders AFGP-2005-0004508, *A Booklet that Tackles the Following Issues: War, Gang War, Codes, Assassinations and Kidnapping, Captured in Afghanistan in 2005*, 2005; IOCF-2003-612992, *Summary of the Three Stages of Guerilla Warfare and Its Effects, from a Mujahidin Perspective*, no date; and AFGP-2002-601078, no date, found in Afghanistan in a building associated with Osama bin Laden.

57. Harmony document folder AFGP-2002-600340, *Guerilla Warfare—Its Nature, Organization, and Training*, no date. See also FBIS SEG20040602000101; Harmony document folder AFGP-2002-600085; and Harmony document folder AFGP-2002-600083.

58. See al-Qurashi, "A Strategic Study of the Pioneer Experience of the Commandos War inside the Cities."

59. Harmony document folder 500MI-2005-RP-MLA00011.
60. Robert Taber, *The War of the Flea* (Dulles, Va.: Brassey's, 1965), 49–50.
61. FBIS GMP20040121000214, "Terrorism: Al-Qa'ida-Affiliated Magazine Analyzes Guerrilla Warfare," Saudi Arabia, FBIS Report, January 15, 2004.
62. Harmony document folder AFGP-2002-60080.
63. See Harmony document folder ISGZ-2005-00000898.
64. Carl von Clausewitz, *On War*, ed. and trans. Michael Howard and Peter Paret (Princeton: Princeton University Press, 1976), 87. Coalition forces captured an Arabic-language copy of Clausewitz's *On War* in Kandahar. See Harmony document folder AFGP-2002-002845, *Brief Book of War: A Military Book by the German General Called Karl the Klosphetise*, 1988.
65. Harmony document folder AFGP-2002-600085.
66. Harmony document folder AFGP-2002-600080.
67. FBIS GMP20030122000038, 2002.
68. Harmony document folder ISGM-2005-001834.
69. See William S. Lind et al., "The Changing Face of War: Into the 4th Generation," *Marine Corps Gazette*, October 1989, 22–26, www.d-n-i.net/fcs/4th_gen_war_gazette.htm, accessed October 15, 2007; Lt. Col. Thomas X. Hammes, "The Evolution of War: The Fourth Generation," *Marine Corps Gazette*, September 1994, www.d-n-i.net/fcs/hammes.htm. Hammes, now retired from the Marine Corps, recently expanded on these ideas in *The Sling and the Stone: On War in the 21st Century* (St. Paul, Minn.: Zenith Press, 2004). Al-Qurashi's article is FBIS GMP20020223000086, "Writer Says New Type of War Suits Mujahidin's Fight against Western War Machine," February 28, 2002. See also MEMRI's Special Dispatch Series no. 344, February 10, 2002, summarizing "Fourth Generation Wars" by Abu Ubayd al-Qurashi in the second issue of *Al-Ansar*. Elsewhere, al-Qurashi has shown some awareness of John Arquilla and David Ronfeldt's concepts in *Networks and Netwars*. Arquilla and Ronfeldt argued that in an asymmetrical environment, decentralized organizations have an advantage over traditional hierarchical structures, and that information and communication are the keys to success. Citing Arquilla and Ronfeldt's article "Cyberwar Is Coming!" al-Qurashi encouraged more effort in strategic communications to counter America and its goal of "Information Dominance." See FBIS GMP20021126000154, 2002. Al-Qurashi also referred in passing to Ronfeldt and Arquilla in FBIS GMP20020614000107, "Pro-al-Qa'ida Writer Expects Failure of US 'Crusade' against Jihad Movements," June 12, 2002.
70. FBIS GMP20031027000226.
71. See FBIS GMP20021001000100. Trevor Dupuy famously applied quantitative techniques to military analysis. Ray Cline was a CIA deputy director for intelligence and later assistant secretary of state for intelligence and research.
72. FBIS GMP20040209000243, "Full Text of Interview Held with Al-Qa'ida Leader Usama bin Ladin on October 21, 2001," Jihad Online news network, January 21, 2003.
73. FBIS GMP20030929000003.
74. See al-Mauritani, "A Practical and Religious Perspective of the Unfolding Events of the Attacks on the U.S."
75. FBIS GMP20041101000236, "Al-Jazirah Site Posts 'Full Transcript' of bin Ladin's Message," November 1, 2004.

CHAPTER 6

Current AQAM Strategic Thinking

Monitoring from afar has the advantage of providing the total picture and observing the general line without getting submerged in the details, which might draw attention away from the direction of the target. As the English proverb says, the person who is standing among the leaves of the tree might not see the tree.

AYMAN AL-ZAWAHIRI LETTER TO ABU MUSAB AL-ZARQAWI, 2005[1]

"Monitoring from Afar"

Salafi jihadist leaders do not constitute a general staff that can promulgate binding strategic guidance to the movement's constituent organizations and to the masses. At best, leaders of individual organizations can exercise significant, though not total, control over their own people. Leaders of the movement often make their wishes known, however, through public statements and internal communications. In addition, the small but vigorous community of Salafi jihadist strategists, who might be likened to Western defense intellectuals, carries on a robust and influential debate in books, journals, and other, primarily Web-based, outlets.

The Internet has been both help and hindrance to the movement. On the one hand, it provides a venue for strategic debate and disseminating lessons learned and new strategic ideas (see chapter 5). On the other hand, by allowing everyone a forum to espouse views and guidance, it enables groups to develop divergent strategic cultures. The virtual method translates into a wider variety of actual strategic behavior than Osama bin Laden, Ayman al-Zawahiri, and other globally recognized leaders of the movement would probably wish.

Nonetheless, it is possible to identify the main points of consensus and debate in AQAM's current strategic thinking. AQAM's formal and thought leaders view the current situation as a religious-political war in which gaining the support of the *ummah* is a goal and a necessity. AQAM intends to achieve its ultimate goal of restoring the Caliphate through two interlocking means: violent jihad and unifying the *ummah*. To that end, they are pursuing two parallel approaches within the mainstream of strategy: an explicitly military campaign and an information operations campaign (*dawah*, discussed briefly in this chapter and in depth in chapter 7). This chapter concentrates on the military track and examines the means by which AQAM's thinkers attempt to neutralize the "Jews and Crusaders" and overthrow the "apostate" local regimes.

Two-Track Strategy

The two-track strategy of violent jihad and uniting the *ummah* is an overarching theme in AQAM's writings. The late Yusuf al-Ayiri insisted that both jihad and a unified *ummah* are necessary to defeat the enemy:

> Peoples of the region [the Middle East] must follow two parallel lines of action. One line is armed jihad against the enemies of God in the region, and especially in Iraq, so that they do not have a chance to catch their breath and attack another country. The other is an effort to strengthen the community's faith and morals on a practical basis, without idealistic theorizing that has never, and will never achieve anything. . . . We must follow the two lines simultaneously without interruption. There must be no new Sufi mysticism that espouses a faith of inaction. We want the community to embark on jihad with all its might, and to embark on reforms with all its might. There is no contradiction between them.[2]

Al-Ayiri was speaking in a broad geographic context, yet the two "lines of action" apply in every jihadist campaign, as shown by al-Zawahiri's 2005 admonition to al-Zarqawi in the context of Iraq: "I stress again to you and to all your brothers the need to direct the political action equally with the military action, by the alliance, cooperation and gathering of all leaders of opinion and influence in the Iraqi arena."[3]

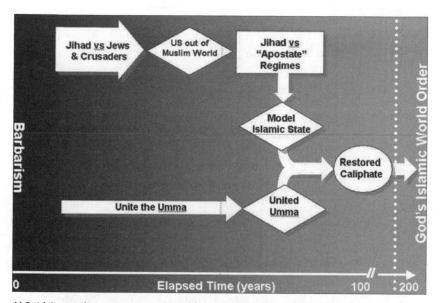

Al Qaida's grand strategy as enunciated from 1996 onward.

Ayman al-Zawahiri was even more specific in March 2006 when he restated the long-standing grand strategy of which al Qaida is merely the most prominent enunciator. The jihadists, he said, should work on "four interrelated fronts":

- The first front is that of inflicting losses on the Crusader West, especially its economic structure, through dealing strikes which will make it bleed for years. . . .
- The second front is that of expelling the Crusader-Zionist enemy from the lands of Islam, particularly from Iraq, Afghanistan, and Palestine. . . . They should leave our lands defeated after the collapse of their economies. This way we can set up the Muslim caliphate state on our land. . . .
- The third front . . . is the front of work on changing corrupt regimes which have sold our dignity and pride to the Crusader West and surrendered to Israel. . . .
- The fourth front . . . is the front of popular missionary action. All clerics, scholars, writers, and thinkers of the Muslim nation should play their role in alerting the nation to the danger it is facing, motivating it to return to Islam, working on implementing the laws of

sharia, and warning it against any course, even if disguised in Islam, that is against applying the rule of sharia or calls for applying the rules of other doctrines and schools.[4]

The Role of the Masses

The unification of the *ummah* is necessary to reach AQAM's goal of restoring the Caliphate. Al-Ayiri was but one of many strategists who believed that the failure of the *ummah* to accept jihad as an individual duty was the reason for the downfall of Islam and that the reversal of this trend would lead to Islam's restoration to its rightful place in the world. "Ever since the community threw its lot in with this world and abandoned jihad," al-Ayiri wrote, "the enemy began to control things in all areas, either directly or through quislings. . . . The only way to reject this humiliation is by raising the banner of Islam. The tree of this faith will not put down roots in our land unless the community waters it with the blood of its sons, as the first believers watered it. It grew for them. No one will do for us what the first believers did unless we ourselves do what they did."[5]

Dawah

AQAM believes that in order to win their global war, they must win the hearts and minds of the global Muslim population, the *ummah*. The mechanism for this is *dawah* (the call). In this context, *dawah* means the use of propaganda and indoctrination to induce Muslims to accept al Qaida's worldview, specifically the enshrining of jihad as, in effect, a sixth pillar of Islam and an individual obligation (*fard 'ayn*) for believers. Having accepted this, believers will come forward to wage jihad—"joining the caravan" in al Qaida's words—and die as martyrs. To AQAM, *dawah* means the full spectrum of information employed to persuade Muslims to reject Western or "apostate" Muslim values in favor of violent Salafism. This persuasion ranges from traditional preaching and print materials to multimedia methods via the Internet and cell phones. *Dawah* applies only to Muslims, and despite occasional influence operations aimed at non-Muslims, the West (*dar al-harb*) appears in AQAM discussions of propaganda only fleetingly (see chapter 6).[6]

In their struggle to attract popular support, the jihadists view themselves as the revolutionary vanguard that will rally the masses. A jihadist thinker writing in 2002 acknowledged the importance of the idea: "Al Qaida placed special emphasis on forming the mujahid vanguard that is the backbone of the jihad operation. This is what has produced such stunning results on all levels."[7] Al-Zawahiri elaborated on this point in a letter to al-Zarqawi:

> If we look at the two short-term goals [in Iraq], which are removing the Americans and establishing an Islamic amirate in Iraq, or a caliphate if possible, then, we will see that the strongest weapon which the mujahedeen enjoy—after the help and granting of success by God—is popular support from the Muslim masses in Iraq, and the surrounding Muslim countries. So, we must maintain this support as best we can, and we should strive to increase it, on the condition that striving for that support does not lead to any concession in the laws of the sharia.[8]

The Military Track: Neutralize or Destroy the Jews and Crusaders

In the explicitly military track of its strategy, AQAM seeks to overthrow the local apostate regimes that stand between it and the Caliphate. However, most jihadists believe that the "Jews and Crusaders"—the United States and its key allies—are actively and effectively propping up these regimes and thus must be dealt with in some way.[9] Al Qaida and many of the other jihadist groups thus maintain that the first priority should be to neutralize or even destroy the United States. They tend to emphasize a variety of measures aimed at doing so, including:

- gathering as many allies as possible in the confrontation with the United States and other forces of infidelity;
- puncturing America's illusion of invulnerability in order to embolden Muslims to join the jihad;
- attacking America's economy, its strategic center of gravity (see chapter 4);
- stripping America of its allies so the full burden of the global war falls on its shoulders alone; and
- inducing the United States to intervene elsewhere in the Islamic world, thereby contributing to America's imperial overstretch.

Gathering Allies

Despite the traditional reluctance of Salafi jihadists to work with those whom they consider to be less pious, many in the movement have been increasingly willing to make tactical alliances against common enemies. In mid-2005, Ayman al-Zawahiri urged such a policy on Abu Musab al-Zarqawi in Iraq:

> I stress again to you and to all your brothers the need to direct the political action equally with the military action, by the alliance, cooperation, and gathering of all leaders of opinion and influence in the Iraqi arena. . . . You and your brothers must strive to have around you circles of support, assistance, and cooperation, and through them, to advance until you become a consensus, entity, organization, or association that represents all the honorable people and the loyal folks in Iraq. I repeat the warning against separating from the masses whatever the danger.[10]

In accordance with this approach, in the early days of the U.S. occupation of Iraq, Abu Muhammad al-Ablaj was willing to envision cooperating with Baathists against the American "invaders": "Allah has turned to [Saddam Hussein] with forgiveness. He declared jihad and did not recognize Israel. There is nothing to bar cooperation with a Muslim who has made jihad his course and way for liberating the holy lands. . . . Al Qaida elements are fighting side by side with the Iraqis."[11] Similarly, in 2004, Hazim al-Madani urged jihadists to form alliances with tribes or other groups with power in society.[12]

In putting forward such proposals, al-Zawahiri, al-Ablaj, and al-Madani were simply echoing the thoughts of the author of the "Five Letters," who years earlier told his correspondent in Somalia that "coordination in practical fields" with other Islamic groups—though not mergers—"will lay the proper groundwork for organizational unity in the distant future" when Salafi jihadism can hold unchecked sway.[13] The author of these letters urged "a comprehensive national front that agrees on general, not detailed, Islamic slogans. That front must lead to an expanded national government approved by the major forces in the country: tribes and political groupings. The slogan acceptable to all is 'Somali Freedom and Islamism.'"[14]

Puncturing America's Illusion of Invulnerability

The jihadists believe that the United States and the global media, including Hollywood, present an image of a nearly invulnerable America, particularly in terms of its military strength (see chapter 4). The strategists thus suggest that successful attacks against the United States, by demonstrating America's actual fundamental weakness, will embolden timorous Muslims to join the fight. Abu Bakr Naji argued that the series of attacks al Qaida mounted against American interests before 2001 "destroyed the people's awe of America and of the lesser ranking Apostate armies."[15] Bin Laden claimed that the Salafi jihadists themselves had a similar epiphany more than a decade ago: "Some of our mujahideen who fought here in Afghanistan also participated in operations against the Americans in Somalia [in 1993]—and they were surprised at the collapse of American morale. This convinced us that the Americans are a paper tiger."[16]

Prominent theorists are not the only ones to divine this idea and its implications. By 2005, jihadist Web sites contained discussions on how to use America's vulnerabilities to puncture the illusion of strength. One jihadist observed that the precipitous drop in stock values that followed the 9/11 attacks demonstrated "the truth of the theory of illusion."[17] Oil is a popular theme in these discussions: "Attacking oil interests will embarrass the U.S. in front of the world, which will realize that the U.S. is not able to secure the oil supplies it alleges," another document purports.[18] More broadly, AQAM has certainly trumpeted the tremendous economic damage done by the 9/11 attacks—bin Laden has estimated it at about one trillion dollars—as embarrassing America in an inspirational (to the jihadists) way.[19]

Attacking America's Economy

AQAM members generally agree that the economy is America's strategic center of gravity (see chapter 4). Al-Zawahiri is certain that the "Crusader-Zionist enemy" will leave "the lands of Islam particularly . . . Iraq, Afghanistan, and Palestine . . . after the collapse of their economies."[20] Therefore, "the first front is that of inflicting losses on the Crusader West, especially its economic structure, through dealing strikes which will make it bleed for years."[21] The author of a 2006 pamphlet published under the aegis of al Qaida in Saudi Arabia urged attacks on oil facilities, observing that "economic jihad in this era is the best method to hurt the infidels."[22]

Lewis Atiyatallah sagely observed that attacks on oil infrastructure can serve the interests of the Saudi government by raising the price of oil. Nonetheless, he urged mounting such attacks anyway because they hurt the American economy and because the struggle against the United States is the global movement's highest priority.[23] Another jihadist argued that it would be better to leave the oil infrastructure intact but prevent the Americans from profiting from this "booty" by impeding their ability to export the oil or by attacking military bases at which American military ships, planes, and armored vehicles refuel.[24]

Whether through a quick decisive shock or as the result of a long campaign, AQAM's strategists have been confident that they can destroy the American economy. A CISR report published in the summer of 2003, for instance, claimed: "The mujahideen . . . knew the enemy's weaknesses. They attacked the pillars of American economy and American weak points. Had it not been for the enormous American information capability and the muscles the United States flexed in several areas to restore some of its prestige and restore some security to its markets, its economy would have collapsed much sooner. The United States is now on the verge of exhaustion and only needs a few blows, which are coming, God willing. God has prepared brave soldiers to bring down calamities on it."[25]

Denying America Allies in Its Struggle

AQAM is aware that the United States is fighting the present global war (not merely the war in Iraq) as part of a broad coalition. They are also aware that, small as they may be, these allies bring critical capabilities and resources to the struggle that America could itself provide only at great cost. These strategists believe, therefore, that it is critical to divide the coalition. Sayf al-Adel observed: "Another important matter is to win the regional political battle so that no country or government is allowed to exercise the same role the malicious Pakistani government played. This is the most dangerous role and had the biggest impact in Afghanistan. Pakistan is the one which provided the land for American military forces to advance from, provided them with intelligence, and also provided them with hypocritical people as an alternative to the Taliban State."[26]

Elements within AQAM have occasionally offered inducements to Europe to opt out of the war, leaving the burden on the United States. On March 15, 2004, four days after the Madrid train bombings for which it claimed responsibility, the Abu Hafs al-Masri Brigade said it was calling a truce in Spain to give the newly elected Spanish government time to fulfill its pledge to withdraw its troops from Iraq.[27] Exactly a month later, bin Laden spoke to the people of Europe: "[I] offer a peace initiative to [the Europeans], whose essence is our commitment to stopping operations

Exiled al Qaida leader Osama bin Laden peers over a map of Afghanistan in 1998, the same year in which he threatened a jihad against the West and allegedly orchestrated bombings at the U.S. embassies in Kenya and Tanzania—links in an expanding chain of terrorist attacks by al Qaida and associated movements. *(AP)*

In the late 1990s the Egyptian Islamic Jihad (EIJ) under Ayman al-Zawahiri (right), shown here with Osama bin Laden in November 2001, merged with al Qaida. Although some EIJ members rejected this shift to a global agenda and dissented on issues of strategy, they remained part of the broader Salafi jihadist movement. *(Reuters/CORBIS/Hamid Mir)*

In May 2003 the bombing of American compounds in Riyadh, the Saudi capital, killed many Muslims and resulted in a strong backlash among the Saudi populace. Here, Saudi Crown Prince Abdullah (second left) and other Saudi officials stand in front of a damaged building. Attackers shot their way into three housing compounds in synchronized strikes and then set off multiple suicide car bombs, killing at least twenty people, including seven Americans. *(AP Photo/Saudi Press Agency)*

The leader of al Qaida in Iraq, Abu Musab al-Zarqawi, conducted a series of attacks over several years that sharply divided the Salafi jihadist movement and horrified much of the ummah worldwide. Zarqawi, who was known for his just-do-it, nonstrategic tendencies, was killed in June 2006 in a U.S. air strike north of Hibhib, Iraq. *(Reuters/CORBIS)*

Until his capture in Pakistan in 2006, Syrian Mustafa Setmariam Nasar, also known as Abu Musab al-Suri, was al Qaida's foremost strategic thinker. Al-Suri opened training camps for incoming jihadists in Afghanistan and is believed to have been one of the chief planners behind the 2004 Madrid train bombings and the July 2005 London bombings. His 1,600-page *Call to Global Islamic Resistance* circulates widely in the jihadist world. *(©Handout/epa/Corbis)*

Elements within AQAM have occasionally offered inducements to Europe
to opt out of the global war on terror, leaving the burden on the United States.
Four days after the July 2004 Madrid train bombings, which killed more than
170 and wounded 500 rush-hour commuters, the Abu Hafs al-Masri Brigade
claimed responsibility and offered a truce to allow time for the newly elected
Spanish government to fulfill its pledge to withdraw its troops from Iraq.
Spain did pull out after its elections, hard on the heels of the attack.
(AP Photo/Paul White)

Some evidence suggests that al Qaida meant to lure the United States into a protracted war against Afghanistan, where the superpower could be ground down, exhausted, and eventually destroyed, as happened to the Soviet Union. Whether or not this was the original intent behind the 9/11 attacks, which killed nearly 3,000 and injured more than 6,290, bin Laden and others convinced themselves that such would be the effect of an American invasion. *(AP Photo/Jim Collins)*

Sanctuaries and secure areas—meaning substantially ungoverned—are important to Salafi jihadist guerrilla operations. Somalia, for instance, has been a key battleground for Osama bin Laden's terrorist group since 1992. Despite recent successes in driving radical Muslims underground and capturing international terrorists, the inability of the government to pacify the capital city of Mogadishu could give Islamic militants another chance to make the country a terrorist safe haven. Here, young men fire assault rifles at the Arbiska training camp, just outside Mogadishu, in September 2006. *(AP)*

against every country that commits itself to not attacking the Muslims or interfering in their affairs—including the U.S. conspiracy on the greater Islamic world."[28]

It is important to understand the anonymous document "Jihad in Iraq: Hopes and Dangers" in this context. This document, which apparently inspired the Madrid train bombings of 2004, contains a sophisticated argument about how the jihadists can win in Iraq against the American-led coalition. The author first observed, "If the United States is defeated this time . . . the doors will open wide to the Islamic tide. For the first time in modern history, we will have an advanced foundation for Islamic awakening and jihad close to [Saudi Arabia] and [Jerusalem]."[29] The author marshaled economic evidence to suggest that the United States can be forced to pull out of Iraq if the cost of war becomes too great. He suggested the best way to increase that cost is to put the entire burden on the United States by inducing all of its coalition partners to leave. Clearly, stripping off the minor allies—each of which contributes only tens or hundreds of troops—is not the best approach; however, the author suggested that inducing one of the major European contributors of the coalition—at that time the United Kingdom, Poland, Italy, and Spain—to withdraw could be decisive. If one of these nations pulled out its troops, others would follow, bringing the minor contributors with them. The entire burden of the war would then fall on America and, more important, its economy. Soon the United States would choose to cut its losses. Most of the rest of the document is devoted to identifying which major European power to attack in an effort to intimidate it into withdrawal.[30] In the course of events, Spain did pull out of Iraq after its elections, which followed hard on the heels of the Madrid bombings, but no other big countries followed suit.

Inducing the United States to Intervene Elsewhere in the Islamic World
Certainly, AQAM seeks to eliminate American hegemony over the Islamic world. Some strategists believe that this end can best be achieved by goading the United States into overt intervention.[31] Here, the jihadists routinely use the idea of imperial overstretch, a term Yale professor Paul Kennedy popularized in the late 1980s in his book *The Rise and Fall of Great Powers*. Only rarely do the jihadists cite Kennedy by name; more often, they simply refer to the mechanism of imperial overstretch.[32]

Though the truth is not clear, some evidence suggests that al Qaida meant to lure the United States into a protracted war in Afghanistan where the superpower could be ground down, exhausted, and then eventually destroyed as happened to the Soviet Union. An American intervention would also demonstrate America's hostile nature to the Muslim masses. Whether or not this was the original intent behind the 9/11 attacks, bin Laden and others in the group convinced themselves that such would be the effect of an American invasion.[33] On the other hand, the jihadists made few concrete preparations for such an invasion, and the loss of Afghanistan occasioned some criticism and self-doubt. Abu Musab al-Suri was disgusted, writing that the 9/11 attacks had given the United States the "pretext" "for realizing its goal to butcher what remained of the core of [the] jihadist movement."[34] Even the staunch Center for Islamic Studies and Research reported: "When retreat followed retreat in Afghanistan on the part of the Islamic Amirate [the Taliban], and it started to lose its territories—cities and power bases—despair began to creep among many of the Muslims, and feelings of impending defeat and the end of the mujahideen there began to overtake them. During the course of these feelings, mutterings began here and there that the mujahideen had made a mistake in their calculations, and that they were taken by surprise by something they had not expected, and that they had been overhasty, and forced themselves into an unequal conflict."[35]

The setback in Afghanistan notwithstanding, the jihadists stand by the idea of imperial overstretch. Abu Bakr Naji provided the most fleshed-out jihadist explanation of the theory, writing in *The Management of Savagery* that superpowers are likely to believe their own media propaganda that they are overwhelmingly powerful and beloved by all because they spread freedom and justice around the world. This leads them into foreign adventurism.[36] However, the domestic societies of the superpowers give priority to worldly pleasures, follow false religions, and are otherwise in a state of moral decay. When these militaries face an "assisting element," the decadent factors "cause the downfall of that superpower . . . no matter how much military power it possesses." Naji claimed that in the case of the Soviet Union, the "assisting element" was the mujahideen who fought in Afghanistan in accordance with the will of God. It should be possible, Naji argued, to do the same thing to the United States.[37]

Many jihadists believe that the United States "strategically extends" itself because it is unable to control its own urges. An al Qaida sympathizer praised the group for successfully changing the "American voice of reason" into a "cowboy mentality."[38] Al-Qurashi thought that "a few hundred strong fighters in constant mobility" would "drive [the U.S. military] crazy."[39] Bin Laden endorsed these opinions of the United States in late 2004 when he enunciated a strategy that operationalized imperial overstretch. "All that we have to do," he said, "is to send two mujahideen to the furthest point east to raise a piece of cloth on which is written al Qaida, in order to make the generals race there to cause America to suffer human, economic, and political losses without their achieving for it anything of note. . . . This is in addition to our having experience in using guerrilla warfare and the war of attrition to fight tyrannical superpowers."[40]

Once the United States is embroiled in a war, it must be kept there so that the costs of overstretch can truly begin to bite. Hence, al Qaida leader al-Atiyah wrote to al-Zarqawi in December 2005 that "prolonging the war [in Iraq] is in our interest."[41] Abu Hamzah al-Muhajir, al-Zarqawi's successor as the head of al Qaida in Iraq, taunted President Bush in November 2006, saying, "I urge you, the lame duck, not to escape quickly as your lame defense secretary did because we have not quenched our thirst from your blood yet."[42] Al-Zawahiri has made similar arguments. After President Bush's January 2007 speech announcing that the United States would "surge" an additional twenty thousand troops to Iraq, al-Zawahiri responded with a hearty endorsement, seeing in the plan a contribution to the imperial overstretch that he hopes will bring down America. "Bush raved in his latest speech," al-Zawahiri mocked, "and among his latest ravings was that he will be sending 20,000 of his troops to Iraq. So I ask him: why send 20,000 only—why not send 50,000 or 100,000? Aren't you aware that the dogs of Iraq are pining for your troops' dead bodies? So send your entire army to be annihilated at the hands of the Mujahideen, to free the world from your evil and theirs, because Iraq, land of the Caliphate and jihad, is able to bury ten armies like yours with Allah's help and power."[43]

Similarly, in October 2006, an al Qaida sympathizer posted a message to several jihadist Web sites summarizing the group's strategy against the United States. Al Qaida's long-term strategy, he wrote, involves "pulling the enemy into direct military engagement and direct fighting in Muslim lands, which economically, morally, and socially exhausts and bleeds America, and mobilizes and recruits Muslims against this enemy. . . . And we all know that this stage successfully began with the American invasion of Afghanistan after the blessed September attack and the great development of the fall of America in the swamp of Iraq."[44] He went on to say that the U.S. government had tried to withdraw from military confrontation with the jihadists, but the jihadists "did not permit" this to happen because the United States "had not yet reached the stage of near total collapse and weakness that Al Qaida wants."[45]

In another post, a jihadist calling himself Mukhaddab summarized eight goals he had deduced from studying al Qaida's writings. These included:

> Pushing Muslims into the camp of truth and Al-Qaida even by exploiting the instincts of survival and self-defense against the assaulting enemy. Anywhere there was a direct conflict with the enemy, people would be forced to take sides: either side with the enemy, which would be pure unbelief, collaboration, and treason . . . or side with those fighting against the assaulting enemy.
>
> 5. By drawing the enemy into direct engagement and conflict, Al-Qaida also wanted to realize an enormous goal: to realize practical and legitimate adequacy in terms of recruiting equipped and trained individuals who would swear allegiance until death in the way of God.
> 6. Al-Qaida also wanted to create areas that Abu Bakr Naji, in his distinguished booklet *"The Management of Savagery"* has called "areas of desolation"—areas in the Islamic world from which the authority of the local infidel central state vanishes. [Afghanistan, Iraq, and Somalia are cited as examples of success.]
> 7. Al-Qaida wanted to shake the Crusader alliance and cause disunion and differing interests among its members as a first step toward disrupting and defeating it.
> 8. Al-Qaida wanted to subject the enemy to a bloody exhaustion—first, to bleed him dry economically, and then to bleed him humanly, socially, and psychologically in a way he cannot bear or compensate.[46]

Jihadist thinkers such as Mukhaddab see American military intervention as more than an opportunity for the jihadists to engage the (allegedly cowardly) American troops in combat; it can also encourage Muslims to join the jihad or otherwise increase their resistance to the enemy. Abu Ubayd al-Qurashi saw such an effect in America's confrontation with Libya: "Weakness and ineffectiveness have marked many of its responses [to terrorism]. For instance, when the U.S. administration wanted to respond to the bombing of the nightclub in Berlin in 1986, which targeted U.S. military personnel, the White House sent aircraft to bombard Libya to deter it for sheltering 'terrorists.' However, what actually happened was the opposite. The bombardment made Libya increase its support for international terrorism, so much so that 15 incidents took place in 1987 and 8 incidents in 1988, and they all had Libya's fingerprints on them."[47]

Making a similar point, Shaykh Abd-al-Aziz bin Rashid al-Anzi commented favorably upon the American military presence in Saudi Arabia and Iraq.

> An open occupation will only help to expose the enemy. An open occupation involves blatant control over the Muslims and triggers fighting, which has already taken place. The enemy's flagrant declaration of the occupation reveals it to the Muslims. . . . Many people who spoke about the military presence of the Crusaders in the country of the Two Mosques realized the meaning of the abovementioned rule. They believed that the arrival of the Crusader forces in the open to protect the oil fields would be in favor of the Muslims. The first who made such a statement was Safar Bin-Salih al-Hawali. In his book *The Traitors Are the Most Disgraceful Deal in the History of Modern Islamic Movements* Abu-Bakr Naji quoted al-Hawali as saying in a study published in the *Al-Mujahid* periodical that "direct Western military intervention in the Muslim countries will be in favor of Islam, God willing, since the peoples will know the truth about the battle between Islam and atheism." He provided the Afghan war as an example and said how it remained weak for several years between the groups and the regime in of the '70s. However, he said, the Muslims waged an uprising to defend their faith after Russia brought in its armies. Only then the Muslims realized the truth about the battle.[48]

Overthrow the Local "Apostate" Regimes

The rhetoric of al Qaida and other Salafi jihadist groups of a global perspective usually gives priority to neutralizing the United States and its allies before trying to overthrow strong "apostate" regimes.[49] Not all agree, however. First, some jihadist groups do not wish to attract the ire of the United States. For instance, some Central Asian groups have reportedly chosen not to attack American interests because they believe doing so would risk American military intervention.[50] Second, whether or not the movement's senior leaders find it desirable, most people are going to act locally even if they do think globally. In fact, a certain degree of conflict is desirable because it inspires the masses and encourages them to join. Finally, the lure of apparently attainable success attracts some people.

Given these facts, and all other things being equal, Salafi jihadist leaders prefer to have the movement operate—and vie for power—in relatively weak states, because the "apostate" governments typically have strong security services (see chapter 3). Al Qaida and its predecessors fought many unsuccessful, even catastrophic campaigns in the "heart" of the Arab world—Egypt, Syria, and more recently against the Saudi regime. Their failure to overthrow strong "apostate" regimes has led to an increasing emphasis on striking at the strategic flanks where the security services are not so strong or may be nonexistent. In other words, AQAM must think not only about how to operate inside particular countries, but how to choose which countries in which to mount insurgencies at all.[51] In 1993 or 1994, the author of the "Five Letters" encapsulated this debate in language reminiscent of Basil H. Liddell-Hart:

> The Somali operation confirmed an important and correct military principle at the tactical and strategic levels, which is the sensitivity and critical nature of action on the flanks. Most battles, if not all, are won or lost in operations on the adversary's flanks. If we go back to the beginning of the Crusader wars, the reasons for their failure are that they tried to strike at the centers of Islam in Syria, Egypt, and the Arabian Peninsula. However when they began via what were called "geographical discoveries" to encircle the Islamic world with military centers on its periphery, then brought under control the international waterways, then began lopping off the remote parts piece by piece, they succeeded in finally reaching the heartland. They now fully control it, including the religious sanctuaries in the Peninsula and Palestine. . . . Before you abandoned the [Central] Asian position under the slogan that you were going to work in the heartland region—the Arab region—you had totally rejected the concept of movement on the flanks claiming that the battle would be decided in the heartland. . . . But now you say you have accomplished a strategic gain. Where? In Somalia? Where is Somalia? Is it not on the southern flank of the Arab world? . . . You went to work in the heartland, yet got involved in the southern flank where you achieved a brilliant victory that could only have been achieved on the flank.[52]

Some ten years later, Yusuf al-Ayiri seems to have internalized this concept as he named "the many routes to jihad":

> There is Afghanistan, which is bordered by Pakistan, Iran, Uzbekistan, Tajikistan, Turkmenistan, and China. There is Chechnya, which is bordered by Georgia, Dagestan, the Ingush Republic, and Russia. There is Palestine that is bordered by Egypt, Jordan, Lebanon, and Syria. There is Kashmir that is bordered by Pakistan, and India. There is Indonesia, which is surrounded by sea from all sides. There is Eritrea that is bordered by Sudan, Ethiopia, and the Red Sea. Look at the Philippines, Macedonia, and other fields of jihad. It is impossible for a believer who is keen on jihad not to find these many routes.[53]

By 2005, Ayman al-Zawahiri too was arguing for a periphery-inward strategic approach to the global war, because "the battles that are going on in the far-flung regions of the Islamic world, such as Chechnya, Afghanistan, Kashmir, and Bosnia, they are just the groundwork and the vanguard for the major battles which have begun in the heart of the Islamic world."[54] The primary means by which AQAM operates in those countries where it chooses to vie for power is guerrilla warfare with a healthy mixture of terrorist violence. Many AQAM strategic thinkers recognize the importance of guerrilla warfare (see chapter 5). The late Yusuf al-Ayiri—a political analyst at heart—thought that guerrilla warfare could defeat the technologically advanced American military.

> The [Middle East] region's people are the third factor. They are a hard nut to crack for the invaders and the governments, for the peoples of the region are beginning to realize that they are a factor in world events. Day after day, they are recognizing that they have a tremendous weapon, one that terrifies everyone and forces everyone to respond to their demands. This weapon is asymmetric war. This weapon is guerrilla war and martyrdom operations. U.S. weapons are useless against this method. Nuclear weapons are useless against it. Arab governments cannot control it. It is a tremendous powerful weapon that draws its power from faith and holding fast by the rope which God stretches out.[55]

Of course, in conducting guerrilla warfare it is important to have a close relationship with the people. Shaykh Abd-al-Aziz Bin Rashid al-Anzi, writing for the CISR, acknowledged this point when he wrote: "The Muslim nation is the strategic depth of the mujahideen in the guerrilla warfare. It provides shelter, refuge, and camouflage during fighting. The Muslim masses are a source of information for the mujahideen. They gather information and help with monitoring and surveillance. Moreover, they provide the mujahideen with fighters and supplies that never end."[56]

After a long period of neglect, it appears that the movement's strategists are increasingly aware of the need to be close to the people. It is true that the al Qaida charter, a document dating to the 1990s, says, "Our path is a path of fighting Jihad and we do not handle matters of aid or things like it."[57] Even in that era, however, some in al Qaida were arguing for a close relationship with the people. For instance, one AQ writer, in a series of letters captured in Kandahar, Afghanistan, said, "I'll mention to you a discovery which is merely thousands of years old. This discovery states that a movement that is isolated from its masses, that is suspicious of its people, and whose people are suspicious of it, can achieve nothing but destroy itself."[58] Hazim al-Madani wrote that the jihadists should put a great effort into preparing the society in which they will fight. The precise nature of these preparations should be subject to the particular nature of the country, but these preparations should include forming alliances with tribes or other groups that have power in the society.[59]

Al-Zawahiri admonished al-Zarqawi in a personal letter to seek public support, reinforcing the importance of the people to the jihad movement:

> If we are in agreement that the victory of Islam and the establishment of a caliphate in the manner of the Prophet will not be achieved except through jihad against the apostate rulers and their removal, then this goal will not be accomplished by the mujahid movement while it is cut off from public support, even if the Jihadist movement pursues the method of sudden overthrow. This is because such an overthrow would not take place without some minimum of popular support and some condition of public discontent which offers the mujahid movement what it needs in terms of capabilities in the quickest fashion. Additionally, if the Jihadist movement were obliged to pursue other methods, such as a popular war of jihad or a popular intifadah, then popular support would be a decisive factor between victory and defeat. . . . In the absence of this popular support, the Islamic mujahid movement would be crushed in the shadows, far from the masses who are distracted or fearful, and the struggle between the Jihadist elite and the arrogant authorities would be confined to prison dungeons far from the public and the light of day. This is precisely what the secular, apostate forces that are controlling our countries are striving for. These forces don't desire to wipe out the mujahed Islamic movement, rather they are stealthily striving to separate it from the misguided or frightened Muslim masses. Therefore, our planning must strive to involve the Muslim masses in the battle, and to bring the mujahed movement to the masses and not conduct the struggle far from them.[60]

Sanctuaries and secure areas are also important to the operations of Salafi jihadist guerrillas. Such secure areas—secure for them meaning substantially ungoverned—are typically found on the strategic flanks of, for example, Somalia, Afghanistan, and Tajikistan. The search for sanctuary has been a particularly pressing problem for AQAM because of the ruthlessness of the "apostate" nations' security services. Sayf al-Adel said that pressure from the local security service was one of the main reasons why he and Abu Musab al-Zarqawi left their native Egypt and Jordan, respectively, and went to Afghanistan:

The security services in both Egypt and Jordan began to recruit spies from these groups [Egyptian Islamic Jihad and the Egyptian Islamic Group]. They succeeded in this field to a large extent for many reasons. . . . Consequently, we felt it was important that the leadership of an Islamic action should be remote from these strikes to enable it to plan effectively and achieve its plans. . . . Communication and integration with trustworthy Islamic individuals and groups would never take place as long as merciless security services existed in these countries. Departure, therefore, was a must.[61]

Similarly, Abu Bakr Ba'asyir and Abdullah Sungkar, leaders of Jemaah Islamiyah, fled to Malaysia in 1985 because Indonesia had become too dangerous.[62]

Al-Zawahiri became aware of the necessity of a secure rear area by being on the receiving end of the tender mercies of the Egyptian security service. He wrote in *Knights under the Prophet's Banner* that the chance to go to Afghanistan came "as a gift on a gold platter" because the repeated security crackdowns in Egypt were making life too difficult for the EIJ. "The problem of finding a secure base for jihad activity in Egypt used to occupy me a lot," he wrote, "in view of the pursuits to which we were subjected by the security forces and because of Egypt's flat terrain which made government control easy, for the River Nile runs in its narrow valley between two deserts that have no vegetation or water. Such a terrain made guerrilla warfare in Egypt impossible and, as a result, forced the inhabitants of this valley to submit to the central government and be exploited as workers and compelled them to be recruited in its army."[63]

Abu Bakr Naji also sees a necessity for sanctuary, though in a more offensive way than other writers. The violent jihad actions that occur during the phase Naji called "Disruption and Exhaustion" serve only as a means to pave the way for the real main effort: the provision of governance in the liberated region(s). For Naji, areas purged of regime influence are valuable as potential sites for establishing a sharia-based administration providing services to the people. If the jihadist "administrative groups" lead the regions skillfully, such pockets can gradually coalesce with other similar regions, moving toward an Islamic state and eventually the Caliphate. Initial success would provide a concrete example drawing additional supporters to side with "the people of truth."[64] Naji's perspective on sanctuary is in harmony with his view of the nature of the jihad writ large: "a major victory is a series of small victories."[65]

The Mujahideen's Humanitarian Efforts

Following the October 2005 earthquake that devastated eastern Pakistan and the disputed territories of Kashmir and Jammu, mujahideen seized the opportunity to help the ravaged communities through relief and aid efforts. Members of Jamaatud Dawa (JuD, formerly Lashkar-e-Tayyiba, a Pakistani group operating in Kashmir and affiliated with al Qaida) claimed that it "initiated relief activities 30–45 minutes after the earthquake."[66] The group cited its knowledge of local terrain as a major reason for its quick reaction. JuD and another prominent militant group, Hizbul Mujahideen, set up hospitals, delivered aid, and provided shelter for victims. Al Qaida leader Ayman al-Zawahiri also repeatedly called on Muslims to help the victims in Pakistan: "Today, I call on Muslims in general, and on Islamic relief organizations in particular, to go to Pakistan and help their Pakistani brothers and withstand the troubles and harm they face for this purpose."[67] In addition to aid for victims, mujahideen used this opportunity to establish madrassas, filling the educational void after the earthquake destroyed many schools. The madrassas will have a lasting influence in these areas because Jamaatud Dawa plans to give all earthquake orphans an "Islamic education."[68]

Pakistan is not the only country to witness a substantial mujahideen response following a natural disaster. After the December 2004 tsunami ravaged much of Southeast Asia, mujahideen to set up relief camps in Banda Aceh, Indonesia. The Laskar Mujahideen posted an English-language sign outside its relief camp that read "Islamic Law Enforcement." The group's members said that they had "been collecting corpses, distributing food and providing Islamic teaching for refugees."[69]

Mujahideen used these tragedies to highlight the ills of society and encourage Muslims to "join the caravan." As victims searched for understanding, the mujahideen explained that God was punishing them for not following the correct path: "My dear brothers, you heard about the Tsunami disaster and the earthquake in Iran. You also heard about what Muslims around the world feel. In Pakistan, a large number of places had to face land sliding causing destruction. Several areas have been affected. Similarly, there is a lot of destruction in Balochistan. My dear brothers, what do you think these disasters are? [Passage from the Koran]: It is the result of our sins. So, keeping in mind these circumstances, we should reform ourselves."[70]

Rethinking the Strategy?

Since 2005, an alternate strategic approach has emerged among some of the intellectual elites of the Salafi jihadist movement in the Arab world. These strategists tend to have much more respect than their colleagues for American military strength; they argue for less centralization and bureaucratization and instead seek a transition to something more closely approximating leaderless resistance. Abu Musab al-Suri led the way in his 2005 book *Call to Global Islamic Resistance.*[71] Al-Suri rejected assessments of many of the strategists and leaders of the movement, assailing them, in essence, for viewing the world through rose-colored glasses. "The condition of the umma at present begs for defeat—that is, if we had no hope in God," he wrote.[72] In fact, the United States "reclaimed" the "initiative" in the war promptly after September 11 and has kept it ever since.[73]

Al-Suri maintained that for a variety of reasons, not least the leadership's inadequacies in propagandizing the masses together with their choice to operate clandestinely, the jihad was not attracting the number of people it needed.[74] In fact, "looking at the jihadist phenomenon and its leaders since its launching over the past four decades . . . we find that their numbers did not exceed several hundred, even in countries of millions like Egypt and al-Sham, and, furthermore, did not exceed even tens in other countries!"[75] Moreover, al-Suri argued, though it may be comforting to imagine the American military as weak, cowardly, and easily defeated, this is a gross underestimation of the enemy. Indeed, confrontation with any organized conventional military is futile.

> Open confrontation with America or any of her military allies is impossible as long as America can maintain complete hegemony with its overwhelming technological capabilities, and particularly with the presence of the collaborating powers who conduct her administration on the ground, besieging jihadist centers and participating in the advance against them. Tora Bora, Afghanistan 2001, Khurmal, Iraq 2003, Jabal Hatat, Yemen 2003, and what occurred in Fallujah while I edit this text, November 2004, demonstrated what Hama, Syria 1982, Tarablous, Tel a-Za'tar, and Beirut, Lebanon 1982, and Nabatiya, Lebanon 2000 proved concerning open confrontation by jihadist bands. The mujahideen confronted in these instances only locally competent armies, so imagine the same with American military might! The futility of open confrontation between small cells and organized superior armies is a well known matter addressed in most studies on guerilla war.[76]

In addition, al-Suri pointed out that the foreigners have the full cooperation of the "current ruling systems in Arab and Muslim lands," which
place their security services and media at the disposal of the infidels.[77] The
net result is a cultural and religious catastrophe because the coalition of
foreign infidels and local "apostates" brings

> programs for social, religious, and cultural transformation comprised of
> methodologies for replacing the Islamic faith and fragmenting the popular
> elements of Arab and Muslim identity, programs for reshaping societies,
> intellectual and cultural elements, educational and research methodolo-
> gies, and media programs—reshaping everything up to the Friday sermon
> on the pulpits of Muslim mosques, including the largest centers of reli-
> gious and intellectual influence such as the Al Haram mosque in Mecca,
> the mosque of the Prophet in Medina the Radiant, Al Azhar in Cairo, and
> a similar influence in Muslim mosques in every Muslim country, city,
> village, and town.[78]

Al-Suri's prescription is simple. The Salafi jihadist movement must
"become a strategic phenomenon, following the model of the Palestinian
Intifada against occupation forces, the settlers, and all who aid them.
However, it should be broadened and embrace all corners of the Islamic
world, reaching with its deterrent arms the heart of the invading United
States and its allies of infidels, from every race and in every place."[79]

Al-Suri characterized this as "system, not organization."[80] The system
should pass on only "general guidance"—"a common aim, a common doc-
trinal program, and a comprehensive educational program." The movement would abandon its bureaucratic infrastructure and its efforts to
impose command and control. The highest leaders would lead only small
cells.[81] The general guidance and common educational program would
entail promulgating material to incite the masses to "resistance" and to
educate them in conducting their struggle. This would mean widely disseminating "military training manuals, and courses, and popular guides to
popular resistance" in Arabic and also translating them into Turkish, Urdu,
Malaysian, and Indonesian, "as well as to other Islamic languages" and
possibly into European languages such as English, French, and Spanish.[82]

As might be predicted, no other member of the jihadist elite has made
an argument as comprehensive as al-Suri's; however, there are indications that at least two strategists are thinking along parallel lines. In the
summer of 2006, Lewis Atiyatallah seemed to urge delay in creating a
model Islamic state—with all the bureaucracy and infrastructure that

al-Suri loathed—even if the jihadists should attain victory in Iraq over the United States. Al-Suri would certainly have agreed with his reasoning: "Establishing a nation in the real meaning (which includes being attached to a certain piece of land with presence of establishments, departments on the land, and the people who are on a certain piece of land . . . etc.) We are not in a hurry for that; it consumes energy and will be an easy target for the enemy (the Americans and their followers have long arms, which are the air weapons and the weapons of mass destruction, we must be aware of that . . . !!)" (ellipses in original).[83]

A New Strategic Method in the Resistance of the Occupier, by Muhammad Khalil al-Hakaymah *Source*: Muhammad Khalil al-Hakaymah, *A New Strategic Method in the Resistance of the Occupier,* SITE Institute, September 29, 2006.

Muhammad Khalil al-Hakaymah, a somewhat controversial jihadist who claims to speak for the Egyptian Islamic Group, has presented a vision much more expansive than Atiyatallah's. In fall 2006 he urged the jihadist movement to find a "new method" of fighting. Previously they had operated in "open battlefields," "prov[ing] that they are incomparable fighters." This brought about great victories in Afghanistan, Chechnya, and Bosnia; however, the jihadists had proven themselves incapable of standing up to American military might in Iraq and Afghanistan because the Americans used "a new fighting technique to which the mujahideen were not accustomed." This included isolating the "victimized country"—a task made easier by co-opting the rulers of nearby countries—and ruthless application of military force through extensive use of local collaborators and "air and missile superiority."

Al-Hakaymah further observed that the local security services are crushingly effective at stamping out clandestine organizations and that the fight against the security services distracts the mujahideen from what should be their highest priority: fighting the "aggressive occupier." Moreover, the "secret organizations" have failed, due to their extensive "rules and regulations," to attract the young men of the *ummah* to "do the duty of Jihad." Finally, of course, the infidel enemy exists in many locations around the world where creating jihadist organizations is not possible.[84]

In place of the current unsuccessful approach, al-Hakaymah suggested something like al-Suri's global resistance, calling it "individual jihad" in the "indirectly occupied countries." This approach has flourished, al-Hakaymah maintained, since Operation Desert Storm and the establishment of the "new world order." He offered as examples the 1990 murder in the United States of Meir Kahane, the murder of some female Israeli students by a Jordanian border guard who thought they were mocking Muslim graves, and an attempted assassination of Hosni Mubarak. Such individual jihads can dislodge the enemy and push him into collapse and retreat, making "the way for desired strategic goals." Through the application of such means, al-Hakaymah claimed, "the British, French, and Italian occupation[s] were defeated"; "everyday and everywhere they met a continuous resistance from the *ummah*'s youth." In order to bring about such results, a small attack every month is more effective than one big attack every year or two.[85]

Conclusion

AQAM has gone beyond dogmatic strategy. The goals of its organizations have been widely published across the Internet and via audio and video messages from leaders such as Osama bin Laden and Ayman al-Zawahiri. Their intent is clear: the Americans and their allies must be driven from Muslim lands in order to create the strategic opportunity to establish the Caliphate. Helpful to Western policy makers are the facts that AQAM needs the open media to reach its followers and has never been shy about proclaiming its goals and objectives. This widely available material also reveals, however, that AQAM's strategic thought is evolving over time; this is bad news for those who would offer simplistic strategies for countering the Salafi jihadist threat.

Notes

1. FBIS EUP20051012374001, "Report: Complete Text of al-Zawahiri 9 July 2005 Letter to al-Zarqawi."
2. FBIS GMP20030929000003.
3. FBIS EUP20051012374001.
4. FBIS GMP20060305535004.
5. FBIS GMP20030929000003.
6. There is little evidence to support assertions by U.S. commentators that AQAM is waging a sophisticated information operations campaign against the West, and al Qaida aims little of its extensive propaganda effort at "infidels."
7. FBIS GMP20031027000226. The book, published by Majallat al-Ansar, consists of four essays by Sayf al-Din al-Ansari, Abu Ubayd al-Qurashi, Abu Ayman al-Hilali, and Abu Sa'd al-Amili.
8. FBIS EUP20051012374001.
9. The salience of specific "Jews and Crusaders" in jihadist discourse varies from place to place. For instance, in the Middle East, the jihadists complain primarily about the United States and its partners: the United Kingdom, France, and Israel. In Chechnya, the primary emphasis is of course on Russia, and the United States is in the background. In East Asia, it is the United States, operating in concert with Australia. In Pakistan, for groups such as Jamaat-ud-Dawa, which focus on the Kashmir problem, the emphasis is on India.
10. FBIS EUP20051012374001.
11. FBIS GMP20030523000158, "Al-Qa'ida's al-Ablaj Issues New Threats against US, West; Says UBL Is Alive," *Al-Majallah*, London, in Arabic, May 25–31, 2003.
12. See Hazim al-Madani, ICPVTR-13453, "The Enemy: Who Is He?" www.al-qaedun. com, November 22, 2004, in the database of Rohan Gunaratna's International Centre for Political Violence and Terrorism Research, www.pvtr.org/coreproj-ects_pathfinder.htm, accessed October 15, 2007.
13. Harmony document folder AFGP-2002-600053, 14.
14. Ibid.
15. Stephen Ulph, "New Online Book Lays Out al-Qaeda's Military Strategy," Jamestown Foundation, March 2005, summarizing Abu Bakr Naji's *Management of Savagery*.
16. FBIS GMP20040209000243001, "Compilation of Usama bin Ladin Statements 1994–January 2004."
17. FBIS GMP20040728000229.
18. FBIS GMP20050210000288, "Unattributed Article Details 'al-Qa'ida's Future Operations,' Threatens Homeland, US Worldwide Interests, Oil Supplies," February 10, 2005. See also Naji, *Management of Savagery*, 19, 41–43, on attacking petroleum targets; FBIS GMP20060328336001.
19. See FBIS GMP20040209000243 for bin Laden's estimate. Abu Hafs al-Mauritani similarly put the losses from 9/11 at more than a trillion dollars, though he may simply have been parroting bin Laden. Document 14419 in the database of Rohan

Gunaratna's International Centre for Political Violence and Terrorism Research, www.pvtr.org/coreprojects_pathfinder.htm, Abu Hafs al-Mauritani, "A Practical and Religious Perspective of the Unfolding Events of the Attacks on the U.S.," November 22, 2004. See also Harmony document folder AFGP-2002-801121.

20. FBIS GMP20060305535004.
21. Ibid.
22. FBIS GMP20060302371003, "Al-Qa'ida in Arabian Peninsula Claims Attack on Oil Installation, Posts Links to Book," March 1, 2006.
23. SITE Institute, "Q&A with Lewis Attiya Allah: Thoughts on Jihad in Saudi Arabia, Legitimacy of Striking Oil Targets, and Mujahideen in Yemen and Algeria," July 28, 2006.
24. Stephen Ulph, "Internet Mujahideen Intensify Research on U.S. Economic Targets," January 18, 2006, www.jamestown.org/news_details.php?news_id=155, accessed March 7, 2007.
25. FBIS GMP20031004000119.
26. IntelCenter, "Al-Qaeda's Advice."
27. "Islamists Declare Spain Truce, Endorse Bush," www.foxnews.com/story/0,2933,114489,00.html, accessed December 29, 2006. It is not clear who was in the "Abu Hafs al-Masri Brigade," but it was named after Mohammed Atef, once the number three man in al Qaida and its military leader, whose nom de guerre was Abu Hafs al-Masri. Atef died in Afghanistan in late 2001 at the hands of the U.S. Air Force. See also FBIS EUP20040317000482, "Abu Hafs al-Masri Brigades Calls Truce in Spain," March 17, 2004.
28. FBIS GMP20040415000029, "Bin-Laden Offers Europe 'Peace,'" April 15, 2004.
29. FBIS GMP20040728000229.
30. Ibid.
31. Abu Musab al-Suri is one of the skeptics. He has argued that the loss of Afghanistan was a disaster because it goaded the United States into open confrontation. See FBIS FEA20060523023251, linked to: CTC/OTA Translation and Analysis, "Abu Musab al-Suri's 'The Call to Global Islamic Resistance,'" February 2006.
32. Abu Bakr Naji referred to Kennedy in *Management of Savagery*, 7. Ayman al-Hilali also referred explicitly to Kennedy, though in a somewhat different context; see FBIS GMP20031027000226.
33. Bin Laden seemed to hint at such a strategy in 1997. See FBIS GMP20040209000243, "Usama bin Ladin Dares US Commandos to Come to Afghanistan"; memo from bin Laden to Mullah Omar, October 3, 2001, quoted in Alan Cullison, "Inside al-Qaeda's Hard Drive," *Atlantic Monthly*, September 2004, 70; Abu Hafs al-Mauritani in Harmony document folder AFGP-2002-801121. Abdullah bin Abdul Muhassen al-Utaibi made a similar argument in 1998, though he suggested luring the United States to intervene in Saudi Arabia; see Harmony document folder AFGP-2002-002883.
34. Al-Suri, *Call to Global Islamic Resistance*, al-Suri's original page 121, hereafter "internal numbering."
35. Quoted in David Cook, "The Recovery of Radical Islam in the Wake of the Defeat of the Taliban," *Terrorism and Political Violence* 15, no. 1 (2003): 33.
36. Naji, *Management of Savagery*, 7.
37. Ibid., 7–9.
38. Center for International Issues Research, 2006.
39. FBIS GMP20020814000145.

40. FBIS GMP20041101000236. In this connection, see also "Former Osama bin Laden Bodyguard in Al-Arabiya TV Interview: I Love Him More than I Love My Own Father," MEMRI Special Dispatch no. 1611, www.memri.org, accessed June 7, 2007.

41. A full translation of Atiyah's letter, "Letter Exposes New Leader in al-Qa'ida High Command," September 25, 2006, can be found at http://ctc.usma.edu/publica tions/pdf/CTC-AtiyahLetter.pdf, accessed September 23, 2007.

42. FBIS GMP20061110668001, "Iraq: Al-Muhajir Pledges Allegiance to al-Baghdadi, Threatens US, Europe," November 10, 2006.

43. FBIS GMP20070123281002, "Al-Zawahiri Calls on President to Send 'Entire Army' to Iraq," January 22, 2007. In the same speech, al-Zawahiri argued that the Taliban was defeating the United States in Afghanistan.

44. Global Issues Report, "Insight on al-Qaida's Strategy to Influence U.S. Midterm Elections," October 31, 2006.

45. Ibid.

46. FBIS GMP20061129281001, "Jihadist Website Analyzes al-Muhajir Statement, al-Qa'ida Strategy," November 15, 2006.

47. FBIS GMP20020614000107, "Pro al-Qaida Writer Expects Failure of US 'Crusade' against Jihad Movements," June 12, 2002.

48. FBIS GMP20060328336001.

49. Western analysts commonly say that al Qaida gives priority to attacking the "far enemy" (the United States) before the "near enemy" (the local regimes). Members of the movement rarely if ever use this terminology, however. We are grateful to two senior terrorism analysts in the intelligence community for first making us aware of this fact, which we have now abundantly confirmed in our own research.

50. Kurt M. Campbell and Richard Weitz, *Non-military Strategies for Countering Islamist Terrorism: Lessons Learned from Past Counterinsurgencies* (Princeton: Princeton Project on National Security, Woodrow Wilson School of Public and International Affairs, Princeton University, 2006), 16–17.

51. Lin Piao, Chinese military leader and onetime heir-apparent to Mao, faced a similar question. He noted that Mao dictated that the revolutionary forces within a country must first capture the countryside surrounding the big cities before taking the cities themselves. Lin suggested that one could consider North America and Western Europe as analogous to cities and that this would suggest focusing immediate revolutionary efforts on the surrounding regions: Asia, Africa, and Latin America. The parallels with AQAM thinking are striking. See Lin Piao, "Encircling the Cities of the World," in Walter Laqueur, *The Guerrilla Reader* (New York: New American Library, 1977), 197–202.

52. Harmony document folder AFGP-2002-600053, 13, 14.

53. FBIS GMP20041112000250.

54. FBIS EUP20051012374001.

55. FBIS GMP20030929000003. The final sentence is a reference to the Qur'an, 3:103. Actual references to "asymmetric warfare" are rare in Salafi jihadist literature. More common are statements such as "the remedy for the Crusader enemy that possess power and technology is to get the enemy to involve his prowess in battlefields where he cannot utilize his weapons, only to find himself defeated in an unconventional war." See Harmony document folder DIAC-2006-000132, *47 Pages of Military Instructions*, no date.

56. FBIS GMP20060328336001, "Terrorism: Al-Qa'ida-Affiliated Book Sets Rules for Attacking Economic, Oil Interests," March 28, 2006.

57. See Harmony document folder AFGP-2002-000080.

58. Harmony document folder AFGP-2002-600053.

59. Document 13453 in the database of Rohan Gunaratna's International Centre for Political Violence and Terrorism Research (Global Pathfinder), www.pvtr.org/coreprojects_pathfinder.htm; Hazim al-Madani, "The Enemy: Who Is He?"

60. FBIS EUP20051012374001.

61. FBIS GMP20050606371001.

62. FBIS SEP20031203000005, "Indonesia: Timeline on Ba'aysir, Bombings, Legal Case," December 3, 2003.

63. FBIS GMP20020108000197.

64. Naji, *Management of Savagery*, 47.

65. FBIS GMP20050810371012.

66. FBIS SAP20060101005002, "Pakistan: Jamaatud Dawa Leader Enumerates Relief Activities in Quake-Hit Areas."

67. FBIS CEP20051024027128, "Al-Zawahiri Urges Pakistan Quake Aid."

68. Jawad Hussain Qureshi, "Earthquake Jihad: The Role of Jihadis and Islamist Groups after the October 2005 Earthquake," International Crisis Group, July 24, 2006.

69. FBIS GMP20050107000189, "Radical Islamic Group Moving into Tsunami-Hit Aceh," January 7, 2005.

70. FBIS SAP20050320000001, "Pakistani Militant Chief Urges Muslims to Spend on Jihad," March 10, 2005.

71. Andrew Black argues that al-Suri is, in effect, enunciating and elaborating upon fourth generation warfare doctrine. See his "Al-Suri's Adaptation of Fourth Generation Warfare Doctrine," in the Jamestown Foundation, *Terrorism Monitor* 4, no. 18 (2006): 4–6.

72. Al-Suri, *Call to Global Islamic Resistance*, 40 internal numbering.

73. Ibid., 64 internal numbering.

74. Ibid., 1438–40 internal numbering, 852 internal numbering.

75. Ibid., 39 internal numbering. Al-Sham comprises Syria, Jordan, and Lebanon—roughly the Levant.

76. Ibid., OSC translation, 66 internal numbering. Al-Suri was already toying with this idea as early as the late 1980s. In his book recounting lessons learned in Syria he wrote: "The battle of Hamah proved beyond a shadow of a doubt, the conventional wisdom that, any revolution that goes into an open all out confrontation in a defined geographical location that needs to be defended, without any intervention by outside forces to aid it, and without starting marginal confrontations in other areas to force the army to relocate some of its forces, and on timing not its own, is doomed to utter failure and destruction. Even though the mujahideen were forced into the battle through a well-orchestrated plan by the regime, this does not change the fact that it led to total failure. A lesson we should take to heart." See Harmony document folder AFGP-2002-600080.

77. Ibid., 30 internal numbering. For al-Suri's views on the invincibility of the security services of the "apostate" regimes, see p. 66.

78. Ibid., 30 internal numbering.

79. Ibid., 1393 internal numbering. On pp. 66 and 67 al-Suri also points to the Iraqi resistance as a prototype for the type of global resistance he was urging.

80. Lia, "The al-Qaida Strategist Abu Mus'ab al-Suri: A Profile," 17.

81. Ibid.

82. Al-Suri, *Call to Global Islamic Resistance*, OSC translation, 1445 internal numbering.

83. SITE Institute, "Q&A with Lewis Attiya Allah: Thoughts on Jihad in Saudi Arabia, Legitimacy of Striking Oil Targets, and Mujahideen in Yemen and Algeria," July 28, 2006.

84. SITE Institute, "Hukaymah's *A New Strategic Method in the Resistance of the Occupier (Means and Goals)*," translation, www.siteinstitute.org, parts I and II. Subsequent publications by the SITE Institute have rendered the author's name as "Hakaymah," the spelling we adopt.

85. Ibid.

CHAPTER 7

Strategic Communication

Back then I believed that Islam is the only true religion, and you could even say that I was an embryonic radical Muslim. But in my mid-twenties—I'm now 34—I changed course in ways that have had a profound and lasting effect on my life. Over a period of years, I grew tolerant of cultural and religious differences. I stopped thinking that I had all the answers, or that my understanding of Islam was somehow better and more perfect than everyone else's. I think there were two basic factors in this change. First, . . . listening to Western music, I found that I loved the albums of the Beatles, U2 and Queen, which included a subtle but very clear message of spirituality, freedom and tolerance. . . . The second was what we call, in Indonesian and Arabic, "tassawuf," or what you call in English "Sufism."

INDONESIAN ROCK STAR, AHMAD DANI, OCTOBER 3, 2006[1]

"The Other Side of the Hill"

Nearly all senior American policy makers consider the "war of ideas"—an expression that subsumes issues of ideology, religion, political vision, and so on—to be a key front in the war on terrorism. Those charged with prosecuting the global struggle against AQAM, military and civilian alike, agree that winning the war of ideas is vital to succeeding against the violent Salafist enemy, and that it is a struggle the United States cannot afford to lose. An almost equally uniform consensus has emerged among top American officials since 9/11 that America is losing that war, that its management of what the U.S. government likes to call "strategic communication" runs a distant second to the impressive capabilities of AQAM.[2]

Therefore, it is important to consider AQAM's views and perceptions of strategic communication—to see how it looks from the other side of the hill, so to speak. Specifically, how does the enemy conceive of strategic communication, what role does it play in AQAM'S strategy and operations, and what is the enemy's assessment of the information battle with the West, specifically with the United States? Although American views on strategic communication in the war on terrorism are well known thanks to frequent public discussions of the issue, AQAM's views are much less known or understood. This chapter elaborates the enemy's view of strategic communication in order to increase understanding of this topic and thereby improve America's analysis and assessment of its performance in the war of ideas. Our discussion is based on perceptions and does not attempt to establish "ground truth" regarding U.S. government performance in the information battle with AQAM; rather, its value is in its elaboration of enemy views and practices regarding strategic communication.

Defining Strategic Communication

During the past decade, the term *strategic communication* has gained currency in both the U.S. government and business circles. Many definitions exist, but American officials use the term extensively without referring to a particular interpretation, particularly since 9/11. AQAM does not use this term.

The American View
For comparative purposes, we will first establish what the U.S. government means by *strategic communication*. The Department of Defense (DoD) has struggled for years to define it, and the definitions have changed over that time, particularly since the 9/11 attacks. A message from the Chairman of the Joint Chiefs of Staff on October 25, 2004, promulgated what was then a new definition. Strategic communication, he said, is "the transmission of integrated and coordinated U.S. Government themes and messages that advance U.S. interests and policies through a synchronized interagency

effort supported by public diplomacy, public affairs, and military information operations, in concert with other political, economic, information, and military actions."[3] In this definition, the U.S. government is the prime mover, and *strategic communication* is a one-way communication from the government to the target foreign audiences. Moreover, "transmission" of government themes is separate and distinct from "other political, economic, information, and military actions." Strategic communication comprises only "public diplomacy, public affairs, and military information operations," not policy or kinetic operations. In essence, even at the highest levels, words and actions are to be handled differently.

The 2006 "QDR Execution Roadmap for Strategic Communication" defines *strategic communication* as "focused United States Government processes and efforts to understand and engage key audiences to create, strengthen, or preserve conditions favorable to advance national interests and objectives through the use of coordinated information, themes, plans, programs, and actions synchronized with other elements of national power."[4] This definition is an improvement, though it remains to be seen when the DoD will fully operationalize it. Strategic communication is no longer a one-way transmission; audiences must be "understood" and then "engaged." It is no longer simply about getting across helpful messages (means); it is also about generating favorable conditions for advancing U.S. interests (ends). Arguably, "synchronizing" words with actions represents an improvement from ensuring that the two operate "in concert," but the change is subtle, at best. This definition still contains a number of weaknesses. In particular, the U.S. government is still the prime mover, and "themes, plans, programs, and products" are still considered distinct from "actions" despite the fact that actions can also "create, strengthen, or preserve conditions favorable for the advancement of U.S. interests."

AQAM's View
Although the enemy eschews American terminology, it too considers the war of ideas important, even imperative, to the success of its global jihad. However, AQAM's concepts of strategic communication are significantly different from American norms in scope, context, and strategic import. AQAM places exceptionally high value on the information battle against the "infidel," considering success in this arena to be a precondition for victory in its jihad to restore the Caliphate. Indeed, the al Qaida leadership considers winning the war of ideas to be the larger part of the struggle, as

explained by Ayman al-Zawahiri: "More than half this battle is taking place in the battlefield of the media . . . we are in a media battle in a race for the hearts and minds of our *ummah*."[5]

AQAM's view of strategic communication centers on the concept of *dawah* (literally "the call"). A common Islamic term, *dawah* is used in this context to mean the use of propaganda and indoctrination to induce Muslims to accept al Qaida's worldview, specifically enshrining jihad as the pinnacle of Islam and an individual obligation for "true" Muslims. Having accepted this, believers will come forward to wage violent jihad— join the caravan—and die as martyrs. *Dawah* to AQAM means the spectrum of information employed to persuade Muslims, particularly angry young males, to reject Western or "apostate" Muslim values in favor of violent Salafism. This persuasion ranges from traditional preaching and print materials to multimedia methods delivered via the Internet and cell phones. In American terms, *dawah* can be considered close to information operations (IO), while jihad corresponds to kinetic operations (KO). It is worth noting that *dawah* applies only to Muslims, and that the bulk of AQAM's strategic communication effort is aimed at Muslims, not at the United States, the West, or "apostate" regimes.[6]

There are several significant differences between AQAM's views of strategic communication and American concepts. First, for the enemy, *dawah* is an inherently nongovernmental activity; in the absence of any state that harbors what al Qaida or other Salafi jihadists consider to be true Islam (nearly every Islamic state today is deeply hostile to AQAM), the enemy relies exclusively on private outlets for its propaganda.

In addition, AQAM considers *dawah* to be inextricably linked to jihad; not only is there no clear dividing line between deeds and words, such a division is unnatural if not unthinkable; operations and information are fully integrated and support each other. "Political and information functions are combined [and] linked in the military function," one al Qaida thinker noted, "and . . . all act together harmoniously to serve the ancestral jihad plan without dominance of one on the other."[7] Instead, AQAM values highly what Westerners have called the "propaganda of the deed" (see chapter 8 for more on operations tied to mobilization efforts). For the enemy, deeds become propaganda, and any *dawah* that departs significantly from what the movement actually does is false and conveys the wrong message. A member of the Abu Sayyaf Group, an al Qaida affiliate in the Philippines, even referred to combat operations as "armed *dawah*," illustrating the deep connection between deeds and words that forms the core of the Salafi jihadist strategic communication: "The coordination of urban mujahideen actions . . . is the principal way of making armed *dawah* to establish the Truth of Islam. . . . These mujahideen actions carried out with specific and determined objectives, inevitably become propaganda material for the mass Communications system."[8]

Abu Musab al-Zarqawi concisely expressed this seamless fusion of *dawah* and jihad when he said that "the sword and the pen will complement one another."[9] This view is in no sense a Salafi jihadist invention; it has deep resonance in Islamic history and harkens back to how Islam was spread by the Prophet himself. "Islamic governments," explains an al Qaida manual, "are established as they [always] have been: by pen and gun, by word and bullet, by tongue and teeth."[10] A senior member of al Qaida explained the strategic purpose of *dawah* and its outcome when properly applied: "We opened the *ummah*'s eyes to its issues and as a result, the youth came forward to fight for the dignity of Islam and Muslims, armed with the hope of becoming martyrs."[11]

Leading thinkers in AQAM, including Abu Bakr Naji, Abu Musab al-Suri, and Ayman al-Zawahiri, emphasize the importance of winning "hearts and minds," a term they actually use.[12] They understand that in the modern era, they must succeed in the media to achieve this. "Once the tools for building public opinion are obtained," Osama bin Laden explained, "everything you ask for can be done."[13] In the late 1990s, he wrote to Mullah Omar illustrating the importance of winning "hearts and minds" to the Salafi jihadist movement, saying that "the media war in this century is one of the strongest methods; in fact, its ratio may reach 90 percent of the total preparation for the battles."[14]

Waging the War of Ideas

There is surprising convergence of opinion between the United States and AQAM that the global struggle between the two constitutes a war of ideas, although the two view this information struggle in very different terms and have reached radically different conclusions about the state of the overall media battle.

U.S. Government Self-Assessment and Perceptions

In the five years since 9/11, it has become received wisdom that the U.S. government is waging its information campaign against al Qaida with lamentable ineffectiveness. No senior official has been more outspoken in condemning American efforts in strategic communication than former defense secretary Donald Rumsfeld, who recently offered: "We probably deserve a D or D+ as a country as to how we're doing in the battle of ideas. . . . We have not found the formula as a country."[15]

Although the U.S. government, particularly the DoD, has frequently explained the importance of strategic communication in the war on terrorism (e.g., "This war is both a battle of arms and a battle of ideas"),[16] most observers still see notable inadequacies. The government has sponsored numerous studies of its strategic communication and related efforts since 9/11. All found American efforts wanting, and some detected near-fatal flaws. The Defense Science Board (DSB) argued in October 2001 that the United States "needs a sustained, coordinated capability to . . . influence foreign publics."[17] The board's major study of strategic communication, released three years later, found significant problems, principally the persistence of legacy ideas and procedures, and concluded: "We need to move beyond outdated concepts, stale structural models, and institutionally-based labels."[18]

Many consider American successes in strategic communication during the Cold War to constitute part of the problem. Faced with a radically different enemy after 9/11, America responded slowly to the challenge. The February 2003 National Strategy for Combating Terrorism (NSCT) asserted, "We will wage a war of ideas,"[19] yet policy makers widely consider that the campaign did not gain significant traction, nor has it notably helped the war on terrorism's efforts to date. A blunt DSB assessment finds that the United States "today is without a working channel of communication to the world of Muslims and Islam."[20]

In addition to organizational problems, a shortage of funds has harmed U.S. efforts in the war of ideas against al Qaida. A 2002 State Department study revealed that the United States was spending only $1 billion to "inform and persuade international audiences," versus more than $30 billion on intelligence and $25 billion on traditional diplomacy.[21] And not all the money spent to persuade foreign populations goes to the war effort. For instance, in Fiscal Year 2003, the United States spent $11 million on Radio Sawa, a new flagship American-style radio program aimed at the

Arab world, but also provided $27 million for anti-Castro broadcasting aimed at Cuba and $80 million for Radio Free Europe/Radio Liberty.[22]

The NSCT states clearly what the U.S. government wants strategic communication to do in the war on terrorism. The United States "will wage a war of ideas to: make clear that all acts of terrorism are illegitimate, ensure [that] . . . conditions and ideologies that promote terrorism do not find fertile ground in any nation . . . kindle the hopes and aspirations for freedom of those in societies ruled by the sponsors of global terrorism."[23] The government espouses a broad concept of strategic communication that encompasses not merely delegitimizing al Qaida and its methods but also undermining terrorism and its theological-cum-political bases in the Islamic world. In this view, strategic communication is the key enabler to curb AQAM's growth while promoting Western political and social values, including American norms regarding freedom and open debate. A lack of progress in strategic communication, in this view, may itself undermine American strategy in the war on terrorism.

America's shortcomings in this vital area are widely believed to be exacerbated by AQAM's robust capabilities in the war of ideas. "What bothers me most is how clever the enemy is," explained Secretary Rumsfeld, who was especially concerned with al Qaida's efficient mendacity in the realm of strategic communication.[24] Senior officials and experts also believe that the enemy is as effective in communicating its ideas as the U.S. government is impaired. Secretary Rumsfeld explained that our enemies are "skillfully adapted to fighting wars in today's media age, but for the most part we, our country, our government, has [sic] not adapted."[25]

AQAM's Self-Assessment and Perceptions
Considering America's pessimistic assessments of its own performance in the war of ideas, one might expect AQAM's leaders to be satisfied and confident that they are winning. Such is not the case. To them, a media victory seems far off and elusive. Indeed, pronouncements by senior jihadists reflect a profound pessimism about *dawah* every bit as deep as U.S. concerns about strategic communication. "However far our [media] capabilities reach," Ayman al-Zawahiri wrote in 2005, "they will never be equal to one-thousandth of the capabilities of the kingdom of Satan."[26] With regard to the Internet specifically, one jihadist lamented in January 2007 that "the enemies possess technological capabilities and information power on the Internet ten times greater than ours."[27]

Salafi jihadist leaders seem to have no idea how to stop the onslaught of Western and Western-style media—above all, satellite television and the Internet—against the *ummah*.[28] Muslim youths today "are swimming in the oceans of pleasure and lust," explained Abu Musab al-Nadji, and the powerful currents are leading them away from the path of sacrifice for Islam.[29] Abu Ubayd al-Qurashi stated that "America is trying to spread fornication among believers, so as to neutralize the largest possible number of Muslims from the ongoing war."[30] The result is fatalism about the limits of *dawah* in an age of ubiquitous images of sex and immorality. Al-Zarqawi lamented that "many faithful believers shun jihad. . . . It is regrettable and horrifying that the infidel Crusader media were able, through the collusion of our countrymen, to influence the personality of Muslims."[31] Al-Zarqawi's statement illustrates two major recurrent themes in jihadist commentary on the problems of *dawah* in the media age: the extent to which Muslims are complicit in the spread of Western images, and the view that a diet of Western-style programming and images via TV and the Internet changes the mindset of believers, thereby rendering thoughts of jihad (as AQAM defines it) implausible if not impossible. To this dangerous challenge AQAM has yet to devise an accepted solution. Although it is becoming a more serious problem as Western-style media increasingly reach the *ummah*, this is not a new issue for AQAM. A leading jihadist reported to bin Laden in 1998: "Regrettably, this movement suffered from great political and informational deficiency. . . . This deficiency is considered one of the killers of the movement."[32]

The profound pessimism of AQAM strategists and leaders regarding the war of ideas is all the more surprising considering the long view the jihadists take of the struggle. In top AQAM circles, the extended nature of the struggle against "infidels" (and, of course, its ultimate triumph) is accepted and unquestioned. "The jihad Islamic movement . . . has not set a specific date for achieving this goal," al-Zawahiri explained in 2001. "It could take several generations to achieve. The Crusaders in Palestine and Syria left after two centuries of continued jihad. . . . The British occupied Egypt for 70 years. The French occupied Algeria for 120 years."[33]

AQAM's considerations regarding the media battle against the West are grounded in Salafi jihadist theology and cannot be fully understood from any Western or secular viewpoint. Al-Zawahiri has sometimes expressed the view that al Qaida's jihad may need to continue indefinitely, a reality other leaders seem to accept. In 2005 he defined the goal of the Salafi jihadist movement and its holy warriors as follows: "Their on-going mission is to establish an Islamic state, and defend it, and for every generation to hand over the banner to the one after it until the Hour of Resurrection."[34] Other AQAM strategists focus on nearer-term though still ambitious goals: "[Al Qaida] aims to liberate global political thought and the current political reality from the fetters of globalization-fueled U.S. hegemony."[35]

It is important to note that AQAM's widespread pessimism regarding its strategic communication, particularly its perceived inability to get its message to the right audience, has little to do with the U.S. government's efforts, to which AQAM pays almost no attention. In effect, official American actions (public affairs, diplomacy, or information operations [IO]) are of modest interest or consequence to al Qaida. The jihadists have essentially defined the interaction of Western cultural norms with the *ummah* as the center of gravity in the media battle. On this crucial ground, U.S. and Western popular or mass culture, and their imitators in the Muslim world, overawe the jihadists. Confronted by *Baywatch* and pop music, AQAM feels itself defenseless, knowing that such Western images have put down roots among millions of Muslims, especially the young men whom the jihadist movement needs to entice to "join the caravan."

Dawah and Jihad

Having defined the concept of *dawah* and al Qaida views of the "media battle," we must explain how these issues affect AQAM strategy and operations, and how they could be seen as jihadist weaknesses and possibly exploited.

Al Qaida's predicament is very simple: without *dawah* there can be no jihad. Yet AQAM faces formal and informal obstacles to preaching its brand of "armed *dawah*" and reaching the Muslim masses. While Salafi jihadists have successfully exploited the Internet in many ways, they lack access to more conventional media, above all television, which they see as a critical shortcoming. Bin Laden himself once observed: "Not a single TV channel has been acquired which can preach Islamic injunctions according to modern requirements and attain an international influence."[36]

This access problem has not improved in the last five years, and the absence of any Salafi jihadist presence on television has become a greater liability given the rising importance of satellite television in the Arab/

Muslim world. This shortcoming is particularly galling to AQAM considering the proficiency of Shia radicals in this arena (e.g., Al Manar, Hizballah's satellite television channel). Contrary to Western perceptions, al Qaida loathes Arab media, which it views as at least implicitly anti-Salafi, almost without exception. AQAM reserves a special hatred for the TV news network Al-Jazirah, a bugbear to many in the U.S. government but perhaps a bigger one to radical Salafists, who consider the Qatari network infected with secularism, nationalism, and dangerous tendencies toward Western-style reporting. To AQAM, there is little difference between Al-Jazirah and Fox News. Any journalists who attempt to cover issues from anything other than a Salafi viewpoint are ipso facto enemies of the movement: "The suspicious role that the piggish [Arabic-language pun on "Al-Jazirah"] television channel and other secular channels play to frustrate Muslims and revive rotten nationalism is revealed, day after day."[37]

Such complaints are common. A poster to a password-protected jihadist Web site warned his brethren to "beware of the secular al-Jazeera Channel . . . they are hypocrites in the first degree. . . . Beware of the Arab media."[38] Irked by media reports about intra-insurgent feuds and atrocities committed by the jihadists, the "Minister of War" for the "Islamic State of Iraq" warned in May 2007 that Islam's enemies "came with 'Al-Arabiya' and 'Al-Iraqiya' and [U.S.-run] 'al-Hurra' and 'Al-Jazeera' and every peddler of a message . . . each trying to convince the people that the soldiers of the nation of Islam are liars who kill innocent and weak people, and they know that what they say is untrue."[39] Similarly, the Indonesian Imam Samudra, one of the Bali bombers, referred to the Western "ape mass media" (the reference to apes being very offensive in Indonesia) and lamented that Indonesian media were now making "apes their mascot" as well.[40]

Image originally posted on a jihadist Web site ridiculing Al-Jazirah as the "RAND Channel for Broadcasting Lies and Discord." The RAND Corporation has become a favorite target for abuse in the jihadist community. *Source*: Center for International Issues Research, "Manipulation of RAND Reports by Extremist Propagandists," *Global Issues Report*, May 15, 2007.

In fact, senior jihadists, including strategists, profess a belief in a comprehensive media conspiracy against them that prevents al Qaida and its brethren from getting their message out (e.g., America's "tremendous media arsenal and hegemony over most, if not all, of the media"). Ayman al-Zawahiri thinks the movement is under a "media siege" and that breaking this siege is an "independent battle that we must launch side-by-side with the military battle."[41] By the same token, the November 2006 inaugural issue of *Technical Mujahid*, an online periodical devoted to technology and Internet security, claimed that the "Crusaders' media and its agent followers in the Muslim lands" had erected a "fence" that prevented them from getting their message out.[42]

While the broader Arab experience clearly shapes such beliefs (for example, most top jihadists come from countries where media are controlled by the state and genuinely free media are rare), there is no doubt that AQAM's fears of a clandestine media cabal that corrupts and co-opts Muslims to Western ways are deep-seated. Muhammad Khalil al-Hakaymah has suggested that much of this is happening at the behest of the U.S. government, particularly its intelligence agencies. He believes that since mid-2003

> Washington has spent tens of millions of dollars to finance Islamic broad-casting stations, television programming, and to prepare a curriculum to be taught in the schools of the Islamic World, and has spent millions of dollars on Islamic thinkers who are looked at as representing the Muslim elite, and on holding political workshops in support of moderate Islam, and has built schools and mosques and carried out programs to save what the journalist described in his report as "the old Qur'an." All of this was planned to be carried out through targeting the Islamic media, the religious leaders, and political parties, and through providing all the money, assets, and human force needed by the American Intelligence service to guarantee the success of its plan.[43]

An al Qaida strategist explained in 1998 that an infidel media conspiracy designed to "spread ignorance among Muslims [comprises] a huge special information system . . . a troop of writers, poets, journalists, anchormen, various television networks and the media in general, as well as dissolute and hypocrite musicians."[44] One jihadist thinker even went so far as to argue that the media are America's single greatest strength: "The United States does not have the power that matches its international position and reputation . . . it mostly depends on the media with which it has fascinated the nations of the world. For years, American TV exported American culture to the world . . . the magicians of the modern-day pharaoh were the media people."[45]

The lens of conspiracy through which radical Salafis view the media struggle leads to conclusions that outsiders often find difficult to comprehend but which nevertheless express feelings strongly held by many jihadists, whose worldview is steeped in "infidel" conspiracies and anti-Muslim secret powers. For instance, "the real intent of these cartoons," a senior Pakistani jihadist explained during the early 2006 Danish cartoons controversy, "is to smear the concept of jihad so that Muslims come to hate it. All over the world, propaganda against jihad is spreading and [it] is called 'terrorism.'"[46]

Western media, according to AQAM, have done their work well. Arab governments are uniformly hostile to Salafi jihadists; entertainers and other public figures are corrupted; and not even the Sunni establishment, the *ulema*, can be trusted to defend "true" Islam. Indeed, the jihadists believe that the *ulema* are almost universally compromised, no matter how impressive their apparently anti-American credentials may be, and are therefore functionally in the enemy camp and not to be trusted. Except for a small number, the *ulema* have generally been the first to disappoint the mujahideen, not only in the Arabian Peninsula but elsewhere.[47] Bin Laden explained in 1998, "When the jihad stopped among the *ummah* for a while, there emerged a generation of religious scholars who had no experience in jihad. They fell under the influence of the U.S. media that invaded the Islamic countries, and were thus defeated psychologically even before engaging in military action. They say: we cannot go for jihad. True, jihad is necessary, but we cannot do it."[48]

Al-Zarqawi expressed a similar sentiment in 2004, typically without mincing words: "The Sunnis are asleep due to lies told by their so-called wise men and *ulema* that drugged the *ummah* and let it down. They were the bridge that the enemies crossed to kill the *ummah*. Whenever the *ummah* wanted to wake up and avenge . . . the humiliation of its religion and honor, they told it: Stay asleep and don't wake up."[49] The AQAM-affiliated Center for Islamic Studies and Research lamented the role of the "apostate" regimes in the corruption of the *ulema*, castigating "hired media and mercenary journalists . . . harping on the theme of ignorance" and assailing "the tyrants' untiring efforts to monopolize the *ulema*, until no one can give a fatwa except someone whom the tyrant selects and appoints, whose fatwas he approves, and whose statements he finds congenial."[50]

Yusuf al-Ayiri, among the most influential jihadists until his death in late 2003, even argued that AQAM's enemies support Sufism, a strain of Sunni Islam that emphasizes the personal and mystical experience of the religion, as a way of suppressing jihad: "The Zionist-crusader alliance has realized that a large number of Muslims will reject secularism. They have given thought to an alternative acceptable to Muslims that will be harmless, ineffective, and passive. They cleared a space for so-called 'spiritual' groups that care only for the 'spirit' and never take any real action. In the Islamic world, such groups are represented by Sufi dervishes. Most of the Sufi brotherhoods in the Islamic world are infidels."[51]

Abu Musab al-Zarqawi described the tribal leaders in Iraq in similar terms, saying that they "are mainly Sufis who have turned religion into a festival of singing and dancing to whatever tune and that ends with a good meal. These people are real opium and sedative, and a source of lies for a nation that is groping its way in the dark. As to the spirit of Jihad and culture of martyrdom and disengagement with the infidel, they are as innocent of them as the wolf is innocent of the blood of Joseph, peace be upon him. Despite all the woes and bad conditions none of them speaks about jihad or calls for martyrdom. They are hopeless and not qualified for anything."[52] The allegedly narcotic effect of Western images, described by al-Zarqawi in 2004, is a regular theme of AQAM propaganda: "The dust of lies and smoke of charlatanry released by the enemies of Allah are only intended to dope and weaken you so that you will not rise as heroes as men do."[53]

AQAM thinkers believe that the Western media have lulled Muslims into believing that peaceful coexistence is possible, thereby denying the need for jihad. Sayf al-Din al-Ansari asserted that the West has "turn[ed] talk of peace into a drug that saps the rage of the oppressed."[54] Abu Ubayd al-Qurashi explained in almost identical language that al Qaida's enemies have turned "talk about peace into a sedative to absorb the anger of the oppressed people," asserting the commonly held notion that Western media and culture actually anesthetize Muslims and steer them away from "true Islam."[55]

AQAM's thinkers commonly believe that the Western media, in collaboration with "apostate" Muslims, conspire to prevent the movement from getting credit for its operations—a major problem given that al Qaida depends on inspirational operations to support *dawah*. More than a decade ago, Abu Hafs al-Masri (also known as Mohammed Atef) believed that the December 1994 Airbus hijacking perpetrated by Algerian jihadists was undercut by the fact that the French "were in total control. . . . They became the sole conduit of information for the world." As a result, the hijackers were unable to get out their message through the world press, and thus the movement could not benefit from the martyrs' action.[56] Sayf al-Din al-Ansari explained in exasperation about the rampant conspiracy theories regarding the 9/11 attacks that "the defeated [Muslims] continue to ask themselves to this day, 'Could Al Qaida really have done this? Or was it just a Jewish deception?'"[57] Such concerns have also arisen in the context of the war in Iraq. In spring 2004, Zarqawi expressed the belief that the United States intentionally misportrayed the Iraqi insurgency as a Baathist effort rather than jihad by "true Muslims" in order to deny al Qaida the propaganda fruits of its sacrifices.[58] Leading jihadists see a hidden hand behind the allegedly inaccurate media coverage of AQAM's operations.

Hard-line Salafi jihadists view even such anti-Western Islamic movements as the Muslim Brotherhood—the progenitor of much modern Salafi activism—as weak. Abu Bakr Naji lamented that it is easier for jihadists to recruit "ordinary people" than members of "the Islamic movement," who "are (already) polluted by the doubts of the evil shaykhs."[59] Despite such obstacles, *dawah* is a vital precondition for AQAM to achieve its goal to establish the Islamic Caliphate and "to educate Muslims that allegiance to Islam and the traditions of the Prophet must precede allegiance to any other framework."[60] Understanding that "restoring" the Caliphate is a long-term project that will have to happen without the support of Sunni governments or *ulema*, al Qaida needs "to establish a generation of mujahid emigrants to carry on our vision after us."[61] Al-Zawahiri explained the role of *dawah* in ensuring that the struggle continues: "The persistence of the resistance will transfer the popular wrath from one generation to another and keep the desire for revenge alive in the people's souls."[62]

In order to pass on that jihad spirit to subsequent generations, AQAM must offer the *ummah* a clear alternative vision. Given the "media siege," AQAM sees great hope in the propaganda of the deed, the idea that actions can convey ideas. By vigorously waging jihad and showing to Muslims the outcome of their operations, Salafi jihadists believe they can overcome or at least mitigate the West's overwhelming media power, thereby ensuring that the movement will continue: "The best thing that mujahideen can offer . . . is a pure jihad, right choices, and mature media. This should raise a generation of the country's citizens and tribes that carry one banner and initiate jihad."[63] This concept is hardly passive, however, and AQAM advocates pushing Western media and Western-style programming out of the Muslim world, kinetically if necessary. The stakes are high and the task is clear: "We have to attack the secular, liberal, and modern, and call on people to boycott their films, newspapers, and Internet."[64]

AQAM's thinkers do not believe that winning the media battle will be easy, as "evil" Western cultural norms have insidiously worked their way into the consciousness of the *ummah*. Of greatest concern to Salafi jihadists is the rise of Western-style content delivered by Muslims for Muslims via television and the Internet. Popular programs such as *Star Academy*, a Lebanese version of *American Idol* starring attractive young Arabs (especially women) wearing "infidel" dress and singing Western-style love songs, have a following across the Middle East and epitomize the enemy's insidious ability to transform Muslim hearts and minds.[65] One Salafi scholar supportive of al Qaida attributed the decline of morals among Muslims in part to "the corruptive media, from 'video clips,' 'Star Academy,' 'Super Star.' More than this are the porn movies and the stench channels."[66] Bollywood movies, popular among Muslims in southern Asia, are another bugbear of the jihadists, who claim the films, though chaste by Western standards, advocate "Hindu polytheism" in addition to immorality.[67] The threat of Westernization via mass media makes "armed *dawah*" particularly important and necessary.

Star Academy contestants. Photo by Faris Jammal.

For AQAM, the need for *dawah*, including its armed variant, is rooted in Islam's deepest history. It goes back to the Prophet himself, who high-lighted the problem of *wahn*, a term commonly translated as "weakness" but which Muhammad defined as "a love of the world and hatred [or dislike] of death." Salafis consider *wahn* the main stumbling-block pre-venting youth from joining the jihad; it is *wahn*—an attachment to this world and its pleasures greater than a desire for martyrdom—that *dawah* aims to discredit and defeat.

Wahn

The Prophet Muhammed described *wahn* in a famous hadith.

The Prophet said: "The People will soon summon one another to attack you as people when eating invite others to share their food." Someone asked, "Will that be because of our small numbers at that time?" He replied, "No, you will be numerous at that time: but you will be froth and scum like that carried down by

> a torrent (of water), and Allah will take the fear of you from the breasts (hearts) of your enemy and cast *al-wahn* into your hearts." Someone asked, "O Messenger of Allah, what is *al-wahn*?" He replied, "Love of the world and dislike of death."[68]

Deep concerns about *wahn* pre-date even the beginnings of al Qaida and have been a constant in the movement. Decades ago, Sayyid Qutb, the intellectual godfather of the Salafist renaissance in the second half of the twentieth century, asked pointedly, "Those who fear torment, pain, martyrdom, and the loss of life, children, and property if they would wage jihad in the path of Allah should take a careful look—what does their submission to that which is not Allah cost them in terms of life, possessions, and children?"[69] In 1988, Abdullah Azzam, the founder of al Qaida, bemoaned the fact that Muslims had abandoned jihad "due to love of this world and abhorrence of death."[70] More recently and bluntly, Abu Musab al-Zarqawi stated in spring 2004, "Everybody has either overlooked jihad, been burdened by the ephemeral bliss of the worldly life demonstrating a dislike for jihad, or renounced jihad because he is afraid and scared of death."[71]

Although *dawah* is simple at its core—its purpose is "to inspire the *ummah* with love of jihad and its people"[72]—and it relies on repetition of a few basic themes, AQAM has a constant struggle getting the message out, not least because the enemy is so adept at countering al Qaida's informational efforts with its own powerful propaganda. "They seek to dissuade people and spread lies and biased propaganda to prevent people from fighting jihad or aiding the mujahideen."[73] The Egyptian strategist Sayf al-Adl explained how *dawah* is supposed to work: "We opened the *ummah*'s eyes to its issues and as a result, the youth came forward to fight for the dignity of Muslims, armed with the hope of becoming martyrs."[74] The informational power of the "infidel" is so great, however, and the threat of *wahn* so pervasive, that *dawah* is a constant uphill struggle.

While Salafi jihadists consider their beliefs and doctrines to be self-evident and take it as dogma that the *ummah* will eventually rally to their cause, their view of strategic communication is in many ways burdened with pessimism seemingly at odds with their unshakable faith that their cause must triumph in the end. While *dawah* does produce martyrs and brings forth young men to wage jihad, AQAM approaches the problem with a high degree of trepidation. The jihadists' view that the whole world is against them, that most Muslims are compromised by the

Westernization of their values, and that the "Zionists and Crusaders" are directing a global media conspiracy to undermine Islam is common in the movement and a source of constant concern. To ranking Salafi jihadists, losing the war of ideas constitutes the greatest threat to the success of AQAM's global jihad.

Slide from a Jemaah Islamiyah PowerPoint presentation. Previous slides showed the atrocities being inflicted on Muslims around the globe. The black text then says, "But we're still busy with *Indonesian Idol*...and hedonism." The blue text is the hadith about *wahn* rendered in Bahasa Indonesian. *Source*: Center for International Issues Research, 2004.

Dawah: Strategy, Methods, and Metrics

AQAM's strategic communication encompasses a broad spectrum of activities, all aimed at encouraging young Muslims to accept the radical Salafi vision of jihad, and thereby obtaining recruits and supporters. In Western business terms, al Qaida possesses an exceptionally well-defined global brand that enjoys proven niche appeal in the Islamic world, particularly among angry young men. "Armed *dawah*" exists to reach potential recruits with the right message at the right time, before youths are corrupted to "infidel" mores and are lost to the cause.

Means
Access to mainstream media constitutes perhaps the main problem in the "war of ideas," according to AQAM sources. The "media siege" inflicted

on the movement by the dominance of Western ideas and content in the global media, which is compounded by the spiritual weakness—if not outright disloyalty—of most Muslim news and entertainment outlets, means that traditional media, particularly television, are simply not viable outlets for the Salafi jihadists. The hostility of the "apostate" governments across the Islamic world adds to the difficulty. To compensate for this weakness, AQAM has turned to new media, principally the Internet, and has enjoyed considerable success at waging its digital jihad.

AQAM has unquestionably benefited from the recent explosion in access to the Internet across the Arab/Muslim world. Islamic rates of Internet exposure, while not yet at Western levels, are rising rapidly. By mid-2004 there were 1,462,000 Internet users in Saudi Arabia, an enormous jump from only 90,000 three years before, and 69 percent of users were between the ages of twenty and thirty-five.[75] Even the poorest and most repressive corners of the Islamic world are seeing strong Internet growth. By 2005, 42 percent of households in Syria owned a personal computer and 10 percent of the population enjoyed home Internet access; a similar pattern is emerging in Pakistan, where by 2006 half of all Internet users were going online at home, compared with 26 percent at Internet cafés and 15 percent at the office.[76] Considering that Internet cafés are ubiquitous in developed areas of the Islamic world, any urban Muslim who wishes to go online has easy access, and increasing numbers of them reach the Internet at home, which will render local government surveillance of Internet activity more difficult.

AQAM's Internet-driven media strategy, which is a decentralized activity executed by individuals or small cells of propagandists around the globe, is based on the simple reality that online efforts enjoy reasonably unfettered access to the key demographic, namely the *ummah*'s young men. "Digihad" is cheap compared with conventional media, and the target audience is comfortable with Internet formats and technologies, which AQAM effectively exploits. Because it is inexpensive, well distributed, and effective, the Internet represents an ideal command, control, communications, and propaganda platform for the radical Salafi movement. Jihadist use of the Internet, including Web sites in many languages, thousands of bulletin boards and blogs, plus "deep Web sites" that are difficult to locate, presents a challenging target for enemies to counter or disrupt.[77] In January 2007, the Global Islamic Media Front even announced the launch of the online Voice of the Caliphate Channel, which uses streaming video to disseminate jihadist content.[78] The Internet itself may be viewed as a de facto sanctuary for AQAM, a factor the technically savvy element of the movement seems to appreciate.

A noteworthy developing aspect of AQAM's use of the Internet for *dawah* is the proliferation of Web-based, cost-free video games aimed at boys and teenagers. Frequently closely modeled on popular Western online games (some are even copied from "America's Army," the U.S. Army's successful online recruiting tool), these games offer action, impressive graphics, and heavy doses of Salafi propaganda to youths. They are frequently realistic and lurid in their depictions of alleged "Zionist and Crusader" atrocities, with some games being based directly on actual events in Iraq (e.g., the battles of Fallujah). All extol the virtues of jihad against the "infidel," and some games define success not solely by killing the enemy, but by achieving martyrdom. In nearly every case, the enemy—increasingly American troops in Iraq—is depicted as employing cruelty, rape, and plunder in its struggle against Islam. Typical is a 2006 video game from al Qaida in Iraq (AQI), or at least its sympathizers, that begins with a voiceover (in American English) by an Iraqi youngster: "I was just a boy when the infidels came to my village in their Blackhawk helicopters . . ."[79] Considering the well-known addictive and persuasive effects of video games on Western youth, it would be naive to assume that AQAM's online games do not have similar impacts on Muslim boys, who are increasingly able to access the Internet at will.

Methods

While methods of delivery for AQAM propaganda are often technologically advanced, Salafi jihadists customarily rely on conventional, indeed traditional, themes and images to bring "armed *dawah*" to the Muslim masses. While religious motifs are constant, as is deep-seated hatred of the "Crusader-Zionist" enemy, issues of shame, honor, and vengeance also feature prominently and serve as powerful motivators for would-be mujahideen.

The theme "jihad as an individual obligation" is ubiquitous in Salafi jihadist propaganda and underpins everything else. A late-2005 AQI online poster exclaimed: "We Want You for Jihad," adding, "Your belief in Allah did not allow you to be defeated and you brought the *ummah* into the light."[80] A jihadist video seized in Toronto in mid-2006 explains it simply: "Come forth and kill the Jews and Americans, for killing them is foremost of obligations and the greatest form of worship."[81]

Overcoming fear of death is an important component of this foundational effort. A Turkish jihadist Web site in 2006, for example, described the glorious acts of martyrs: "They kept their promise and gave up their lives for Allah. Which side are we on?"[82] An Iraqi jihadist Web site frankly lists among the things that detract from faith "cowardice and fear of death and imprisonment."[83] Encouraging youths to abandon earthly pleasures and embrace a martyr's death, thereby overcoming the dreaded *wahn*, is a regular feature of AQAM *dawah* messages, with Muhammad himself regularly quoted to encourage young men to join the caravan. An Uzbek jihadist video released in late 2005 proclaims: "The Prophet said, 'He who dusted his feet on the path of jihad—Allah will preserve him walking through fire.' Don't consider those who died on jihad dead, for they are with Allah."[84]

Another near-constant theme in AQAM *dawah* is honor, with emphasis on how the enemy's actions humiliate and shame the *ummah*. Individual Muslims must avenge this stain through action and sacrifice. "The roots of humiliation cannot be destroyed without a barrage of bullets. . . . Without sacrificing blood, the degradation will never cease," asserts a 2005 AQI video. "I am for death and not for dishonor. My blood cries for Islam!"[85] Such appeals to honor seem to resonate effectively with AQAM's target audience, and likely explain why accounts of martyrdom frequently extol the dedication and youth of those who give their lives in the jihad. Jihadist propaganda regularly criticizes the lethargy of Arabs in fighting the enemy, thus making clear that only dedicated mujahideen from AQAM can avenge the honor of the occupied and oppressed. The title of an online visual study of the Iraqi resistance posted by a jihadist group in 2006 is revealing in this regard: "The Third Year of Disgrace, Weakness, Defeat and Arab Disappointment in Pictures."[86]

Another regular theme in AQAM *dawah* is personal vengeance for the alleged crimes committed by the enemy, with angry Muslims offering accounts of suffering at the hands of "infidels" that can be avenged only by jihadist action. As an eight-year-old boy explained in a 2006 video: "When I grow up I want . . . to kill American soldiers because they killed my father when they shelled our house more than a year ago. My mother always tells me that I have to grow up quickly, to seek revenge for my father, for whoever killed him and destroyed our house and made us live in my grandfather's house. I will do so when I grow up."[87]

Sexual shame and degradation constitute another powerful theme Salafi jihadists use in their effort to rouse hatred in Muslims so they will join the ranks of jihad. Much of this propaganda is exceptionally lurid and includes sensationalist allegations of mass rapes by U.S. military personnel, "Crusader" use of mosques and holy sites as brothels or bars, and allegations of U.S. forces sexually compromising Muslim women, including forcing them to participate in "unnatural" acts. In a typical case, a 2004 Afghan leaflet shows an alleged U.S. soldier searching the groin area of a burqa-clad woman, with the accompanying text: "Is this harmless sister also a terrorist? To the Afghan mujahideen: Where is your courage? Tomorrow the same thing will happen to your daughter or sister."[88] The leaflet continues: "They try to take things over. They hope to install Satanic rule. . . . America's Satanic soldiers try to search our helpless and innocent Muslim women, as you can see in the picture. Our mujahideen sit silently by. You sit like cowards and do nothing. Afghan mujahideen, your grandfathers defeated the British. You defeated the Russian superpower. Today against the Americans, why do you just sit by silently? Are you afraid of death and becoming a martyr according to Allah's path? Martyrdom is a gift from Allah. Death comes regardless."[89]

Image from a pro-Taliban propaganda letter. The text on the graphic says in Pashtu: "Is this harmless sister also a terrorist? To the Afghan mujahideen: Where is your courage? Tomorrow the same thing will happen to your daughter or your sister." An unshown caption reads in part: "The above picture shows the American animals searching one of our countrywomen. An innocent Muslim woman. Through their 'searching' they seek to see the women's bodies." *Source*: Harmony document folder AFGP-2004-005632.

AQAM propaganda commonly employs explicit sexual imagery for dramatic effect. "These sons of monkeys and pigs raped us. . . . Kill them so that we may rest," exclaims an al Qaida in Iraq video that highlights a letter supposedly sent by an Iraqi woman "martyred" at Abu Ghraib (a venue that features prominently in AQAM propaganda, especially regarding matters of sexual shame). The 2006 video, which extols a mujahid who reputedly martyred himself in a revenge attack on U.S. forces, explains that the man "decided to get revenge for Fatima and every Muslim woman" by joining the mujahideen and attacking the occupier.[90] While such propaganda may seem excessive to outsiders, it appears to be quite effective at rousing hatred of the enemy, especially among those predisposed to AQAM's message, and it would be unwise to assume that the lurid and sensationalist nature of such media compromises its message or messenger in Muslim eyes.

The same can be said of the broader issues of alleged "Crusader" atrocities as they appear in Salafi jihadist *dawah* efforts. U.S. and Western military operations are presented simply as a cruel war on Islam, with the "infidel" enemy deliberately targeting Muslim civilians. AQAM videos, now found on most jihadist Web sites, show graphic images of dead civilians, frequently children, allegedly killed by "Crusaders"; visitors are often explicitly asked to avenge the children cruelly murdered by the enemy. "What did these children do that they deserve to be killed?" asks an Iraqi jihadist video that details the alleged killing of civilians by U.S. forces near Bilad, Iraq, in 2006.[91] While some of these videos and images are actual "collateral damage" inflicted by coalition forces, many are exaggerations or outright fabrications. This does not appear to concern radical Muslims, who are a receptive audience for graphic anti-Western propaganda, and few AQAM *dawah* efforts seem to have failed by being too explicit or condemnatory of "infidels."[92]

Avenging such crimes is another prominent feature of AQAM propaganda, which includes lurid videos depicting attacks on U.S. and coalition forces in Iraq, usually delivered via popular Salafi jihadist Web sites. The graphic footage, often of bombings and shootings that kill "infidels," is accompanied by Qur'anic inscriptions and chants glorifying jihad, invariably including the *tekbir*, "Allahu akbar!" "This work serves the jihad in a new style," exclaims a 2006 video from al Qaida in Iraq that hails the deeds of snipers, who are a subject of adulation on AQAM Web sites. The sniper video is among the most popular propaganda items for al Qaida currently. "Relying on Allah, we will snipe a pig," says one video. Another that extols the famous "Sniper of Fallujah," Abu Azzam, who was reputed to have killed many coalition troops, explains the jihadist view of sniping: "It was not you who killed them, it was Allah [working through you] who killed them."[93]

AQAM's propaganda also highlights suicide bombers who attack coalition forces in Iraq. These formulaic videos customarily depict the bomber before the operation, often quoting the Qur'an, followed by alleged action footage of the suicide operation. Exaggerated claims of "Crusader" casualties ("forty pigs were killed") are standard fare in these videos.[94] Web-delivered videos of improvised explosive device (IED) attacks on coalition forces in Iraq, frequently carefully choreographed and professionally filmed, are increasingly prominent in AQAM's *dawah* efforts.

High-ranking or famous al Qaida martyrs receive special attention in Web-based propaganda, and the deaths of well-known jihadists are usually accompanied by insta-tribute sites online that celebrate the achievements of the fallen fighter and demand that his example be followed or his death avenged. The June 2006 killing of Abu Musab al-Zarqawi by U.S. forces resulted in the launch of several such sites, with customary incantations: "All over the world people are crying at such a loss. . . . [He was] smart, bright, loyal, kind-hearted, generous, and he adored his mother."[95]

In contrast to such flowery language, AQAM propaganda includes invective aimed at Muslims who refuse to toe the Salafi jihadist line or, worse, are considered "slaves and servants to the Crusaders."[96] Typical is the language used in a 2006 jihadist video from Waziristan: "You often see in the news how the mujahideen are accused of being terrorists, and how the American stooges, Pervez [Musharraf] and [Hamid] Karzai, hand them over to Jews and Crusaders for a paltry price."[97]

While Salafi jihadists are reluctant to show unintentional Muslim casualties of the jihad, and assiduously avoid depictions of mujahideen-inflicted "collateral damage" in their propaganda, they revel in demonstrating what happens to co-religionists who betray "true Islam." AQAM videos frequently portray the execution of traitors, loosely defined as Muslims who have served the "infidel" in some manner, in a positive light, as a service to the *ummah* and a necessary bloodletting. An early 2006 video from Afghanistan depicts the killing of two alleged "spy-bandits" and reports that it was a "happy occasion for anyone who saw or heard the executions."[98] Videos depict "Allah's punishment" quite graphically in what are essentially snuff films; according to the formula, a captive Muslim confesses to serving the "infidel" and is then killed ritually, usually with shots to the head. Close-ups of the lifeless body are customarily included along with Qur'anic texts justifying the killing. The fate that befalls "traitors to the *ummah*" serves as a control mechanism and deterrent for an organization that is concerned with spies, provocateurs, and betrayal (see chapter 3).

Alternatively, however, Salafi jihadists go to pains to demonstrate their self-proclaimed compassion toward fellow Muslims. AQAM messages emphasize the movement's deeply held belief that as Islam is the natural state of mankind, Salafism is the natural state of Muslims; those who reject al Qaida's view of the faith and the world do so out of ignorance or because their minds have been corrupted by the "infidel." "If one takes the time to understand our aims, one will embrace them," explained one AQAM thinker, thus highlighting the commonplace line that average Muslims will turn to radical Salafi ways after they are properly exposed to them. Even those taken hostage by the jihadists frequently accept their beliefs and hail the virtues of the holy warriors, according to the movement's propaganda. For example, Sudanese hostages—fellow Muslims seized in Iraq in early 2006 and released after they "repented for their crimes"—were said to have embraced "true Islam" thanks to their experience. "They have treated us like angels would treat people," one of the former hostages proclaimed. "This is the character of the mujahideen. We will support their cause."[99]

AQAM messages nevertheless make clear what happens to Muslims who reject Salafi ways or are enthralled by "infidel" values and morality. Accidents and natural disasters are regularly portrayed as the wrath of Allah fallen on those who failed to support the jihad. Militants depicted the catastrophic December 2004 Asian tsunami as Allah's vengeance for the alleged immorality on display in ostensibly Muslim nations such as Indonesia. A Chechen jihadist explained: "Everyone knew of the mass prostitution that went on there, but no one issued a strong rebuke. Prostitution became a common occurrence, and there was no one to stand up against this immorality."[100]

For all their heavy-handed and frequently crude portrayals of the enemy, and their harsh messages aimed at fellow Muslims, AQAM's propagandists can be surprisingly sensitive to cultural nuances. Their messages emphasize that their movement, while Arab-led, is a global enterprise in which

Muslims from all nations and cultures are welcome. While most al Qaida propaganda is in Arabic, a language that enjoys primacy throughout Islam, AQAM's *dawah* is multilingual and is available in many languages— Turkish, Bosnian, Indonesian, Urdu, and Pashtu, among many others, and increasingly in English. Videos often demonstrate sensitivity to the cultural and ethnic diversity in AQAM ranks, and movement agitprop makes efforts to highlight the jihadist accomplishments of non-Arab "brothers." Arab themes are overrepresented but not necessarily dominant, and AQAM's propaganda is increasingly adept at blending local and traditional customs with Salafi jihadist messages (e.g., explaining the need for jihad in Afghanistan in terms of both Pashtun tribal ways and the requirement to fight the infidel per Salafi beliefs). Some propaganda can appear almost "politically correct" in its desire not to offend fellow fighters. For example, a Turkish jihadist Web site refers to the glorious accomplishments of the mujahideen in Chechnya while encouraging "Muslims in Turkey" to join the struggle—a formulation designed not to exclude Kurds.[101]

Metrics

Does AQAM's propaganda (or strategic communication) work? There can be no doubt that many thousands of young Muslims have answered the call, responding to "armed *dawah*" by joining the jihad. Clearly, al Qaida's strategic communication effectively exploits rich religious and cultural themes deeply embedded in Islamic faith and civilization. Moreover, AQAM's propaganda is growing more sophisticated, and its methods of dissemination are unquestionably impressive, exploiting state-of-the-art and cost-effective technologies with widespread access to the *ummah*. Since 9/11 it has successfully gotten its message to increasing numbers of Muslims in every corner of the globe, winning unprecedented sympathy for its views and actions.

Whether this is sufficient to maintain the jihad is another question. It is understood in jihadist circles that the war of ideas underpins the movement's grand strategy, and that without effective *dawah* the jihad will fail through attrition and inertia. Some members of the movement have examined its manpower needs, and not all have been pleased with the results of their analysis. In 2005, Abu Bakr Naji offered the assumption that 500,000 mujahideen would be necessary "for our long battle and to achieve the results we want."[102] While a half-million jihadists represents a large absolute number—and something the movement has not come close to reaching—it is small against the backdrop of the *ummah*. Given a global Muslim community of not less than 1.2 billion, a half-million recruits would be only .04 percent of the total population, a figure that hardly seems unrealistic.

AQAM's inability to muster even a tiny fraction of 1 percent of the *ummah* underlines the marginal nature of its appeal. How far AQAM is from reaching that goal was laid bare by Abu Musab al-Suri's recent analysis. Al-Suri is perhaps the most perceptive strategist in the movement, and in 2005 he noted that al Qaida had done decidedly poorly at actually winning recruits: "Numbers did not exceed several hundred, even in countries of millions like Egypt and [Syria], and . . . did not exceed even tens in other countries!"[103] Aukai Collins, an American convert to Islam who fought in the jihad in Chechnya and elsewhere, offered a similarly pessimistic view in 2002. Defining the mujahideen as "the Muslims of the world who answer the call of jihad and fight," he wrote that "no one knows for sure, but the mujahideen generally agree that there are actually fewer than ten thousand of us spread throughout the world."[104] A jihadist posting to a Web site in 2006 marveled at the damage that the mujahideen could do to the United States if only "one person out of 100 thousand men went out to do jihad."[105]

Conclusion

Just as the American military is acutely aware of the role strategic communication plays in modern warfare, so too are the jihadists. In one sense, however, the latter's understanding of the role of information in the global war is more correct than that of the U.S. military. They have correctly identified what they must do to achieve victory—namely, attract the Muslim masses to their cause—and they bend the vast majority of their informational efforts in that direction. The United States has not correctly identified how information fits into the strategic picture of the war against the Salafi jihadists. It, too, tries to attract the support of the Muslim masses, not realizing that merely denying the masses to the enemy would be adequate.

The jihadists have also correctly identified the main information threat they face. It is not the efforts—white, gray, or black—directed by the U.S. government. Rather, the jihadists are alarmed by the narcotic effect of the complete information environment that surrounds most Muslims, particularly young people. From the Salafi jihadist point of view, school curricula, Friday sermons at the mosque, television channels, radio stations, most of the books and poetry and songs, and most of what is on the Internet are fundamentally anti-Islamic. The increasingly global availability of secular information places the jihadists at a tremendous strategic disadvantage.

Notes

1. Ahmad Dani, quoted at the Liberty for All Web site, October 3, 2006, www.lib forall.org/programs-educational-campaign.html, accessed January 30, 2007.
2. Former defense secretary Donald Rumsfeld once said that losing the information battle to AQAM is "the thing that keeps me up at night." See Robert Burns, "Rumsfeld: Terrorists Manipulating Media," Associated Press, August 28, 2006, www. washingtonpost.com/wp-dyn/content/article/2006/08/28/AR2006082800879_ pf.html, accessed December 14, 2006.
3. Chairman of the Joint Chiefs of Staff, "Decisions on Strategic Communication," Joint Staff/J-5 (Plans and Policy Division) message, U.S. Department of Defense, October 25, 2004.
4. U.S. Department of Defense, "QDR Execution Roadmap for Strategic Communication," Office of the Secretary of Defense, Washington, D.C., September 25, 2006, 3.
5. FBIS EUP20051012374001.
6. Little evidence supports American commentators' claim that AQAM is waging a sophisticated information operations campaign against the West.
7. Harmony document folder AFGP-2002-003251.
8. Harmony document folder 500MI-2005-RP-MLA00011.
9. FBIS GMP20040615000107.
10. *Al-Qaeda Manual*, no date.
11. IntelCenter, "Al-Qaeda's Advice."
12. For Naji's references to "hearts and minds," see his *Management of Savagery*, 46; for al-Suri's reference, see Harmony document folder AFGP-2002-600080; for al-Zawahiri's reference, see FBIS EUP20051012374001.
13. FBIS SAP20010929000001, "'Exclusive' Interview with Usama bin Ladin on 11 Sep Attacks in US."
14. Bin Laden was responding to Mullah Omar's criticism that he was a publicity seeker in granting interviews to Western media from his Afghan haven. See Harmony document folder AFGP-2002-600321, *Letter from Usama bin Laden to Mullah Omar*, late 1990s.
15. Donald Rumsfeld, "Remarks by Secretary Rumsfeld at Army War College, Carlisle Barracks, PA," DoD press release posted directly to the Internet, March 27, 2006, www.defenselink.mil/transcripts/2006/tr20060327-12710.html, accessed December 14, 2006.
16. U.S. Department of Defense, "Quadrennial Defense Review 2006," Office of the Secretary of Defense, Washington, D.C., February 2006, www.defenselink.mil/ pubs/pdfs/QDR20060203.pdf, accessed December 14, 2006.

17. U.S. Department of Defense, "Report of the Defense Science Board on Managed Information Distribution," Office of the Under Secretary of Defense for Acquisition, Technology and Logistics, Washington, D.C., October 2001, www.acq.osd.mil/dsb/reports/mid.pdf, accessed December 14, 2006.

18. U.S. Department of Defense, "Defense Science Board 2004 Summer Study on Transition to and from Hostilities," Office of the Under Secretary of Defense for Acquisition, Technology and Logistics, Washington, D.C., December 2004, www.acq.osd.mil/dsb/reports/2004-12-DSB_SS_Report_Final.pdf, accessed December 14, 2006.

19. U.S. National Security Council, "National Strategy for Combating Terrorism," The White House, Washington, D.C., February 2003, www.whitehouse.gov/news/releases/2003/02/counter_terrorism_strategy.pdf, accessed December 14, 2006.

20. U.S. Department of Defense, "Defense Science Board Task Force on Strategic Communications," Office of the Under Secretary of Defense for Acquisition, Technology and Logistics, Washington, D.C., September 2004, www.acq.osd.mil/dsb/reports/2004-09-Strategic_Communication.pdf, accessed December 14, 2006.

21. U.S. Department of State, "Building America's Public Diplomacy through a Reformed Structure and Additional Resources," U.S. Advisory Commission on Public Diplomacy, Washington, D.C., 2002, www.state.gov/documents/organization/13622.pdf, accessed December 14, 2006. These numbers are, of course, outdated and to some extent subjective. Nevertheless, it remains that the United States spends hundreds of billions of dollars on the military, tens of billons of dollars each on intelligence and diplomacy, and billions of dollars on efforts to sway foreign populations.

22. U.S. Government Accounting Office, "U.S. Public Diplomacy: State Department and the Broadcasting Board of Governors Expand Efforts in the Middle East but Face Significant Challenges," Washington D.C., February 10, 2004, www.gao.gov/new.items/d04435t.pdf, accessed December 14, 2006.

23. U.S. National Security Council, "National Strategy for Combating Terrorism."

24. Robert Burns, "Rumsfeld: Terrorists Manipulating Media," Associated Press, August 28, 2006, www. washingtonpost.com/wp-dyn/content/article/2006/08/28/AR2006082800879_pf.html, accessed December 14, 2006.

25. Donald Rumsfeld, "New Realities in the Media Age: A Conversation with Donald Rumsfeld," Council on Foreign Relations, February 17, 2006.

26. "Letter from al-Zawahiri to al-Zarqawi," October 11, 2005, www.dni.gov/press_releases/letter_in_english.pdf, accessed June 7, 2007.

27. Center for International Issues Research, "Internet Militants on the Defensive; Part 1 of 2: Threat Assessments," *Global Issues Report*, February 9, 2007.

28. In the 1990s, Algerian jihadists specially targeted satellite TV dishes, which they saw as conduits for evil and termed *paradiaboliques*, a play on *antenne parabolique*; see Luis Martinez, *The Algerian Civil War 1990–1998 (New York: Columbia University Press, 2001)*. Similarly, a flyer found after the battle at Tora Bora includes advice for parents to "protect [your child] from the poison of the TV channels and guard him from viewing movies of violence, crime, sex, and drugs." See Harmony document folder AFGP-2002-001122-HT-NVTC, *How to Raise Children*, 2001 or earlier.

29. Paz, "Reading Their Lips."

30. FBIS GMP20021126000154.

31. FBIS GMP20040706000164.

32. Harmony document folder AFGP-2002-003251.
33. FBIS GMP20020108000197.
34. FBIS GMP20040615000107.
35. FBIS GMP20031027000226.
36. FBIS SAP20010929000001.
37. FBIS GMP20040518000261, "Al-Zarqawi's al-Tawhid Group Claims Responsibility for Iraqi Assassination." For another example of criticism of Al-Jazirah, see FBIS GMP20060929342006, "Mujahidin Shura Council Addresses 'Fallacies' in Al-Jazirah's 'Top Secret' Program," September 27, 2006. In this piece the Mujahideen Shura Council, a Salafi jihadist group dominated by al Qaida in Iraq, complains that a particular broadcast had supported the "traitorous Arab governments against the honest mujahideen," exposed the mujahideen's secrets, and shown them in a frivolous light.
38. SITE Insitute, "Continued Campaign across Jihadist Forums to Support Fatah al-Islam and the Mujahideen in Lebanon," May 22, 2007.
39. SITE Institute, "Abu Hamza al-Muhajir, Minister of War of the Islamic State of Iraq, Releases Audio Message Calling for Sunni Unity," May 5, 2007.
40. FBIS SEP20041222000085. The reference to the "ape mass media" may also be a reference to the Jews, whom extremists sometimes refer to as the "descendants of pigs and monkeys."
41. FBIS GMP20020108000197.
42. SITE Institute, "First Issue of the *Technical Mujahid*, a New Periodic Magazine Related to Technology and Internet Security Published by al-Fajr Information Center," November 28, 2006.
43. FBIS GMP20061012281001.
44. Harmony document folder AFGP-2002-002883.
45. FBIS GMP20031004000119.
46. Center for International Issues Research, "Muslim Groups Mobilize against Pakistani and Western Governments," *Global Issues Report*, February 23, 2006, www.globaliwatch.com, accessed June 14, 2006.
47. FBIS GMP20040420000246.
48. FBIS GMP20010921000115, "Al-Jazirah TV Broadcasts Usama bin Ladin's 1998 Interview."
49. FBIS GMP20040406000138.
50. FBIS GMP20031004000119.
51. FBIS GMP20030929000003. Abu Musab al-Suri said the Sufis, along with the reformist and Tablighi groups, have "increased in absurdity and distance from Muslims' reality." See FBIS FEA20060523023251.
52. FBIS GMP20040615000107.
53. FBIS GMP20040406000138.
54. FBIS GMP20031027000226.
55. FBIS GMP20020918000173, "Al-Ansar Write Views Goals, Religious Grounds of September Attacks," September 18, 2002.
56. This document was likely among the first to coin the term *air-martyrdom operations*; see Harmony document folder AFGP-2002-600069, *French Plane Incident in Algerian Airport in December 1994*, December 30, 1994. In an eerie precursor of the 9/11 attacks, the hijackers had intended to crash the plane into the Eiffel Tower.
57. FBIS GMP20031027000226.
58. FBIS GMP20040406000138.

59. Naji, *Management of Savagery*, 22.
60. FBIS GMP20040109000138, 2004. The GSPC publicly declared fealty to al Qaida in September 2006.
61. See Harmony document folder AFGP-2002-002953, *Computer Disks* [3½" Floppy] *Seized from Mes Ainak Jalalabad on 1/31/02*, late 1990s to December 2001.
62. FBIS GMP20020108000197.
63. FBIS GMP20050601712008.
64. SITE Institute, "The Global Islamic Media Front Presents an Article: 'What after the Denmark Happenings . . . a Work Plan,'" February 10, 2006.
65. Authorities found documents criticizing *Star Academy* in materials recovered from a cache of documents associated with Saudi jihadist Abdallah al-Muqrin. See Harmony document folders SA-RIY-040721-90010-60564, no date; and SA-RIY-040721-90010-60854, no date. The former contains a fatwa against the show issued by (possibly pro-government) Saudi clerics. More generally, a religious lecture recovered in 2006 at a site associated with al Qaida in Iraq rails against the tendency of Muslim youth to watch satellite television. According to the speaker, the enemies of Islam use television to keep the youth immersed in worldly matters and divert them from worship, thus turning them into powerless men who cannot and will not fight the infidels.
66. SITE Institute, "Sheikh Hamed al-Ali Evalues the Danger and Effects of a Variety of Dissolutions Which Have Beset the Muslim Nation," November 14, 2006. *Super Star* is a Middle Eastern television program akin to *American Idol*. See also Harmony document folder ISGZ-2004-602178, *Post by al-Mis'ar on the Al-Ansar Islamic Forum about a Demonstration by the Jihad Youth in Kuwait*, May 7, 2004, which contains materials found in Fallujah criticizing *Star Academy*.
67. For a typical critique, see Muqtadir Abdul, "Bollywood or Bust," Islamic Awakening.com, August 29, 2006, www.islamicawakening.com/viewarticle. php?articleid=1234, accessed December 14, 2006.
68. See www.islaam.net/main/display.php?id=1448&category=164, hosted by Islamic Network, a U.K.-registered charity, accessed January 29, 2007.
69. FBIS GMP20031113000204.
70. Azzam, *Join the Caravan*.
71. FBIS GMP20040107000001, "Al-Qa'ida's Abu-Mus'ab al-Zarqawi Deplores Muslims' 'Renunciation' of Jihad."
72. SITE Institute, "The Global Islamic Media Front Presents an Article."
73. FBIS GMP20031027000226.
74. IntelCenter, "Al-Qaeda's Advice."
75. FBIS GMP20060606415001, "Media Aid 6 Jun: Saudi InterMedia Survey 2006."
76. FBIS GMP20050613368001, "Media Aid 13 Jun: Syria InterMedia Survey 2005"; and FBIS SAP20060105372001, "Media Aid 5 Jan: Pakistan InterMedia Survey 2006." Satellite and cable television are even more commonplace in the Muslim world; 19 percent of Pakistani homes have cable access (48 percent in urban areas), and 80 percent of Syrian homes have a satellite TV receiver; FBIS GMP20050613368001; FBIS SAP20060105372001. Although this may not be good news for AQAM, it indicates that any radical Salafi activists who might gain access to satellite TV channels would enjoy immediate entry into many Muslim homes and the strong majority of Arab ones.
77. "Deep Web sites" cannot be located with normal search engines such as Google or Yahoo.

78. SITE Institute, "Announcing the Start of Broadcasting the Programs of the Channel of 'The Voice of the Caliphate,'" January 20, 2007.

79. Center for International Issues Research, "Jihadi Video Game Posted on Hostile Web Forums," *Global Issues Report*, January 31, 2006, www.globaliwatch.com, accessed June 13, 2006.

80. Center for International Issues Research, "Condolences from the Mujahideen Shura Council in Iraq to the Islamic *Ummah* and Chechen Mujahideen on the Martyrdom of Shamil Basayev," *Global Issues Report*, July 12, 2006, www.globaliwatch.com, accessed June 13, 2006.

81. Canadian Broadcasting Corporation, "Jihadist Video Aimed at Muslim Youth," *CBC News*, June 20, 2006, www.cbc.ca/story/2006/06/20/video20062006.html, accessed January 30, 2007.

82. Center for International Issues Research, "Videos on Hostile Turkish Websites Solicit Financial Support for 'Jihad' in Chechnya," *Global Issues Report*, February 1, 2006, www.globaliwatch.com, accessed June 12, 2006.

83. Center for International Issues Research, "The Role of Iraqi Women in the Jihad Phase," *Global Issues Report*, June 14, 2005, www.globaliwatch.com, accessed June 13, 2006.

84. Center for International Issues Research, "Latest Video from 'Soldiers of God' Targets Recruitment of Uzbeks and Features Islamic Movement of Turkistan Leader Tahir Yuldashev," *Global Issues Report*, June 27, 2005, www.globaliwatch.com, accessed June 13, 2006.

85. Center for International Issues Research, "GIMF Releases a New Video Featuring a Day in the Life of a Mujahid," *Global Issues Report*, January 30, 2006, www.globaliwatch.com, accessed June 13, 2006.

86. Center for International Issues Research, "Baathist Website Claims U.S. Violation of Islam and Women in Iraq," *Global Issues Report*, April 14, 2006, www.globaliwatch.com, accessed June 13, 2006; "The Third Year of Disgrace, Weakness, Defeat and Arab Disappointment Shown in Pictures," www.baghdadalrashid.com/vb3/showthread.php?t=14093, March 21, 2006.

87. Center for International Issues Research, "'Sniper of Falluja' Hailed in a Recent Hostile Propaganda Campaign," *Global Issues Report*, January 18, 2006, www.globaliwatch.com, accessed June 13, 2006.

88. Harmony document folder AFGP-2004-005632, *Propaganda Letter against the US*, August 2004.

89. Ibid.

90. Center for International Issues Research, "Video of Suicide Attack Responds to Alleged Abuse of Iraqi Women," *Global Issues Report*, February 28, 2006, www.globaliwatch.com, accessed June 13, 2006. For an example of pornographic sexual imagery, see Harmony document folder ISGQ-2005-M0001988, *Winds of Victory* (video), 2005.

91. Center for International Issues Research, "Hostile Web Forum Posts a Video Exploiting Fears of Iraqi Children," *Global Issues Report*, May 17, 2006, www.globaliwatch.com, accessed June 13, 2006.

92. AQAM propaganda portrays U.S. forces as evil and also castigates them as cowards for their casualty aversion and reliance on technology and firepower. U.S. leadership is similarly viewed as evil, but also corrupt and inept. President George W. Bush is regularly depicted as cruel and incompetent; for instance, in a manipulated video loop, popular on jihadist Web sites, showing him saying, "This Crusade is gonna take a while." A 2005 online Christmas card from al Qaida in

Iraq greeted U.S. forces with "Merry Christmas Pigs—from Iraqi Resistance," and included a satirical graphic of the president with the title "Errorist." See Center for International Issues Research, "Hostile Website Posts an Ugly Christmas Card to Coalition Forces," *Global Issues Report*, December 22, 2005, www.globaliwatch.com, accessed June 13, 2006.

93. Ibid.
94. Center for International Issues Research, "Mujahideen Shura Council in Iraq Releases New Martyrdom Video," *Global Issues Report*, June 7, 2006, www.globaliwatch.com, accessed June 13, 2006.
95. Center for International Issues Research, "Zarqawi Supporters Rapidly Produce 'Martyrdom' Propaganda," *Global Issues Report*, June 8, 2006, www.globaliwatch.com, accessed June 13, 2006.
96. Center for International Issues Research, "Militant Websites Post Video Justifying the Killing of Iraqi Civilians," *Global Issues Report*, July 14, 2005, www.globaliwatch.com, accessed June 13, 2006.
97. Center for International Issues Research, "Latest Ummat Studio Urdu Video Supports Insurgency in Waziristan," *Global Issues Report*, May 18, 2006, www.globaliwatch.com, accessed June 13, 2006.
98. Center for International Issues Research, "Hostile Turkish Web Forums Post a Video Depicting Execution of 'Spies' in Waziristan," *Global Issues Report*, March 27, 2006, www.globaliwatch.com, accessed June 13, 2006.
99. Center for International Issues Research, "Video of Released Sudanese Hostages Posted on Hostile Website," *Global Issues Report*, February 14, 2006, www.globaliwatch.com, accessed June 13, 2006.
100. Center for International Issues Research, "Dagastani Militants Launch 'Voice of Mahachkala Television,'" *Global Issues Report*, February 23, 2006, www.globaliwatch.com, accessed June 13, 2006.
101. Ibid.
102. FBIS FEA20060523023251.
103. Ibid.
104. Collins, *My Jihad*, xii.
105. SITE Institute, "America's Bitter Harvest Following 9/11 and Wars in Afghanistan and Iraq," September 14, 2006.

CHAPTER 8

Joining the Caravan

The men who know are few, those who act are even fewer. Those who perform Jihad are rarer and scarcer, and those who remain steadfast on this path are hardly sufficient to be mentioned.

ABDULLAH AZZAM, *JOIN THE CARAVAN*, 1988[1]

The Enigma of Membership

In his study of the global Salafi jihad, Marc Sageman concluded that "recruitment is still a mystery."[2] It can also be said that membership remains an enigma, wrapped in the riddle of motivations. Membership is a poorly defined concept in any discussion of AQAM. For example, Khalfan Khamis Mohamed, arrested and interrogated by the FBI about his part in the 1998 Tanzania embassy bombing, admitted his role in the bombing but denied that he had ever heard of an organization called al Qaida.[3] Indeed, the security services in the West have worked hard to identify al Qaida's leadership structure. While captured records from training camps and safe houses may offer a glimpse of the administrative side of al Qaida (or other Salafi jihadist organizations)—trainee evaluations, employment contracts, examinations, and oaths—they give us at best a misleading and incomplete understanding of "membership" as a whole in the global jihad, especially as it has evolved since 2001.[4]

The ground truth of membership generally lies somewhere along the spectrum between those who are highly educated and may have deep

Qur'anic knowledge and those who have little or no education.[5] The "youth" who respond to the call and enlist come from diverse backgrounds and include people with university degrees and others from humble madrassas. Al-Suri observed in his evaluation of lessons learned in Syria that "during the course of a revolution and armed struggle many faithful join the fight from different backgrounds and various party affiliations and ideologies." The dangers and hardships of war unite this mixture of backgrounds into brothers-in-arms seeking the same goal.[6]

It is better, perhaps, to view AQAM membership as a matter of situational perspective. Al Qaida strategists view those under them as their brothers (in religion and in arms), their cadre, their trainees (while in camps), their personal army of martyrs (*shahid*), and mujahideen, but less often as "members" per se.[7] Foot soldiers often have their own existentially based image of their path. For example, Nasir Ahmad Nasir Abdallah al-Bahri (also known as Abu Jandal, bin Laden's former bodyguard from the foot-soldier ranks), boasted that "Usama bin Ladin chooses his elements from the steel and fire. They are not political elements with official jobs and university diplomas."[8] Followers are indeed recruited while they are at universities, including Western and particularly European ones. In fact, many foot soldiers probably have no idea who their worldwide compatriots truly are; the increasingly virtual nature of al Qaida's global jihad means that most of its leaders and members will never meet face-to-face. In many cases, all they know for sure is that they are fellow Muslims following a similar "path to jihad." Put another way, there is an important distinction between joining the caravan of jihad—the reality of the foot soldiers—and recruiting new members into clandestine terrorist organizations, which typically is the prerogative of the strategists, who tend to emphasize secrecy and operational security. Fear of betrayal militates against taking in all comers to this part of the movement.

The discourse on joining the Salafi jihadist movement is part of the larger narrative that al Qaida and associated movements tell about themselves. It is an evolving dialogue that members—current and prospective—share and build upon to legitimize and strengthen the movement as a whole. It is particularly important to listen to these voices of jihad on recruitment issues, because this realm is a crucial one in the "war of ideas." Former U.S. secretary of defense Donald Rumsfeld noted in 2005 that "this struggle cannot be won by military means alone. . . . And since, ultimately, what they need to survive is the support of those who they can indoctrinate, this is an ideological battle as well. . . . This war has required not only the vigorous pursuit of known terrorists, but finding ways to stop extremists from gaining recruits and adherents. It is this ideological component, I suggest, that is the essential ingredient for victory."[9]

Al Qaida strategists concur with the secretary's conclusion that recruits are necessary for victory. Ayman al-Zawahiri believes that during the three decades before September 11, 2001, the movement succeeded in Egypt, at least, "in outlining to the youths issues that were absent from the minds of the Muslim masses, such as the supremacy of the Shari'ah, the apostasy of the rulers who do not rule according to God's words, and the necessity of going against rulers who are affiliated with the enemies of Islam."[10] It is the operations side of the movement, according to al-Zawahiri, who put their beliefs into practice, that "has strongly influenced the Muslim youth" and enabled the movement to grow and progress.[11] In other words, operations are the ultimate narrative device, a story directed at prospective recruits and others in the *ummah* who sit passively on the sidelines of the jihad. As for the "need to attract the nation's best men," one strategist wrote, "the best way to do that is through justifying the operations rationally and through the sharia."[12]

AQAM expends a great deal of time and energy encouraging Muslims to join the caravan of jihad.[13] This chapter considers recruitment issues from the perspective of AQAM's strategists and foot soldiers, illustrating the key areas of mobilization, methods, motivation, and momentum. Captured documents, interrogations, and Internet discussions (those not intended for public dissemination) reveal the internal narrative, while audio, videos, books, speeches, and other published data illustrate the carefully crafted external narrative directed at the *ummah*.

U.S. government and academic analysts have extensively studied al Qaida recruitment. For example, Quintan Wiktorowicz's work on Salafi jihadists in Western Europe notes the role of alienation and describes specific processes of recruitment.[14] In *Understanding Terror Networks*, Marc Sageman observed that before 9/11, a remarkably high proportion of hard-core Salafi jihadists worldwide attended one of twelve mosques or schools. Sageman also emphasized the "bunch of guys" bonding dynamic among displaced Muslim young men—many of them middle class and educated—and the importance of kinship and friendship ties to joining al Qaida.[15] Jessica Stern interviewed hundreds of terrorists and drew her own conclusions about al Qaida's place within the larger paradigm of terrorist recruitment. Her work focuses on the sense of rage and helplessness that often compels individuals to join terror groups.[16]

What follows is an effort to delineate the concepts and concerns, as defined by the global Salafi jihadists themselves, and place them into a framework for further analysis and application in the Long War. If this is to be a "war of narratives, fought on the battlefield of interpretations,"[17] then it is imperative that the U.S. government base its actions on as accurate an interpretation as possible. Key to understanding the ideological component is understanding those who would be indoctrinated and those who do the indoctrinating.

Mobilization: Answering the Call

AQAM'S strategic thinking begins and ends with the proposition that "there is no solution without jihad."[18] If jihad is the solution, then the *ummah*—the worldwide body, or nation, of Muslims—is the key. According to al-Zawahiri, "the mujahid Islamic movement will not triumph against the world coalition unless it possesses a fundamentalist base in the heart of the Islamic world."[19] In other words, al Qaida served as the catalyst for igniting jihad, but sustaining it requires much broader and deeper support throughout the *ummah*. The masses are the "growth medium" for further replication of the jihadist movement.

Recruiting message: a "call" encouraging others to "join the caravan" in Iraq. *Source*: U.S. Military Academy, Combating Terrorism Center, Imagery Project, http://ctc.usma.edu/imagery/imagery_nature.asp#camel, accessed September 23, 2007.

AQAM's strategists have been focusing on mobilizing the *ummah* for some time, with the aim of readying Muslims to respond to whatever call to action may come from the Salafi jihadists' elites. In 1997, bin Laden stated that "what we are interested in is our people's awareness of the dimensions of the current battle and the need for them to join the mujahideen and get ready for the day of the decisive confrontation, with its heavy costs in terms of money and lives."[20] Before 9/11, Ayman al-Zawahiri wrote that for there to be a truly global jihad, the vanguard must rally the *ummah* to the cause and awaken within them, especially the "sons of Islam," a new awareness.[21]

Both bin Laden and al-Zawahiri have the inherent advantage of speaking as authorities on the modern-day fighting of jihad from their experiences as "Afghan Arabs" in the 1980s.[22] Throughout the 1990s, when they spoke of mobilizing all Muslims to fight the forces against Islam, they expected to be taken seriously. Bin Laden made his most direct call to all Muslims in a 1998 fatwa: "The ruling to kill the Americans and their allies—civilians and military—is *an individual duty for every Muslim who can do it in any country in which it is possible to do it.* . . . We—with Allah's help— *call on every Muslim* who believes in Allah and wishes to be rewarded to comply with Allah's order to kill the Americans and plunder their money wherever and whenever they find it" (emphasis added).[23]

Nonetheless, the calls remained largely unanswered. The high status accorded to bin Laden and his close associates was not enough to inspire a truly global jihad. Admittedly, word of mouth and a recruiting process in select mosques, study groups, and madrassas brought thousands of "sons of Islam" to al Qaida's training camps, but the top strategists had aimed for much greater numbers. To that end, actions against the "Zionist-Crusader" enemy served as their recruiting posters. A bold attack on the American homeland was the culmination of their efforts to gain, and it was hoped hold, the attention of prospective mujahideen.[24]

Much as anarchists in the late nineteenth century spoke of "the propaganda of the deed," Salafi jihadists talk about the proselytizing effect (*dawah*) of terrorist violence. The "blessed raid" of 9/11 expressed what words could not: "Those young men . . . said in deeds, in New York and Washington, speeches that overshadowed all other speeches made everywhere else in the world. The speeches are understood by both Arabs and non-Arabs—even by Chinese."[25] Bin Laden marveled in a videotaped discussion at the beneficial effect the attacks had upon interest in Islam. His companion replied that this "huge event" turned doubters into joiners.[26]

The 9/11 operation amplified al Qaida's call to jihad throughout the world. It immediately earned al Qaida recognition in many regions and made Osama bin Laden a folk hero and an icon for a multitude of grievances against the West. But did it mobilize the *ummah* as al Qaida had hoped and claimed it did? The strategists acknowledge the myriad problems involved in harnessing popular support. First is the dichotomy of being a member of the movement's vanguard while remaining close to the masses. Al Qaida trainer Abu Hudaifa privately warned bin Laden that "it is important to have a popular jihad, not the jihad of the elite, which can be surrounded, hit, and liquidated."[27] For his part, al-Suri has expressed concern that too often the movement's efforts at "incitement" have been a "fiasco" because they have been "elitist and complicated," not to mention "uncompromising, threatening, impassionate, and rigid."[28] Al-Zawahiri's prescription for elitism is to actively engage the masses: "The mobilization of the nation, its participation in the struggle, and caution against the struggle of the elite with the authority: The jihad movement must come closer to the masses, defend their honor, fend off injustice, and lead them to the path of guidance and victory."[29]

A New Strategic Method

In 2006, a call for a "new strategic method" by al-Hakaymah of the Egyptian Islamic Group pointed out that overreliance on the methods of "suicidal operations and car bombs" was creating an unnecessary distance between the mujahideen and the *ummah*: "This has to prevent the *ummah* from participating in the fateful battle which we launch against the enemy. From this point we had to find and apply simple methods and less costly methods which could be available and learned everywhere, just to provoke the *ummah*'s sons to participate in today's battle through individual jihad tactics. Otherwise the *ummah* will still play the role of fan or spectator during the entire battle which may take a long time."[30]

Al-Zawahiri, in his July 2005 letter to al-Zarqawi, used the Taliban's experience in Afghanistan as an object lesson for AQI: "We don't want to

repeat the mistake of the Taliban, who restricted participation in governance to the students and the people of Qandahar alone. They did not have
any representation for the Afghan people in their ruling regime, so the
result was that the Afghan people disengaged themselves from them."[31]
Popular support is so important, al-Zawahiri instructed al-Zarqawi, that
"the Islamic mujaheed movement would be crushed in the shadows" in
its absence. "Therefore, our planning must strive to involve the Muslim
masses in the battle, and to bring the mujaheed movement to the masses
and not conduct the struggle far from them."[32]

Al Qaida strategists believe that the Muslim masses—defined by
al-Zawahiri as those "who do not know how to theorize, make philosophical remarks, and do not use big words or boast"—need to be educated
as well as led.[33] The strategists have counted on the *ulema* to play the
pivotal role of educators in the call to jihad, but in this expectation they
have been sorely disappointed (see chapter 1). As a result, the strategists do
not leave education solely to Sunni scholars. They view themselves as the
keepers and purveyors of the true knowledge and application of jihad, in
addition to being guardians of sharia. Al-Zawahiri cautioned al-Zarqawi:
"The mujahid movement must avoid any action that the masses do not
understand or approve, if there is no contravention of sharia in such avoidance, and as long as there are other options to resort to, meaning we must
not throw the masses—scant in knowledge—into the sea before we teach
them to swim."[34]

Bin Laden began educating the masses about the actions to come in
the mid-1990s. It was only later, however, that grand unifying themes
for the call, such as the Palestinian cause and the all-consuming hatred
for the United States and Israel, came to the fore.[35] Al-Zawahiri realized
that unless members of the *ummah* were under the threat of invasion,
they were unlikely to respond to the call. He instructed al-Zarqawi that
"the Muslim masses . . . do not rally except against an outside occupying
enemy, especially if the enemy is firstly Jewish, and secondly American.
This, in my limited opinion, is the reason for the popular support that the
mujahideen enjoy in Iraq, by the grace of God."[36] Al-Suri concurred, arguing in 2005 that successful incitement should be organized around a "fundamental idea" that is "religiously deep-seated" and "comprehensible" to
the masses. In his mind, this idea was "preventing foreign aggression . . .
[and] defending . . . Muslims and their homeland."[37] Thus, the narrative of
the call—aside from the central tenet that jihad is an individual duty—

is flexible and changes according to real circumstances or perceived grievances, whichever will gain the jihadist leadership the most leverage in mobilization.

The strategists envision a "big tent" mobilization for jihad. Al Qaida's leaders resolutely believe in the universal appeal of jihad and are certain that many Muslims from around the world will be mobilized, however loosely, under their command because it is God's will.[38] Previous theaters of jihad, most notably in Afghanistan in the 1980s, gave them a taste of jihad's multinational and multiethnic possibilities as well as a sense of empowerment when the mujahideen from around the world responded to their call.

Indeed, the difficulties of regional jihads such as those in Afghanistan and Bosnia with respect to unity of purpose were never resolved once translated into the global jihad; rather, the difficulties were magnified on a grander scale. Recently, voices have been indicating a need—possibly reflecting the strategists' real worry about the response to their narrative— for more support and, more important, for unity. Strengthening morale and stiffening backbones continues to be an integral part of the call. In December 2005, al-Zawahiri voiced an "appeal to Muslims everywhere, especially in the neighboring countries, to back their brother mujahideen in Afghanistan, Iraq, and Palestine with funds, men, *dawah*, and every-thing that is within their power. I appeal to them to unite and join the blessed jihad and refrain from dispersion. Unity is the way to victory."[39]

Nevertheless, though Salafi jihadists often couch support in all-or-nothing terms, they acknowledge that popular support is usually a matter of degree.[40] A 2002 essay on the "blessed raids" of 9/11 is an example of such thinking. To emphasize the decisive "human factor" in this struggle for the "souls of men," Abu Sa'd al-Amili categorized supporters and non-supporters within the *ummah*. The former group is "highly disciplined and organized."[41] Then there are the nonsupporters, who do not follow the "path to jihad." One group of these consists of "hypocrites and defeatists."[42] This group, "famous for its prattle," is not just content to "shirk" jihad; rather it seeks "to dissuade people and spread lies and biased propaganda to prevent people from fighting jihad or aiding the mujahideen."[43] Other nonsupporters include those in the "middle of the road," who need to be reminded of their obligation to join the jihad and are liable to change their minds or join the defeatists, and the "spectators," who adopt a wait-and-see approach. Al-Amili recommended that "the correct attitude toward these people is to maintain a ray of hope that they will join the ranks of the supporters. We must maintain good relations with them through fruitful cooperation, kind words, hard work, and ongoing sacrifice in the hopes that this will eventually win over their hearts and bring them over to the truth. This is a far better and surer method than declaring war on them."[44]

Abu Bakr Naji took this range of Muslim opinion into account and offered some important qualifiers in 2005 to the traditional notion of popular support: "Notice that when we say that the masses are the difficult factor, our meaning is not that we make our movement dependent on them. We know that they not generally dependable on account of what the Taghuts created in their structure. (We also know) that there is no improvement for the general public until there is victory. (As for) whoever ignores the masses and presumes [or] expects that they will (represent) the majority, the role of media politics is to gain their sympathy, or at the very least neutralize them."[45]

Putting out the call for mobilization is one step, albeit an important one, on the path to global jihad. The next phase, when the jihadist rhetoric meets reality, involves the foot soldiers' response to the call and their methods for joining the caravan.

Methods: Recruitment versus Joining

AQAM has problems with both the quantity and the quality of its recruits. Ramzi Yousef, currently serving a life sentence in the "Supermax" prison in Colorado, is living proof of AQAM's need for selectivity in recruitment. In 1995, Yousef, fresh from masterminding the attack on the World Trade Center in 1993 and at that time planning simultaneous attacks on trans-Pacific airline flights, used a "cold pitch" to recruit a South African student at a Pakistani university. Instead of joining Yousef's conspiracy, the student went to the police, who arrested Yousef.[46] This is not the only such incident. More recently, three naturalized U.S. citizens in Ohio had their plans for jihad in Iraq disrupted when they approached a fellow Muslim and former member of the American military and asked him to train them. Instead, "the trainer" turned informant, and federal authorities arrested the three men.[47]

Not surprisingly, then, smart, organized jihadists use a discernible and careful methodology in their mobilization efforts to avoid being betrayed by a clumsy recruiting "pitch." This methodology includes both targets and methods. We will consider the target audience for recruiting messages before analyzing the strategists' preference for a formalized recruitment process and the foot soldiers' experience of joining.

At first glance, the focus for the call to jihad may appear ill defined; for example: "O Muslim youths: Be helpers of Allah. O scholars, be helpers of Allah. O seekers of learning, be helpers of Allah. O businessmen, be helpers of Allah. O officers and soldiers, be helpers of Allah. O writers, thinkers, teachers, journalists, and men of professions, be helpers of Allah. O every male and female Muslim, be helpers of Allah. Rise in the name of truth in the cause of God."[48] Al-Zawahiri's method in this December 2005 speech is to appeal to a broad but segmented range of potential supporters. This message underscores the belief that everyone can be "helpers" and all have a specific role to play. He is also proving that, although strategists often make broad public appeals, they often have more narrowly focused support needs beyond "foot soldiers."[49]

While al Qaida strategists make general appeals to the *ummah* to support jihad and rally them to action, they also have an intended target audience and therefore fashion their messages to Muslims on a more personal level. This is not surprising given the central tenet of their movement: jihad is an expression of faith and obedience, and it is an individual obligation (*fard 'ayn*) of every Muslim. A would-be mujahid must feel that bin Laden or al-Zawahiri is speaking directly to him for this appeal to have any success. One writer on a jihadist Web site described this empathy and underscored the operational necessity for this part of the joining narrative—open indoctrination—to occur in public. "Whoever listens to the calls of Osama bin Laden senses in his words his care for the indoctrination of the supporters of the Jihadi current, like for example in the Gulf States, in order to target the oil fields. The Sheikh, I think, could direct the mujahideen through personal secret messages. However, he wanted the indoctrination to be public, in order that the crowds of people, who wait for his speeches through the TV channels or the Internet, would internalize his targets and follow them."[50]

The pool of potential recruits is a small subset of the entire *ummah*. The call applies only to Sunni Muslims, and of those Sunnis, only to those who are Salafis—one estimate puts the number of Salafis worldwide at thirty-five to fifty million—and finally, only to those who believe that Islam presently demands violent jihad against its enemies.[51] Each layer becomes more exclusionary and further radicalized the closer it gets to the strategists' vision of the ideal foot soldier.[52] Despite the tiny number of candidates for recruitment, Abu Musab al-Suri maintained that "no member should be recruited if he is not fully qualified in terms of doctrine, discipline, and Islamic behavior."[53] In addition to religious beliefs, the target audience also self-selects according to age and gender. The focus of "agitation" is primarily young males.[54] "If we thoroughly examined the issue," bin Laden once lectured, "we will find that the sector between 15 and 25 years is the one that has ability for jihad and sacrifice. This was what we observed in the jihad in Afghanistan."[55]

Though there is no codified method of recruitment into a Salafi jihadist terrorist organization, strategists have left trails of evidence outlining their preferences for an elite cadre. One document captured in Afghanistan details the recruitment process. It discusses six phases for recruiting members to the movement and emphasizes caution and the gathering of a great deal of information about potential recruits.[56] The initial phases call for "observation and categorization" to be followed by "investigation and information gathering." Only then can a relationship be established with a recruit. Subsequent phases involve "preparation" (education and training, i.e., indoctrination), "follow-up" (further evaluation for suitability), and "reprimands" if needed due to security breaches.[57]

The anonymous *Encyclopedia for the Insurgents on How to Become a Good Terrorist* captured in Iraq lays out a similar process in the section "How to Gain a Brother to Jihad."[58] The measures outlined in this document are also designed with security uppermost in mind. They are intended for those "brothers" in a "totalitarian regime" where they cannot openly "com[e] out for jihad."[59] The "precautionary steps" call for closely examining potential recruits and for determining who is "more beneficial to Muslims."[60] The author recommended mosques as a "good place to hunt, and that is why intelligence services fear mosques greatly." Orphanages ("at least we do not have the parents problem to deal with"), high schools, and universities "are [also] fertile grounds despite the numerous eyes of intelligence agents in those places."[61]

The document recommends a carefully scripted recruitment pitch, down to the precise phrases and even the best lighting conditions for showing videos. It reminds recruiters, "Do not forget the three main things we always need: money, knowledge and power." Finally, "Let this be done slowly, there is no need for a rush."[62] Perhaps reflecting the exigencies of manning an insurgency in Iraq and replacing the resultant losses, the author stated (quite contrary to al-Suri's recommendation) that "it is not important if [a potential recruit] was not proper or devout in the popular meaning. . . . It is possible for a person like that to enter the jihad path and excel to make up for his shortcomings."[63]

Consistent with the adage that "people are like a hundred camels; you look for one good for travel, but you do not find any,"[64] Abu Musab al-Suri is adamant that "the highest level of vetting and caution should apply to the nomination of each new member; he should be subjected to a trial and observation period."[65] His preference is for foot soldiers who exhibit the maturity required for jihad and thus are unlikely to cause the kind of problems he observed in Syria:

> The problem of undisciplined out-of-control members . . . was difficult to identify during the battle; the ranks included members who joined the fight without going through the maturity process required in Moslem thought. . . . They joined because of their bravery, zeal, and sympathy to the cause, or for other marginal and unknown reasons, they did not exhibit any negative signs during the battle, they fought valiantly but when they moved abroad their personality traits and real characters started surfacing, they reverted to their old patterns of behavior and . . . many moral transgressions and undisciplined practices took place.[66]

Al-Suri is also concerned about controlling the rate of growth beyond what the jihadist movement can handle: "The rule of thumb 'quality before quantity' should be observed at all times."[67] One of the shortcomings of the Syrian jihad of the 1970s and 1980s was the "inability to replenish the trained cadres that fell in the first round of fighting: There was no specific plan to deal with this eventuality; the pace of events prevented them from remedying the situation, and they adopted a policy of 'open door' recruitment which caused more harm than good."[68]

The quantity versus quality debate is largely a function of the opposing natures of the movement's instrumental leadership (strategists) and its noninstrumental followers (foot soldiers) (discussed in chapter 2). Strategists such as al-Suri keep an eye on the strategic endgame and think instrumentally, hence concerning themselves with the processes of manpower recruitment, attrition, and retention; the foot soldiers see only their role in joining the caravan and view their own personal endgame as the act of fighting—and dying—for the cause.

The joining mindset leads inevitably to the "open door" recruitment that al-Suri warned against. Standards for foot soldiers also relax in times of desperate need for warm bodies to engage the enemy, particularly in Iraq since 2003. As the insurgency intensified, there was evidently no plan in place to replace experienced cadre systematically when the narrative failed to inspire recruits. Message after message from al-Zarqawi in Iraq was an appeal for manpower, such as the following from April 2004:

> I address you as a compassionate man, as an admonisher, and as a sad person who is puzzled as to why people such as you failed to join the caravan and lagged behind to stay alive. You failed to mobilize even though the Crusaders came to you fully equipped and in huge numbers and fought you in unison. Where is the talk of old times, the nightly chats, the wounds of the days, and the sighs of those who yearn to jihad, paradise, and black-eyed maidens? . . . Where are the lions that are capable of experiencing inconvenience, the knights of the field, the heroes of monotheism, and the men of the creed?[69]

Al-Zarqawi's words reflect what has become a defining characteristic of Salafi jihadist recruiting since the destruction of the Afghan training camp system: not enough men are willing to make the long journey to a foreign battlefield, no matter how urgent the need in the view of the strategists. They are willing only to act locally, often without regard to the larger strategic picture. "Joining" does not equate to "going." Much has been made about European jihadists coming to fight in Iraq, but in all likelihood, many more are staying put and becoming part of the home-grown threat to Western nations.[70] Although the movement's leaders may rationalize this trend as spreading the jihad through "cells" in various countries and claim that they planned this all along, the reality is that the strategists' call to come and fight the global jihad, as they have defined it, is still being largely ignored.[71] In the end, this may force the strategists to further refine their mobilization calls and change their recruiting methods and preferences.

Abu Musab al-Suri, a member of the "glass half empty" school of jihad appraisals, blames part of the problem on the unfocused attitude of Muslim youth who lack the "will to fight": "These are humiliated, confused, impotent youths! They waver in religious sentiment and swallow losses and bitterness, then commit unpraiseworthy acts in reaction. This sentiment has not transformed into a fighting will—except with an insignificant few hundred here and there, perhaps tens or single individuals in some Arab and Islamic countries."[72]

Part of al-Suri's book *Call to Global Islamic Resistance* can be understood as starting that process of refining, or even redefining, global jihad. It acknowledges the past failures of jihad and attempts to craft a strategy that accurately reflects "the reality of Muslims today."[73] To that end, it calls for a decentralized global jihad comprised of small cells or individuals and built upon al-Suri's earlier preference for quality over quantity.

An influx of new members can quickly get out of control, turning a jihad into "a fishing ground for moles and spies."[74] An al Qaida document describes the importance of maintaining the "purity of the ranks": "In order for a birth of the movement without deformity or disruption, the founders must put their utmost efforts in creating the core of the group and its cadres. Moreover, for the movement to continue without deadly diseases or injuries that may lead to amputations, it has to pay attention to its recruiting and put great effort into keeping the purity of its ranks from penetration that can lead to its death or end."[75] The strategists have always feared betrayal by infiltrators, particularly those in the movement's clandestine organizations. There is a direct, causal relationship between "security," in al Qaida's view, and the success of recruitment efforts: "A large number of youth turn away from Jihad when they continuously see their activities being exposed, and casualties increase in the ranks of the movement. On the other hand, the same youth are attracted to the Jama'ah when it succeeds in surprising the enemy while enduring minimum casualties."[76]

In the past, the solution was to carefully vet those allowed to join al Qaida in the camps.[77] Al-Qurashi contended that the "training camps provided the best possible jihad preparation." Though tens of thousands of people went through them, he said, "only a small number of them with exceptional faith and mental, psychological, and physical ability were approached and asked to join al Qaida." This selectivity was in part intended to prevent infiltration.[78] The multiphased nature of camp curricula meant that leaders and instructors carefully analyzed trainees before selecting them for the next phase. Despite all this, it was still possible to find agents in the camps, according to a document discussing the training of "foreign enlistees," especially among those who came "far from the official channels."[79]

Arguably, al Qaida strategists unleashed much more than they bargained for in September 2001. By attacking the United States and seeking to mobilize the *ummah*, the dynamic of their organization changed dramatically and irrevocably, and not always in the strategists' favor. One of the clearest indicators of this change is found in those who identify with their cause, especially those who now favor the "just do it" approach to global jihad. What the strategists may have gained in numbers and notoriety they lost in control of the "membership," however it is defined, and to a certain extent lost their ability to steer the caravan as well. Control is a highly prized strategic requirement perhaps underappreciated by those who study al Qaida. Al Qaida has now entered a new era of forced adaptation characterized by an increasing number of freelancers and those who act on impulse.[80] Sayf al-Ansari warned in 2002 that "a feeling of individual responsibility regarding the issue of jihad should not give rise to a kind of improvised behavior that translates jihad into a kind of spontaneous activity and makes the issue an undisciplined current in which everyone weaves on his own loom. A feeling of responsibility does not mean embodying jihad in scattered individual actions. The feeling needs to be deepened by striving for well-planned action emanating from a position of collective activity."[81]

Motivations and Barriers: The Path to Jihad

Some analysts posit rage, hopelessness, and resentment as prime motivating factors to join al Qaida; however, these must be counterbalanced by the strategists' requirement that foot soldiers should not act impetuously. While anger may be a motivation for joining, the actions the leadership desires against its Western enemy call for clear-headed thinking. We will now consider the hardships along the path to jihad and the motivations of those who choose it, as well as barriers to "answering the call" to "join the caravan."

Hardships of Jihad

The "path to jihad" is a physical and spiritual journey for those answering the call to arms. Upon reading the autobiography of American jihadist Aukai Collins, one reviewer aptly commented, "one gets the idea that 90 percent of jihad is just getting there."[82]

As previously noted, al Qaida's early infrastructure for training and recruitment grew out of the jihad against the Soviets in Afghanistan. Foreign fighters filtered into the war zone through established routes. The caravan metaphor was apt then and continues to be so today. The journey is exciting, especially for those who meet other like-minded foot soldiers at guesthouses (the "way points" for the caravan), which in turn reinforces the sense of brotherhood that is so important in the joining and retention process.[83] While the literal paths into Iraq and Afghanistan still garner much of the Allied forces' attention, the strategists deem the figurative path more worthy of time and attention. Ninety percent of jihad is probably emotional preparation—itself at the heart of what is termed "motivation." Much of what internal critics of the state of jihad like al-Suri rail against concerns those who are not spiritually prepared or truly motivated for the journey and exhibit a shallowness of belief.[84] This insufficient faith is another form of betrayal that must be guarded against.

Many of the most prominent Salafi jihadist leaders have warned of the difficulties on the road—literal and figurative—to jihad. Years ago, Abdullah Azzam cautioned that "the path of jihad is long and arduous, and . . . it is not easy for most people to continue the journey, even if they were very eager at the start."[85] Al-Zawahiri quoted Sayyid Qutb to similar effect: "Brother, push ahead, for your path is soaked in blood. Do not turn your head right or left but look only up to heaven."[86] Yusuf al-Ayiri warned in 2004 that "Muslims should not think they will easily reach the territory of jihad. Muslims are exposed to dangers that they have to overcome. No Muslim should expect that his enemy would strew the way of jihad with flowers and would tell him: Come to the satisfaction of God and to paradise."[87] Abu Musab al-Zarqawi addressed the foreign fighters in Iraq in 2004, reminding them of the hardships involved: "[The] missions of *dawah* have never been a road lined with roses and sweet basil; the price of *dawah* missions is heavy, and the price of bringing principles to the land of reality is a lot of torn limbs and blood."[88]

Motivations

One of al Qaida's greatest successes to date lies in tapping various undercurrents of discontent within the *ummah* and harnessing youthful motivations to meet its strategic needs. These motivations include the desire for young Muslim men to appear religious, to be honorable in the eyes of family and friends, to engage in sanctioned violence, and to feel as though they are valued and important. Consider the view expressed by now-deceased Saudi al Qaida leader Yusuf al-Ayiri, attributed first to Azzam, which focuses on deeply rooted convictions over emotions:

"The image that brings people to jihad is different from the image that they come away with." The meaning is that some people embark on jihad based on purely emotional motivation, such as when they see a picture of a Muslim man being tortured or a Muslim woman being raped. This is good. However, what is better is for the mujahid to embark on jihad out of a deep conviction and belief in this path and its close link to the creed of monotheism. The ultimate aim is to promote this sense among people and establish a state that is committed to its implementation.[89]

The strategists insist that religious motivations play a major role, if not the foremost one, in a foot soldier's motivation. The religious component is strategically necessary because it raises jihad to "the status of a sacrament," as one scholar put it, and turns the act of a suicide bomber from a sin to one of martyrdom and worship, thereby justifying violence and making a virtue of it.[90] Strategists also recognize the appeal of honor and the avoidance of shame as powerful motivators; hence, frequently they appeal to recruits' desire to avenge the honor of their religion, their women, their lands, and so on. *Join the Caravan* proclaims that "jihad protects the honor of the nation and lifts shame from it."[91] On the other hand, some prospective mujahideen may simply be looking for outlets for violence and are relieved to learn from al Qaida's leadership that "it's specific in the Koran that jihad is about fighting."[92]

Others find joining al Qaida or another associated movement to be the solution to their feelings of unimportance, their alienation from society, or their resentment toward Western policies and culture. Omar Bakri Mohammed, former leader of al-Muhajiroun in the United Kingdom, opined that "if there [were] no discrimination or racism, I think it would be very difficult for us."[93] One trainee complained about his inability to use his degree in architectural engineering suitably after he immigrated to Canada in the early 1990s: "I found many job opportunities, but the most important were closed. Others were dirty jobs reserved for immigrants. The social and economical life in North America is a jungle governed by ferocious beasts, represented by Jews and their allies."[94]

Barriers
The dual physical and spiritual nature of the path to jihad is vital to understanding the importance of barriers, both formal and informal, that potential recruits face. There is much in a potential mujahid's life that

prevents him from making the decision, many obstacles he must over-come. Al-Amili noted that

> many people claim to fight jihad and want to inflict harm on the enemy. But few of these people have sufficient courage to overcome the material and moral obstacles to carry out their claims. A Muslim may want to join a jihad group or organization, especially one on the level of al Qaida, but when he gets the opportunity, he finds himself reviewing his calculations and connections with this world. At the last moment, he pulls out. He cannot overcome the first barrier. If he does manage to overcome it, he finds himself facing a second barrier—the barrier of exile. In most cases, he must leave his job, his profession, his family, and his tribe to join the ranks of the mujahideen. Very, very few people have the courage needed to overcome this second barrier. If he overcomes this successfully, he will find himself facing a third barrier—joining the battle in deed and in act, rather than in word. This is the highest summit of Islam.[95]

Even those of sufficient faith with a relatively clear physical path still face numerous informal barriers, which can be categorized as familial, economic, social/societal, and psychological. Most of these barriers embody the notion of what the strategists call "loving life too much." In late 2005, al-Zawahiri declared that "our battle is with hesitation, inability, fear, personal accounts, and with the concern for the position, power, family, children, and wealth. Our battle is with our preference for small gains, making it an excuse to abandon the sacrifice for the sake of God."[96]

One such barrier is the pull of family, about which bin Laden commented in 1998.[97] A British Muslim confessed to a reporter that these were precisely the factors that kept him in the United Kingdom. "Every day I think of going there [to Iraq]. But Allah has to choose me. I pray to Allah that I can go there one day and help them. We are torn between these two worlds: a love for life, and a love for death. I have four children. I can't leave them. My children will be led astray if I leave them."[98]

Family members themselves may either encourage or stand in the way of jihad. Some women strongly encourage the male members of their family to take the path; one detainee's sister said he was "not a man unless he participated in jihad."[99] Mothers and fathers also have a role to play in the contentious issue of parental permission. Some potential mujahideen hide their jihad-minded plans from their parents; others seek their families' blessing or have to fight strong parental disapproval. A pro-jihad propaganda document captured as part of Operation Enduring Freedom in Afghanistan makes a direct assault on familial obstacles and other informal barriers:

> Let us ignore our satanic and sensual urges and tell your parents, brothers, sisters, and your relatives who are opposing our jihad and tell them explicitly that we have severed ourselves from the infidels, hypocrites, and evildoers and joined the of vanguards of jihad. As it said in the 24th verse of Chapter 9 in the Holy Qur'an: Oh believers! If you believe that your parents, children, brothers, spouses, tribes, fortunes you accumulated, trades you are afraid to lose, and homes you enjoy—are dearer to you than the love of God, his Prophet, and a jihad waged for the sake of God; wait for God's orders. God will not guide those who are debauched.[100]

Another such urge or barrier is economic, especially for those desiring the comfortable life and Western material culture. Foot soldiers' financial situations could be at either economic extreme or anywhere in between. Those too poor to afford to travel, those deemed too rich and successful, and those in the middle classes—especially the diaspora in the West—give up jobs and opportunities to pursue jihad. Yet many others turn aside to provide for themselves and their families. This dangerous, generationally transmitted attitude concerned strategist Abu Bakr Naji: "Where are the role models that those sons will emulate? You are supposed to be an example for your sons. If you sit back and do nothing, they will do the same. They will carry out the so-called jihad of economic growth and abandon fighting, just like their fathers."[101]

In the case of social or societal barriers, it may not be actual circumstances as much as a perception of being at a disadvantage—encountering obstacles that cannot be surmounted alone—that deafens potential foot soldiers to al Qaida's call. Such barriers are arguably the easiest for al Qaida to overcome. The strategists already have an established counternarrative to the messages from the West—a mix of Islamic religious reformation; self-redemption; and anti-Western, anti-Semitic, anti-American views—for these perceived secular societal ills.[102] The barriers in this case are not between the individual and jihad, but between the individual and the society in which he lives ("apostate" Arab governments, those in the West, Europe, or America). What Western analysts call "cognitive openings"—such as revulsion to the non-sharia societies in which they find themselves forced to live—play upon these barriers.[103] Efforts at assimilation are doomed, according to Omar Bakri Mohammed, the former head of the Finsbury Mosque in London: "People are looking for an Islamic identity. You find someone called Muhammed, who grew up in Western society, he concedes a lot so people accept him. He changes his name to Mike, he has a girlfriend, he dances, he has sex, raves, rock and roll, then they say, 'you are a Paki.' After everything he gave up to be accepted, they tell him he is a bloody Arab or a Paki."[104]

The last type of barrier, the psychological, is unique to each foot soldier. First and foremost is the obstacle of *wahn*, the love of life and fear of death (see chapter 7). In a captured letter to bin Laden from the late 1990s, Abu Hudaifa included as an important strategic goal (in this case, a strategy against the Saudi government) "breaking the barrier of fear and hesitation from the minds of the mujahideen for participating in jihad activities."[105] In a sentiment reminiscent of "the only thing we have to fear is fear itself," onetime al-Zarqawi mentor al-Maqdisi, quoting Qutb, wrote:

> Those who fear torment, pain, martyrdom, and the loss of life, children, and property if they would wage jihad in the path of God should take a careful look—what does their submission to that which is not God cost them in terms of life, possessions, and children? Beyond that, what is the cost in morals and honor? The costs of jihad in the path of God and against the tyrants on this earth will never be as great as the cost of submitting to those who are not God. Once that has taken place, all is humiliation, filth, and shame![106]

Jihad's arduous path may mean that only a select few within the *ummah* are psychologically suited to pursue it. The emotions that play a role in motivating youth to join the caravan must also be carefully channeled. Abu Musab al-Suri noted similarities between al Qaida's foot soldiers and other revolutionaries, with undesirable qualities actually working to a mujahid's favor: "Many books discussed the psychological characteristics of a revolutionary; our experience has shown that a lot of those characteristics are present in the Moslem revolutionary. . . . In general the revolutionary is: idealistic, stubborn and opinionated, impatient and prone to extremism, favors radical solutions that employ violence, impulsive, emotional, easily affected, and willing to sacrifice for his cause. Nothing works better than Islam at containing the negatives and transforming them into positives."[107] Al-Suri warned that "those negatives should be refined and controlled by the leadership through instruction, psychological preparation, and behavioral guidelines."[108] To that end, it is the responsibility of the jihad's older generation to pass on their hard-earned wisdom as well as to provide firm guidance to the next generation of mujahideen.

Momentum: The Next Generation of Jihadists

Foremost on a strategist's mind is the importance of momentum and convincing future generations to join the jihad before "any lull in the war puts the revolution at a dangerous crossroad."[109] Azzam named this concept "the steadfast Jihad" and called it "one of the innermost constituents of this religion."[110] Al-Zawahiri worries that the global jihad's momentum may be lost by political compromise ("What will motivate my son to take up my weapons after I have sold these weapons in the bargains market?")[111] or by a lack of cohesiveness: "If the mujahedeen are scattered, this leads to the scattering of the people around them."[112]

Concern over the state of jihad's next generation has preoccupied al Qaida's leaders since the first war in Afghanistan. The veterans of those days and of subsequent jihads eventually grayed and their ranks had to be replenished with the new blood of Muslim youth; this will remain an ongoing concern for AQAM if the vanguard is not to be made up solely of the "old guard." Even bin Laden concedes that the veteran mujahid "becomes mentally mature, but his ability to make sacrifices becomes weak."[113]

French edition of *Join the Caravan. Source*: www.terrorisme.net/p/article_133.shtml, accessed June 3, 2006.

In addition, the eagerness of youth who do answer the call to jihad is diffi-cult to sustain. Azzam reported that many young men came to Afghanistan "zealous, but then their zeal steadily diminished, until they began disput-ing the very ordinance of jihad."[114] Al-Suri observed a similar waning in the Syrian jihad: "Many of the new recruits were not keen on 'Islamic commit-ment and perseverance'; their zeal and enthusiasm diminished as the battle went on and eventually faded as they left the country."[115]

A lack of enthusiasm either to take up or to continue jihad, in the strategists' view, leads to a dangerous pause in its course and a betrayal of the cause. The *ummah*—and more significantly, the *ulema*—can become sidetracked, misled, or just plain forgetful of their duty. Al-Zarqawi's frus-tration in 2004 was in part rooted in his fear of such a pause: "If the torch of jihad is extinguished, if the breath of jihad weakens, and if the pockets of jihad in Iraq are closed, the Islamic nation will not rise until God wills it to rise."[116]

Current and future generations of Salafi jihadists are made rather than being born to it. Preparation begins at an early age and includes both formal education and informal training within the home. In a captured document partially titled "How We See Our Children What We Want from Them," an unknown writer from the first Afghan jihad succinctly stated the goal from the early 1990s: "To establish a generation of mujahid emigrants to carry on our vision after us and to undertake its pursuits in view of our intentions for the general good and our pursuit of being closer to God's pleasure and the opportunity for success; to carry our message, our thoughts and the benefits of our trials, and to arm them with what they need to go the distance. We want to establish the leadership of the future. In order to do so they need to be educated in Islamic law and in culture, literature, and behavior in line with God's will."[117]

A poster from a jihadist forum in 2005 emphasizes the need for fami-lies to follow the example of the Prophet Muhammed and their ancestors: "The Prophet . . . said: 'Everything with which Adam's children play is for-bidden except for three: arching [*sic*], horses, and family.' Two of the three are in favor of jihad. . . . Ancestors used to teach their children the skills of war. [Unfortunately,] erroneous concepts have prevailed among people concerning their children's education including the concept of keeping children away from scenes of violence and blood. Is there religious ascrip-tion to this effect? Actually, it is quite the opposite."[118]

What the Salafi jihadists cannot control, however, is the content of a nation's educational curricula, which they universally condemn as detrimental to their long-term goals. In recent years, the U.S. government has urged changes in the educational curricula of a number of Muslim countries, most notably in Saudi Arabia.[119] While the United States has not interfered in curricula to the conspiratorial degree that al Qaida leaders imagine, both sides recognize that the "war of ideas" is also being waged in classrooms throughout the Sunni Muslim world (see text box titled "Curriculum Reform"). AQAM believes that the educational curriculum is extremely important in shaping the lives and the spiritual fate of young Muslim children, particularly in *preventing* young people from joining the jihad. Asked about the degree of influence the general society has in shaping young people, Abu Bakr Ba'asyir, the alleged spiritual head of Jemaah Islamiyah, said, "In Islam, environment is very important, especially in educating children about religion. From this environment, children learn to be good or bad."[120]

Curriculum Reform

The United States advocates curriculum changes that run directly counter to those AQAM seeks.[121] Bin Laden believes that "one of the most dangerous interferences in our affairs" is the Western attempt to reform the curricula in schools in Muslim countries.[122] He observed in 2004 that "the Americans' intentions have also become clear in statements about the need to change the beliefs, curricula, and morals of the Muslims to become more tolerant."[123] "Even in our educational curriculums, the objective is to erase the nation's character and westernize its sons, which is an old project that began decades ago in Al-Azhar's curriculums in Egypt. America then demanded that the remaining collaborator countries change their curriculums to dry up the fountains of knowledge. . . . All this took place over a decade and a half before the New York and Washington attacks."[124]

In fact, some AQAM observers see this U.S.-led reform effort as the core of a broad strategy to destroy Islam and perhaps even to replace it in the hearts of the people with Christianity.[125] Abu Ayman al-Hilali wrote in 2002 that among the key elements of the American strategy is "educational globalization [which] involves direct intervention in curricula to shape minds and raise people with U.S. values."[126] Sayf al-Din al-Ansari spoke in similar terms about the alleged U.S.-led "Crusade": "Neither charitable foundations nor religious school curricula escaped unscathed. Islam itself is the target."[127] Abu Ubayd al-Qurashi, reflecting his emphasis on military matters, sees this interference in Islamic education as an intrinsic part of the American military's concept of "information dominance" from the "Joint Vision" documents.[128]

In short, from AQAM's point of view, America and the West have already corrupted the education systems in Muslim countries and are trying to make them worse. Therefore, AQAM must not only stop the encroachment of "infidel" ideals into Muslim schools, but must also roll back the curriculum to support its own goals.

Conclusion

The call to jihad will persist, in some form or fashion, for years to come. Al Qaida will continue to develop and further refine the joining narrative to broaden jihad's appeal to current and future generations of fighters. As we have seen, strategists such as bin Laden and al-Zawahiri understand the dynamics of support within the *ummah* (although they cannot control them as they would like) and are excellent exploiters of theological and psychological levers to gain adherents. This knowledge is at work in the aforementioned aspects of mobilization, methodology, motivation, and momentum, which taken together form the global jihad joining phenomenon.

The act of "joining the caravan" is a mixture of responding to Salafi jihadist doctrine and the power of its ideas (especially that jihad is *fard 'ayn*, an individual responsibility); connecting through existing social networks (kinship, friendship, actual recruiters); and holding an amalgamation of personal beliefs including anti-Americanism and anti-Semitism, cultural and societal alienation, and grievances against one's own government. Above all, for the foot soldiers, it is about choosing to follow the "path to jihad" and trying not to look back.

The joining narrative itself fills a void in the minds of young Muslim men that is difficult for a counternarrative to address. Nonetheless, al Qaida and its brethren movements have substantial concerns about mobilizing, joining, and perpetuating the jihad. Opponents of Salafi jihadists may be able to use these in their counterstrategies. Like much else revealed about AQAM's strategy through their own words, the hopes and fears of the strategists regarding joining is also found within their writings, where, perhaps surprisingly, they do not try to sugarcoat the hardships of jihad. Even before the 9/11 attacks, Abu Hudaifa wrote to bin Laden that "the cause is overwhelming; the march is long; obstructions, and frustrations, and disappointments surrounding jihad activities are many and persistent. What is worse is that some brothers failed to support other brothers on this road."[129]

In the final analysis, al Qaida's leading thinkers know that the key to their enemy's success is to reduce the appeal of the joining narrative enticing "brothers" to start down the path of global jihad in the first place: "God guarantees the reward for leading the path of jihad since He knows that it is difficult for two reasons. The first is the suffering that a mujahid faces when he forsakes his family and property. The second is the fact that it is easier for the enemy to prevent Muslims from taking the path of jihad than killing mujahideen after taking [up] their weapons."[130]

Notes

1. Azzam, *Join the Caravan*.
2. Sageman, *Understanding Terror Networks*, 171.
3. Cozzens, "Approaching al-Qaeda's Warfare." See also the transcript of the trial at http://cryptome.org/usa-v-ubl-19.htm, accessed September 23, 2007.
4. Examples of administrative elements mentioned can be found in the Harmony database. See Harmony document folders AFGP-2002-003249, *A List of Names, Ages, and Professions of al Qaida Members or Recruits*, no date; AFGP-2002-004322, *Training Camp Regulations and Personnel Information*, no date; AFGP-2002-600047, *List of 125 al Qaeda Members, Some with Nationality, by Country of Deployment*, no date; AFGP-2002-600177, *Al-Qaida Leadership List by Location: Afghanistan, Africa, and Asia*, no date; AFGP-2002-600048, *General Structure of al Qaeda Leadership, Bylaws and Objectives*, no date; AFGP-2002-800437, *Recruitment Conditions*, no date; AFGP-2002-000078-FT, *Breakdown of al Qaida Committee Leadership Responsibilities*, no date; AFGP-2002-000080, *Al Qaida Organizational Charter and Duty Descriptions for All Members and Their Qualifications*, no date; AFGP-2002-600045, *An Employment Contract that Describes al-Qaeda Belief, Objectives, and Sphere of Activity, Including Requirements for Joining, Regulations, and Instructions*, no date; AFGP-2002-600175, *Al-Qaida Constitutional Charter, Rules and Regulations*, no date; and the equivalent of a nondisclosure agreement in AFGP-2002-600160, *Form for Sworn Oath of Secrecy of Training*, no date. Some are also available at www.ctc.usma.edu, accessed September 22, 2007.
5. Sometimes combinations of the aforementioned types are used: the 9/11 operation used both university-educated individuals (most famously religious-minded urban planner Mohammad Atta) and "muscle" types from Saudi Arabia, "most [of whom] were unemployed with no more than a high school education. . . . Some

were perceived as devout, others as lacking in faith" (*9/11 Commission Report*, 231–32).

6. See Harmony document folder AFGP-2002-600080, 1989.

7. *Member* is a term applied much more often by those in the West; likewise *foot soldiers*.

8. FBIS GMP20040803000039, "Bin Laden's 'Bodyguard' Interviewed on al-Qa'ida Strategies."

9. Donald H. Rumsfeld, "Budget Testimony as Delivered by Secretary of Defense Donald H. Rumsfeld, Senate Armed Services Comittee," February 17, 2005, www.defenselink.mil/transcripts/transcript.aspx?transcriptid=1717, accessed September 23, 2007.

10. FBIS GMP20020108000197.

11. Ibid.

12. Naji, *Management of Savagery*, 46.

13. This holds true for other terrorist groups as well. "Recruitment pools are one of the most important requirements for terrorist groups to survive over time. Groups need new members both to grow in strength and to replenish losses and defections. . . . Al Qaeda expend[s] considerable resources on recruitment activities"; from Kim Cragin and Sara A. Daly, *Dynamic Terrorist Threat: An Assessment of Group Motivations and Capabilities in a Changing World* (Santa Monica, Calif.: RAND, 2003), 34–35. This is not to say that al Qaida has recruitment "drives," quotas, or an overarching recruitment strategy, according to Sageman, *Understanding Terror Networks*, 123.

14. Quintan Wiktorowicz, *Radical Islam Rising: Muslim Extremism in the West* (Lanham, Md.: Rowman and Littlefield, 2005).

15. Sageman, *Understanding Terror Networks*, 108–9, 115, 125. See pages 107–13 for his discussion of friendship and kinship social affiliations that influence joining jihad. Although Sageman used "terror networks" in the title of his book, he also understands that al Qaida is at the head of a "violent, Islamist, revivalist social movement held together by a common vision of a Salafi state." See www.fpri. org/enotes/20041101.middleeast.sageman.understandingterrornetworks.html, accessed September 23, 2007.

16. Quintan Wiktorowicz's article "Joining the Cause: Al-Muhajiroun and Radical Islam," 1997, www.yale.edu/polisci/info/conferences/Islamic%20Radicalism/ papers/wiktorowicz-paper.pdf, no date (accessed October 11, 2007), later expanded into the book *Radical Islam Rising*, is a study of the al-Muhajirun movement at the Finsbury Mosque in the United Kingdom. Marc Sageman's groundbreaking *Understanding Terror Networks* is widely read and quoted within policy circles. His most detailed chapter on recruitment is "Joining the Jihad." Jessica Stern's *Terror in the Name of God* looks at groups other than Salafi jihadists.

17. Marc Sageman, "Winning the War of Ideas," brief, no date, www.bfrl.nist.gov/ PSSIWG/presentations/ Winning_the_War_of_Ideas.pdf, accessed March 28, 2007.

18. FBIS GMP20020108000197.

19. Ibid.

20. FBIS GMP20040209000243, "Availability of Compilation of Usama bin Ladin Statements."

21. FBIS GMP20020108000197. The terms *awareness* and particularly *awakening* are loaded with meaning for the Salafi jihadists, who are in essence campaigning for the great "awakening" that will take the Islamic world back to the time of the

pious forefathers, the Salafis. Conservative Saudi Muslims in particular mark the early 1990s as the time of "Islamic awakening" within the kingdom.

22. These combat veterans are also referred to as *ghazis* (warriors). Whether they possessed the religious authority to declare jihad is another matter entirely.

23. FBIS GMP20040209000243, "Compilation of Usama bin Ladin Statements 1994–January 2004," February 9, 2004.

24. FBIS GMP20031027000226. "The raid aroused the feelings of the mujahideen and their supporters, hardening their resolve to sharpen their skills and seek out the enemy's weak spots. This was missing in the past, when the mujahideen suffered from dejection, fear, and a feeling of inferiority."

25. FBIS GMP20011213000201, "Al-Jazirah Reports on Pentagon Videotape on bin Ladin Role in 11 September Attacks." A full transcript is at www.defenselink.mil/news/Dec2001/d20011213ubl.pdd, accessed February 29, 2007.

26. Bin Laden related stories from an Islamic center in the Netherlands ("the number of people who accepted Islam during the days that followed the operations were more than the people who accepted Islam in the last eleven years") and from the United States for the increased demand for Islamic books. "Transcript of Usama bin Laden Video Tape," December 13, 2001, www.defenselink.mil/news/Dec2001/d20011213ubl.pdf, accessed September 23, 2007. This anecdotal evidence served only to underscore his belief in the strong horse/weak horse theory ("by nature, [people] will like the strong horse"). FBIS GMP20011213000201.

27. Harmony document folder AFGP-2002-003251, 2000.

28. FBIS FEA20060523023251, 1439–40 original numbering.

29. FBIS GMP20020108000197.

30. SITE Institute, "*A New Strategic Method in the Resistance of the Occupier,* Prepared by Muhammad Khalil al-Hukaymah."

31. FBIS EUP20051012374001.

32. Ibid.

33. FBIS GMP20051211552001, "Al-Zawahiri Says Victory 'Imminent,' bin Ladin, Mulla Omar Leading 'Resistance.'"

34. FBIS EUP20051012374001.

35. FBIS GMP20031004000119, "The Operation of 11 Rabi al-Awwal: The East Riyadh Operation and Our War with the United States and Its Agents," August 1, 2003. "The Palestinian issue became the issue of the Islamic World, the issue of every Muslim, and part of the religion that could not be separated from the Muslim conscience—and this is a fact." Al-Zawahiri noted: "The one slogan that has been well understood by the nation and to which it has been responding for the past fifty years is the call for the jihad against Israel. In addition to this slogan, the nation in this decade is geared against the U.S. presence. It has responded favorably to the call for the jihad against the Americans." FBIS GMP20020108000197. Al-Zawahiri observed that "the animosity to Israel and America in the hearts of Islamists is genuine and indivisible. It is an animosity that has provided the 'al Qaida' and the epic of jihad in Afghanistan with a continuous flow of 'Arab Afghans.'"

36. FBIS EUP20051012374001. In December 2005, al-Zawahiri announced to the "Islamic nation everywhere: 'I am calling on everyone to rise up to support their brothers in Palestine, Afghanistan, and Iraq with their souls, money, prayers, experience, and knowledge. This is the time. Rise up.'" FBIS GMP20060222371001, "Mujahidin News Posts Links to al-Zawahiri Message Calling Bush to Islam,

Asking Muslims to 'Rise Up,'" Jihadist Web sites, OSC Report in Arabic, February 21, 2006.

37. Al-Suri, *Call to Global Islamic Resistance*, OSC translation, 1443 internal numbering.

38. Strategist Abu Ubayd al-Qurashi predicted in late 2002 that "certainly, the Crusader campaign will be opposed by many sincere Muslim youths who will flock to the tent of faith." See FBIS GMP20030122000038.

39. FBIS GMP20051207507001, "Al-Qa'ida's al-Zawahiri Predicts Failure of US 'Crusade' against Muslim States," Jihadist Web sites, FBIS Report in Arabic, December 7, 2005.

40. FBIS GMP20040507000179, "Al-Muqrin Calls on Youth to Follow Example of 'Martyrs of Yanbu,'" Jihadist Web sites, FBIS Report in Arabic, May 7, 2004. The former head of Saudi al Qaida, al-Muqrin, lamented that "not everybody that knows the truth supports you in the fight for it."

41. FBIS GMP20031027000226.

42. Ibid.

43. Ibid.

44. Ibid.

45. Naji, *Management of Savagery*, 21.

46. Sageman, *Understanding Terror Networks*, 109. The "Bojinka plot" was discovered on a computer in a burning apartment in Manila.

47. A federal grand jury indicted all three on conspiracy charges on February 21, 2006. Liza Porteus, "Three Charged in Plan to Attack U.S. Military in Iraq," FOXNews.com, February 22, 2006, www.foxnews.com/story/0,2933,185551,00. html, accessed September 22, 2007.

48. FBIS GMP20051207507001.

49. Some within the *ummah* are excused from jihad—temporarily or permanently—due to infirmity, age, or financial hardship. One captured document states: "Sayyid Qutb means by disallowing abrogation is that we should not demand from the indigent what we expect from the affluent and capable people. The indigent has an excuse not to participate in jihad; it is sufficient for him to donate as much as he can to this effort. However, this should be considered a temporary situation whereas the above person should strive to change it and reach a level of affluence and capability by which he can apply the final stage of jihad." See Harmony document folder AFGP-2002-00089, *Misc: Guerilla War, Jihad, Qadhafi*, no date. That does not excuse, in the jihadists' view, an obligation to serve jihad: "Those who cannot pursue Jihad physically, should not fall short from using money, pen, and words in favor of jihad." See also FBIS GMP20060427538001, "FYI—Comparison of bin Ladin's Full Audio Message with Al-Jazirah.net Text," OSC Report in Arabic, April 27, 2006.

50. Paz, "Reading Their Lips," 4.

51. See Paul Jabber, "The Threat of Jihadi Terrorism: The Role of Ideology and the War of Ideas," presented at the Helsinki Chiefs of Mission conference, October 2006.

52. Sageman, *Understanding Terror Networks*, 54–55, also noted the self-selecting, increasingly radicalized nature of a global Salafi jihad as it progressed after 1989.

53. Harmony document folder AFGP-2002-600080.

54. Ibid. One comment on a jihadists' Web site referred to youth as "unused petrol." Paz, "Reading Their Lips," 4.

55. FBIS GMP20040209000243, bin Laden quotation dated from December 1, 1998. Another top al Qaida leader, Sulayman Abu-Ghayth, referred to Muslim

youths as the "mainstay and cherished hope of the nation everywhere." See FBIS GMP20040723000200, "Compilation of al-Qa'ida Leadership Statements November 1993–June 2004."

56. Harmony document folder AFGP-2002-600174, *Part of a Series Obtained from Abu Hafs's House in Kandahar, Af; Includes the Basis for Establishing Any Religious Movement, as Well as, the Recruitment and Training of Members to Become Agents*, no date. This document was found in Abu Hafs's house in Kandahar, Afghanistan, possibly November 2001. It states there are always two purposes for recruiting: "1—Recruit members for the movement. 2—Cooperation with local people to obtain services"; that is, gaining intelligence from agents and collaborators. Ken Conboy described a comparably complex process for joining Jemaah Islamiyah; see his *Second Front: Inside Asia's Most Dangerous Terrorist Network* (Jakarta: Equinox Publishing, 2006), 84–85.

57. Harmony document folder AFGP-2002-600174.

58. Harmony document folder MNFV-2005-000436, *An Encyclopedia for the Insurgents on How to Become a Good Terrorist*, November 11, 2005.

59. Ibid.

60. Ibid.

61. Ibid. Although not mentioned here, prisons—particularly those in the West—are good "hunting grounds."

62. Ibid.

63. Ibid.

64. This saying is attributed to Muhammed and is quoted in Abu Hudaifa's letter to bin Laden. See Harmony document folders AFGP-2002-003251 and MNFV-2005-000436, 2005; and Abdullah Azzam's *Join the Caravan*.

65. Harmony document folder AFGP-2002-600080.

66. Ibid.

67. Ibid. His reasoning: "a group of organized and trained mujahideen (between ten and twenty) could cover a large section of the city and keep the regime busy as if they were thousands of fighters, whereas organized groups in the hundred could be exposed and expensive to run."

68. Ibid.

69. FBIS GMP20040107000001; see also al-Zawahiri, in FBIS GMP20040723000200.

70. Michael Taarnby, *Recruitment of Islamist Terrorists in Europe: Trends and Perspectives*, report funded by the Danish Ministry of Justice, January 14, 2005, http://www.globaldefensegroup.com/pdf/recruitment_in_europe.pdf, accessed September 23, 2007.

71. Al Qaida leadership has not moved beyond the need to call on followers to go on jihad wherever they command them to go. In April 2006, bin Ladin released a statement calling for jihad in Sudan: "I encourage the mujahideen and their supporters, in general, and in Sudan and around it, including the Arabian Peninsula, in particular, to prepare for managing a long-term war against thieves and Crusaders in western Sudan" (FBIS GMP20060427538001).

72. Al-Suri, *Call to Global Islamic Resistance*, OSC translation, 39.

73. Ibid., 1.

74. Ibid., 39.

75. Harmony document folder AFGP-2002-600174.

76. Harmony document folder AFGP-2002-600005, *Al-Qaeda Security Memo: Intel, Storing Materials and Secrets, Counter-intel*, no date.

77. *The 9/11 Commission Report*, 67. "Thousands flowed through the camps, but no more than a few hundred seem to have become Al Qaida members. From the time of its founding, Al Qaida had employed training and indoctrination to identify 'worthy' candidates."

78. FBIS GMP20031027000226.

79. Harmony document folder AFGP-2002-003732, *Al Qaida Procedures in Recruiting and Hiring People*, no date.

80. A captured Abu Sayyaf Group document also warns the "urban mujahid" against "precipitous action": "The urban mujahid who commits this loses patience, suffers an attack of nerves, does not wait for anything, and impetuously throws himself into blind action, suffering untold reverses" (from Harmony document folder 500MI-2005-RP-MLA00011). Abu Bakr Naji also warned against "excessive zeal" in *Management of Savagery*. His prescription: "This can be remedied by upgrading the level of the young men's religious scholarship. The more they learn, the less evident the problem of excessive zeal will become."

81. FBIS GMP20020307000167, "Fighting in Jihad against Unbelievers Seen as Duty of Every Individual Muslim" (Internet), *Al-Ansar*, February 27, 2002.

82. Refers to Aukai Collins's *My Jihad*. Collins, an American, went on jihad in the early 1990s and fought in Chechnya and Bosnia. His perspective, he admitted, was changed by the birth of his son, to whom the book is dedicated. See James S. Robbins, "Accidental Jihadist," January 21, 2002, National Review Online, http://www.nationalreview.com/robbins/robbins062102.asp, September 22, 2007.

83. This is especially true for jihadis in the West. See Taarnby, Recruitment of Islamist Terrorists, 38; and Sageman, *Understanding Terror Networks*.

84. FBIS GMP20041112000250. Al-Ayiri warned in a posthumous article, "The Illuminations on the Path of Jihad: The Road to the Battle Ground," published in *Sawt al-Jihad* in November 2004: "Let everyone who is convinced of joining jihad know that self-conviction alone is not enough," which, he explained, means that there were generations before who "did their best" and remained "faithful to God" when they were "tired, afraid, and hunted down." Note that this is different from the "inner struggle" definition of jihad that many Muslims believe is the proper definition and use of the term. This "spiritual" aspect is the mental preparation to take part in the physical jihad.

85. Azzam has no comparable modern-day counterpart, according to Sageman, *Understanding Terror Networks*, 123: "Nothing comparable to Azzam's work exists in the present global Salafi jihad."

86. FBIS GMP20020108000197.

87. FBIS GMP20041112000250, "*Sawt al-Jihad* Articles on Difficulties of Jihad."

88. MEMRI, "Al-Zarqawi's Message to the Fighters of Jihad in Iraq on September 11, 2004," Special Dispatch Series no. 785, September 15, 2004.

89. FBIS GMP20031211000267, "'Orator of the Peninsula': Compilation of Essays in Tribute to Saudi 'Martyr' Yusuf al-Ayiri," Internet version at http://www.cybcity.com/news/index.htm, in Arabic, August 1, 2003.

90. Jeffrey B. Cozzens, "Identifying Entry Points of Action in Counter Radicalisation: Countering Salafi-Jihadist Ideology through Development Initiatives—Strategic Openings," DIIS Working Paper no. 2006/6, Danish Institute for International Studies, Copenhagen, 2006, 10.

91. Harmony document folder AFGP-2002-602402, *Join the Caravan*, April 4, 1987. See also www.religioscope.com/info/doc/jihad/azzam_caravan_2_preface.htm, accessed September 23, 2007.

92. Brandon and Thorne, "The Sidewalk Where Terror Breeds." Unidentified American convert to Islam referring to Osama's message.

93. Wiktorowicz, "Joining the Cause," quoted in author's interview with Omar Bakri Mohammed, head of the Finsbury Mosque in the United Kingdom, in 2002.

94. Harmony document folder AFGP-2002-800073.

95. FBIS GMP20031027000226.

96. FBIS GMP20051211552001.

97. FBIS GMP20040209000243001. The domestication of hard-core terrorists, in the case of former al-Fatah Black September members, is the subject of Bruce Hoffman's December 2001 *Atlantic Monthly* article, "All You Need Is Love: How the Terrorists Stopped Terrorism."

98. Brandon and Thorne, "The Sidewalk Where Terror Breeds."

99. Women, whom Marc Sageman called the "invisible structure of the jihad," can actively encourage the men in their lives to undertake jihad. One woman told of her initial hesitation for her husband to go on jihad in Bosnia, but changed her mind after listening to a religious sermon. See MEMRI, "An al-Qaeda Love Story," Special Dispatch no. 984, September 9, 2005, www.memri.org, citing *Al-Sharq al-Awsat*, London, June 17, 2005. Terrorist cell members arrested in Toronto, Canada, in June 2006 had wives who insisted they perform jihad. See "Hateful Chatter behind the Veil," *Globe and Mail*, June 29, 2006. "[Zakaria] Amara's wife had considered adding a clause to her marriage contract allowing her to divorce her husband should he not pursue jihad in support of the Muslim *umma*."

100. Harmony document folder AFGP-2005-0003057, *Pro Jihad Propaganda*, no date.

101. Naji, *Management of Savagery*. In other words, "It is totally unacceptable that our enemy works persistently to fight Islam while Muslims think God will grant them victory when they are sitting on their couch." See FBIS GMP20050214000276.

102. One example among many is an article by Yusuf al-Ayiri that roundly denounces the secularism and unrestrained freedom of the West: "We see how they live today in the United States and in Europe—people in decay, unrestrained by any boundaries, serving only their desires, moved only by desire, opportunistic and ugly, driven only by self-interest, even at the cost of millions of human deaths" (FBIS GMP20030929000003).

103. Wiktorowicz, *Radical Islam Rising*. Wiktorowicz defined cognitive openings as when "an individual becomes receptive to the possibility of new ideas and world views." See Wiktorowicz, "Joining the Cause," 1.

104. Wiktorowicz, "Joining the Cause," citing quote from Lebor.

105. Harmony document folder AFGP-2002-003251.

106. FBIS GMP20031113000204.

107. Harmony document folder AFGP-2002-600080.

108. Ibid.

109. Ibid.

110. Azzam, *Join the Caravan*.

111. FBIS GMP20020108000197.

112. FBIS EUP20051012374001.

113. FBIS GMP20040209000243001.

114. Azzam, *Join the Caravan*.

115. Harmony document folder AFGP-2002-600080.

116. FBIS GMP20040406000138.

117. Harmony document folder AFGP-2002-601110, *Lecture Given concerning Proper Islamic Education for Children of Mujahideen and Emigrés*, no date.

118. FBIS GMP20050214000276.
119. See U.S. House Concurrent Resolution 432, introduced (not passed) June 2002; U.S. State Department's International Religious Freedom Report, 2004.
120. Abu Bakr Ba'asyir, unpublished interview by Scott Atran and Taufiq Andrie, Cipinang Prison, Jakarta, Indonesia, August 13 and 15, 2005. Provided by Montgomery McFate, JAWD.
121. FBIS GMP20040406000138.
122. FBIS GMP20041216000222.
123. FBIS GMP20040209000243001. On this topic, see also Hazim al-Madani, "Jihad as We See It and Want It," document 13449 in Rohan Gunaratna's International Center for Political Violence and Terrorism Research database, www.al-qaedun. com, ICPVTR-13449, www.pvtr.org/coreprojects_pathfinder.htm, November 23, 2004.
124. FBIS GMP20041216000222.
125. Harmony document folder AFGP-2002-601110; see also FBIS GMP20031027000 226.
126. FBIS GMP20031027000226.
127. Ibid.
128. FBIS GMP20021126000154.
129. Harmony document folder AFGP-2002-003251.
130. FBIS GMP20041112000250.

CHAPTER 9

Policy Implications

SO WHAT AND NOW WHAT?

Many Salafi jihadists are dismayed that the *ummah* have refused to join their cause in substantial numbers. They see this as a major setback for their movement if not an actual failure. Their discourse reveals a number of reasons why the movement has not succeeded in attracting a mass following: some are associated with external barriers, some with what the jihadists believe are failures of other Sunnis, and some with internal policy differences. These reasons point to possible vulnerabilities in the movement that can be exploited.[1]

This chapter has three objectives:

1. To summarize Salafi jihadists' descriptions of the external barriers, failures of other Sunnis, and internal policy differences that point to possible vulnerabilities to the movement[2]
2. To propose an approach to exploit vulnerabilities—an approach that could be effective in the midterm to keep the Salafi jihadist movement separated from the broader *ummah*—and to propose supporting actions the United States and other governments can take to exploit these vulnerabilities
3. To describe the institutional understanding that needs to be created within the United States to be a more effective counter to the Salafi jihadist threat in the future

External Barriers

The Power of Apostate Regimes and Their Security Services

Some Salafi jihadists believe that one reason for their failure to mobilize the masses and carry out attacks stems from the power and efficacy of existing states in the Islamic world—especially of their respective security services. According to some, security services—in Algeria, Egypt, Syria, Jordan, and elsewhere—effectively deny the movement a safe haven from which to operate and limit its ability to appeal to the people.[3]

Salafi jihadist thinkers also clearly see the danger of infiltration by enemy intelligence services and the potential consequences for recruitment. Repeated failure resulting from penetration by security services makes it difficult to attract new members and retain old ones (see chapter 3).[4]

The Power of the Media Allied with the United States

Although the consensus in the U.S. government is that the West is losing the media battle, the jihadists take the opposite view (see chapter 7). Salafi jihadists see a number of problems with the media, including:

- a perceived lack of access to television to get the jihadist word out;
- a belief that the media malign jihadists;
- a belief that the United States controls the media or has the media on its side; and
- a belief that even Arab and other non-American media are against the jihadists.[5]

As we have seen, the jihadists even see media institutions such as Al-Jazirah as deeply threatening despite their often critical stance toward the United States.

Failures of Other Sunnis

The Opposition of Senior Islamic Scholars

Salafi jihadists think that most senior Islamic scholars (the *ulema*) oppose them. The jihadists give a number of reasons for such opposition, including that authorities have bribed the scholars, that authorities have intimidated them, that the Western media have brainwashed them,[6] or that the scholars oppose Salafi jihadism out of ignorance and error. The jihadists see this opposition as a major barrier to creating an effective vanguard and a mass movement.

Salafi jihadist strategists have even bluntly discussed the best way to get rid of "informer" sheiks and scholars. Abu Musab al-Suri described his position on the subject as follows:

> The killing of some of the informer Moslem sheiks and scholars (like Sheik Mohammad Shami, Sheik Tawoos, and others) created a public relations nightmare due to their status as scholars among the simple-minded Muslims. The killing of informer sheiks should be dealt with as part of a carefully orchestrated public relations campaign that puts people on notice yet controls the damage and negative fallout. When Sheik Mohammad Shami was killed, the mujahideen did not publicize the operation or take credit for it, so the masses did not know if he was killed by us or by the regime.[7]

Lack of "Sufficient Faith" by Other Sunni Groups

Salafi jihadists' opinion of other Sunni groups and individuals has at times seemed worse than their opinions of Arab and apostate leaders.[8] Most members of AQAM believe that any organization that enters the political realm cannot be a part of their movement. Salafi jihadists have, for example, voiced their hatred for Sufi groups and the Tablighi Jamaat, and they have criticized HAMAS for joining the political process in Palestine.[9] Salafi jihadists hold a special disdain for the Muslim Brotherhood. Abu Bakr Naji described the perceived threat posed to the Salafi jihadists by these political groups when he cautioned that the Muslim Brotherhood's "intellectual infiltration of the jihadist group is serious and dangerous."[10]

An *Ummah* Corrupted by Western Influence and Distracted by "Worldly Concerns"

Salafi jihadists see "man's law"—be it secularism, nationalism, democracy, communism, or any other "ism"—as opposing "God's law." AQAM's strategists warn their public that, "although the slogans [of the 'isms'] look attractive, the contents are destructive and evil."[11] They further point out that democracy has failed Muslims in Algeria and Palestine (after HAMAS's victory at the polls in 2006), among other places.[12]

Another explanation the jihadists offer for why the *ummah* have failed to join the Salafi jihadist caravan is that these Muslims are distracted by worldly concerns (pop culture, jobs, families, marriage) and have a love of life and "hatred of death"; in other words, they are afflicted with *wahn* (see chapters 7 and 8). Their natural desire to settle down, have a family, and stay at home competes with the jihadists' desire to create a new generation of warriors.

AQAM is further concerned that Muslim parents are not raising their children to embrace jihad and violence. They see parents as a potential barrier to youth who want to take up the banner of jihad and consistently stress that their defensive jihad is an individual obligation and youths do not need their parents' permission to go.

Salafi jihadists also see school curricula as a key battleground between the ideology of "true Muslims" and the corrosive ideas of enemy Crusaders and Zionists intended to divert potential young recruits from joining the caravan. They fear that children will be taught a curriculum that will "erase the nation's character and westernize its sons."[13] They are convinced that a direct connection exists between curriculum and the desire to join the caravan, and they adamantly resist any hint of Western influence in the curriculum.[14]

From TV game shows to music to soccer games, AQAM has voiced frustration with the entertainment distractions members of the *ummah* allow themselves. Jemaah Islamiyah admonished those who watched the popular TV show *Star Academy*, a program similar to *American Idol*. Abu Musab al-Suri also criticized an *ummah* he believes are unwilling to "get off the couch" and "join the caravan." He lamented that although Muslims see "scenes of death, destruction, shame, and injury that the television screens transmit . . . [t]hey see these images, and flip the channels between them and pornographic films, cartoons, fashion shows, competitive sports, music and dance parties, and the 'Star Academy' competition!"[15]

Internal Policy Differences

Violence—its role, effectiveness, and targets—is the source of major internal policy differences. Three of these are summarized below.

Using Violence against Muslims

Salafi jihadists disagree over the extent to which they should avoid spilling Muslim blood. Some wish to avoid it at all costs. For instance, Abu Muhammed al-Maqdisi stated that "mujahideen should refrain from acts that target civilians, churches, or other places of worship, including Shiite sites."[16] Others share the sentiment of Abu Bakr Ba'asyir, who said in an interview about the Bali nightclub bombings: "If there happen[ed] to be a few Muslims there, it was their own fault—what were they doing there?"

AQAM strategists also disagree on methods for killing. Al-Zawahiri, in particular, has pointed out that the gruesome televised beheadings of captives carried out by al-Zarqawi had a negative impact on public opinion within the *ummah*.[17] But al-Zarqawi has not been the only proponent of gruesome and publicized killings. In 2005, Abu Bakr Naji described them as one way to free captured mujahideen. He suggested that diplomats be taken hostage and killed in a "horrific manner to plant fear in the hearts of the enemies and their collaborators."[18] Other AQAM thinkers believe the atmosphere of terrorism and brutality caused by these acts will destroy the noble reputation of the jihadist.

Some of AQAM's strategists, including al-Zawahiri, Abu Bakr Naji, and Abu Bakr Ba'asyir, have concluded that killings (accidental or intentional) of other Sunni Muslims have at times weakened support for the movement.[19] Certainly, the 2005 attacks on hotels in Amman, Jordan, seriously hurt al Qaida's popularity in that country.[20] After the attacks, one blogger on a jihadist Web site stated that one could "go to Amman and hear, unfortunately, a lot of people cursing Zarqawi everywhere." He continued, "with this act, al Qaida destroyed its great assets of Jordanian appreciation for its jihad in Iraq."[21]

The condemnation and killing of the Shia is another aspect of the issue of the counterproductive effects of violence. Salafi jihadist feelings toward the Shia run from indifference to absolute hatred. Indeed, before the war in Iraq took on such a starkly sectarian nature, references to the Shia in the Salafi jihadist literature were rare. Many still largely ignore the Shia, but there is also a school of thought represented by the late Abu Musab al-Zarqawi, who called the Shia of Iraq "the lurking serpent, the cunning and vicious scorpion, the waylaying enemy, and the deadly poison."[22]

Unfortunately for AQAM, many, probably most, Sunni Muslims object to killing fellow Muslims, regardless of sect. The spectacle of Sunni extremists denouncing Shiites as infidels, Persian imperialists, or Zionist and American agents at the same time that Shia Lebanese, under Hizbollah's banner, were willing to fight and die against the Israelis has raised questions of credibility and of simple good sense among the *ummah*. Although Salafi jihadists think that a conflict with the Shia will happen sooner or later, al-Zawahiri wrote to al-Zarqawi, "the majority of Muslims don't comprehend this and possibly could not even imagine it."[23]

The Importance of Connecting to Muslims by Means Other than Violent Jihad

Salafi jihadists agree on the necessity of violent jihad—and perhaps also that it is, as Osama bin Laden put it, the "top duty after faith." But some AQAM strategists also recognize that the softer side of the movement can be a way to gain the trust and support of the *ummah*. Figures such as al-Zawahiri, al-Qurashi, and Abu Musab al-Suri have at times stated the belief that proselytizing, sermonizing, relief work, education, and charity can win the *ummah*'s "hearts and minds," and that AQAM has not done enough in this regard.

Agreeing on the Strategic Focus of Jihad

AQAM members differ on the best focus for their jihad. Some focus on the United States (what some Western analysts call the "far enemy"), others focus on the apostate regimes (the "near enemy"), and others believe that both fights are important. Abu Ubayd al-Qurashi probably best represented the "U.S. first" strategy when he said in *Majallat al-Ansar*:

> The choice to target the United States from the beginning was a smart strategic choice for the global jihad movement. The struggle with the United States' hangers-on in the Islamic region has shown that these hangers-on cannot keep their tyrannical regimes going for a single minute without U.S. help. This is why we must strike the head. When it falls, it will bring down the rest. The choice to target the United States is understood and accepted throughout the Islamic community because everybody knows the crimes the United States has committed against Islam and Muslims. This is what ensures popular sympathy and support.[24]

Abu Hafs al-Mauritani expanded on al-Qurashi's thoughts: "If the strike was against a target outside America say an embassy or so then the losses would not amount to that of Sept. 11[;] moreover, the American security agencies would try to avoid shouldering any responsibilities to save some of its accountability and credibility. Add to that, America would blame the country in which the embassy lies[;] besides the attack might cause serious damage to the locals more than the Americans."[25]

Others have more pressing concerns than attacking the United States. They are fighting locally or believe that fellow jihadists should focus on fighting in a particular region or state. Al-Zarqawi, for example, issued calls for jihadists to go to Iraq: "O nation of Islam, come to the rescue of the jihad in Iraq before the infidel majority besieges the mujahideen. O by God, who holds my soul, if the torch of jihad is extinguished, if the breath of jihad weakens, and if the pockets of jihad in Iraq are closed, the Islamic nation will not rise until God wills it to rise."[26] Still others argue that Iraq is not as pressing a priority as the fights in Saudi Arabia and Algeria.[27]

An Addition to the Strategy for Combating Terrorism

The previous section presented how AQAM discusses its own frustrations and failures. Understanding these frustrations and failures in turn illuminates which actions are likely to frustrate the enemy and which actions—although perhaps important to America—will have little effect on them. This section discusses the current American strategy for combating terrorism—based on long-term and short-term approaches—and the opportunity to complement the two with an approach that could be effective in the midterm. The "National Strategy for Combating Terrorism" (September 2006), which describes the U.S. campaign against terrorists and terrorism, portrays the American strategy as comprising two parts:

- A long-term approach: advancing effective democracy to defeat terror in the long term
- A short-term approach: four priorities of action providing protective measures to contain terrorism and create the space and time for the long-term solution to take root:
  1. Prevent attacks by terrorist networks
  2. Deny weapons of mass destruction (WMD) to rogue states and their terrorist allies who seek to use them
  3. Deny terrorists the support and sanctuary of rogue states
  4. Deny terrorists control of any nation they would use as a base and launching pad for terror

Beyond this long-term approach and the four near-term priorities to support it, the statements of Salafi jihadists presented above point to a third approach that could be effective in the *midterm*. This approach attempts to influence other Sunnis to reject and deny legitimacy to the Salafi jihadists as a way of reducing the number of new adherents to the movement and increasing attrition among those already in the movement.

This approach is not new and is similar to the idea of "rolling back" communism during the Cold War. Rather than simply containing communism, some argued for a more offense-oriented approach, an approach that would not only contain the spread of communism but roll it back. But direct military action was seen as too dangerous, so the United States generally limited rollback to "political warfare" and cultural and economic measures to influence the people held captive by Soviet rule.

Unlike communism during the early Cold War, Salafi jihadism is at a weak stage in its development and is ripe for rollback. Creating an environment within the *ummah* that is inhospitable to violent extremists would take advantage of weaknesses the enemy has already identified: (1) the inability to recruit enough people to join the caravan and so create an effective vanguard in the face of a currently apathetic or hostile *ummah*, and (2) the inability to gain a sanctuary within the *ummah* and so be freer from interference by the security forces of the apostate governments and the United States.

To date, the Salafi jihadists' explanations for their failures reveal how they see their own defeat: rejected by an overwhelming majority of the world's Muslims, unable to recruit a vanguard, living in a hostile environment without sanctuary, and limited to executing isolated and ineffective operations. So rolling back the Salafi jihadists could also lead to their defeat, even without the arrival of effective democracy (which, desirable as it may be, is not a prerequisite for ensuring that Muslims remain hostile to Salafi jihadism).

The following principles are particularly important in guiding actions for rollback:

- The aim is to discredit Salafi jihadism so that the movement becomes weak, isolated, and a pariah existing only on the fringe of Sunni Islam.
- The contested ground is the *ummah*—those Sunni Muslims to whom AQAM is appealing.
- The aim is not to convince the *ummah* of the West's rightness, but rather to stop them from supporting and joining the caravan.
- The nucleus of true believers in Salafi jihadism cannot be deterred or converted, but simply killing and capturing them will not alone bring victory.

Actions the United States and Its Partners Should Take

U.S. strategic communication policy, words, and actions should concentrate on rolling back the movement and separating Salafi jihadists from the ummah.[28] To date, U.S. strategic communication activities have not effectively delegitimized the Salafi jihadists.[29] The "shared values" campaign of 2002 was an unfortunate example of a condescending message ("Some of my best friends are . . .") delivered to a suspicious Muslim audience. Many Sunnis oppose American interests, loathe Israel, are hostile to Western military operations in the Middle East, and are appalled by the postmodern Western way of life. But many of the same people are or could also be hostile to Salafi jihadism, and they could be de facto allies in the struggle against it.

An important American objective should be to get Sunni Muslims to dislike AQAM and thus not support or join the movement. (It is desirable, but not necessary, that they dislike AQAM more than they dislike the United States.) Highlighting AQAM's attacks that kill Muslims is an important part of this, but this must be done without making Muslims feel that non-Muslims are telling them what their religion stands for. The evidence suggests that the vast majority of the world's Muslims reject AQAM's ideology. Many Muslims (e.g., Shia) and Muslim organizations (e.g., Tablighi Jamaat, the Muslim Brotherhood) are by definition enemies of Salafi jihadism. The United States should not lecture others about Islamic values. Rather, al Qaida and its methods must be shown to be unattractive, ineffective, objectively at odds with universal human values, and implicitly at odds with Islamic values and Islamic law regarding war and jihad.

The United States should acknowledge the limits of its strategic communication capabilities. Nongovernmental words and images constitute a greater informational threat to the Salafi jihadists than anything Washington can do. A refocused strategic communication effort against AQAM must enable nongovernmental processes and third parties, including nontraditional partners. For instance, the U.S. government should not impede the growth of Arab and Muslim "new media" such as Al-Jazirah and its imitators, which are anti-American to varying degrees, yet whose style of journalism AQAM sees as a serious threat, a dangerous rival for the attention of the Muslim audience.

The United States should encourage Western-influenced television shows in the Muslim world. Locally produced TV programs, constructed on Western lines yet employing Muslims in an Islamic cultural milieu, constitute a competing vision for the *ummah.* One example is *Alam Simsim,* the Egyptian variant of *Sesame Street,* which is popular with Egyptian children in both urban and rural areas. Like its American model, it promotes cultural sensitivity, education, and gender equality—demonstrating that modest American support can deliver considerable dividends.[30]

The United States should support in each Islamic country popular local traditions and interests that Salafi jihadists abhor. The Salafi jihadists' brand of Islam often contrasts sharply with the interests and traditions of many other Sunnis. For instance, soccer has been a source of conflict between Salafi jihadists and other Sunni Muslims, as has the tradition of kite fighting in Afghanistan. The United States should take advantage of this natural tension.The goals of such support are to remind Sunni Muslims of what Salafi jihadists want to take from them, further separating the *ummah* from the Salafi jihadists, and to create more positive feelings toward the United States.

Military operations against al Qaida must always be evaluated as information operations; at a minimum, deeds (bad visuals on TV) should not undermine words. In the strategic communication war, capturing a Salafi jihadist is preferable to killing him in an air strike that results in civilian casualties. Some military operations, specifically humanitarian aid and relief efforts, can be a relatively inexpensive way to get Muslims to view the United States more positively, and might even move them to reject AQAM and its actions. Poll results in Indonesia after the December 2004 tsunami and in Pakistan after the October 2005 earthquake indicate that U.S. relief efforts and humanitarian aid had a striking impact on Muslims in the stricken countries, resulting in more positive views of the United States and more negative views of AQAM's legitimacy.[31] America should take two steps to exploit this impact:

1. Ensure timely and attributed delivery of humanitarian assistance to countries with significant Muslim populations. This will produce at least transient benefits.
2. Ensure that there is a plan for a sustained follow-up by the country team to help consolidate the immediate gains from the humanitarian assistance. This plan could involve projects through the U.S. Agency for International Development, U.S. libraries in local universities, and so on.

U.S. strategic communication should operate on the following principles:

- Emphasize rejecting the enemy and its violence rather than liking the United States. Emphasize that Salafi jihadists are akin to a cult or hate group and that they despise nearly everyone (non-Muslims, non-jihadi Salafists, Shia, Sufis, nationalists, communists, and socialists—anyone in the political realm).

- Leave theology to theologians. Do not engage in arguments about who is or is not a good Muslim and what is "true" or "false" Islam. If individuals or a group declare war on America and plan mass murder in the name of religion, America should not debate the finer points of said group's religion.

- Recognize the power of Western-influenced television (to both attract and repel a Muslim audience).

- Recognize that deeds are at least as important as words in the realm of strategic communication.

The United States with its partners should interfere with AQAM media and communication.[32] To deny AQAM a voice and make it less effective, U.S. government operatives, depending heavily on partners from foreign countries, should disrupt AQAM communications with its members and like-minded individuals and influence the direction of its conceptual evolution by entering jihadist debates on the Internet both as contributors and as hackers.

To deny AQAM a voice, the United States and its partners should plant doubts about the utility of the Internet for disseminating information. U.S. operatives can hack jihadist Web sites and subtly alter their content so that Web site operators cannot be certain that the content on their site is what they posted. America can sow confusion about the message voiced by Salafi jihadists by posting misleading and contradictory Internet messages aimed at the *ummah*, at AQAM's internal constituency, or both. Visitors should not be able to trust that the content of such messages is legitimate and truly represents jihadist thinking and actions. For instance, a document could be subtly altered to project a particular slant (such as that bin Laden or AQAM members see other Muslims as "expendable"), or entirely fictitious messages could be posted.

The United States and its partners should enter jihadist Web sites covertly as contributors with the objective of encouraging less useful strategy and tactics, and disparaging good strategic thinking. AQAM could likely gain more recruits if it proselytized or did charity work, so these U.S. "contributors" could discourage such a course and deride groups that support it. These contributors could also encourage policy differences (e.g., toward more ideological purity), start rumors regarding betrayal by other Web members, make claims that some Web sites are fronts for the apostate security services and the Americans, and encourage jihadists to believe that effective measures (e.g., forming coalitions) are contrary to their religion.[33] AQAM Web sites that the United States or its allies do not manipulate or control should be quickly shut down.

The United States should disrupt AQAM messages being delivered in American prisons by adopting an approach like the one that the United Kingdom has taken in its "Countering International Terrorism" strategy: "The Police Advisors Section has encouraged HMPS [Her Majesty's Prison Service] to develop strategies to identify and combat radicalization within the prison population. The officers have been working with HMPS and other Police and community specialists to establish a unique mentoring program, which seeks to identify those Muslim prisoners potentially susceptible to radicalization or extremist views and which supports them upon their release from prison to integrate them back into their local community."[34]

Actions the United States Should Encourage Other Governments to Take

In states with majority Sunni populations, open up media access to nonviolent or anti-AQAM viewpoints in order to get out alternative messages. A government's main advantage in countering AQAM is not in its "public diplomacy" efforts but in the power of local-language media—TV, film, and other—to counter AQAM's harsh message of violence, hatred, and intolerance. Arabic-language networks such as Al-Jazirah and Al-Arabiyya, for example, carry a powerful message that challenges the extremists. Although those two networks are hardly "fair and balanced," and are usually harsh on American policy, their underlying message supports anti-AQAM positions of relativism, open debate, and of giving opposing points of view a chance to be heard. Al-Jazirah's use of Israeli commentators, for instance, was revolutionary in a media setting where the Israeli was seen as either nonexistent or subhuman.

Governments should support the open-minded currents in their own societies by giving platforms to local folk traditions, tolerant views of Sufism, and popular preachers who extol a religion in accordance with the desires of educated young people and the modern world. Salafi jihadists find all of these to be pernicious influences, and all offer alternatives to Salafi jihadist ideology. The United States should encourage these governments to allow open debate and creativity in the media. America should also support its partners in covertly funding and enabling individuals and organizations that promulgate anti-AQAM views. For instance, the United States could help its partner governments fund and enable Sufi brotherhoods and other organizations that reinforce traditions of tolerance and nonviolence.

The United States should encourage governments to support local filmmakers and screenwriters. Films and soap operas are popular everywhere, and their Middle Eastern creators, such as the Egyptian director Yousef Shahine, often find themselves under attack by extremists, clerical obscurantists, the authorities, and others who condemn ideas opposed to their own. U.S. efforts to encourage governments should include direct support of directors and writers, with exchanges and visits encouraging those who propagate messages of tolerance.

Finally, the U.S. government need not lecture the Egyptians, Saudis, Moroccans, or others on the danger posed by violent extremism. These governments are well aware of the threat. Rather, it should encourage them to use their existing media strengths against the extremists and to avoid inadvertently serving the AQAM cause. For example, they should arrest hate speech in their media, not because such speech is offensive but because it fosters the climate of extremism and violence dear to AQAM and gives AQAM's views an outlet to their audience.

Reduce sources of legitimacy for AQAM by establishing norms for schooling and public religious messages. A ninth-grade Saudi textbook tells its readers: "The clash between this *ummah* and the Jews and Christians has endured, and it will continue as long as God wills."[35] Such educational materials can instill bigotry in the target audience. This type of curriculum, combined with teaching practices that do not tolerate alternative ideas, can lead to a culture of hate. To avoid this "gift" to AQAM, the United States should encourage other governments to create a culture of tolerance in their education systems. Educational reform should reinforce traditional norms—such as emphasis on obeying one's parents—that are beneficial both to society and to the fight against AQAM. The United States could offer teacher exchange programs, textbooks, and free educational training to foreign Muslim teachers.

When religious leaders and other voices of authority vocally support jihad, AQAM gains adherents. Some clerics, both in states with Muslim majorities and in Western democracies, still publicly advocate violence against America and its allies. Since authorities in most states have some control over what is said in public by religious leaders, the United States should press for governments to prevent expressions of violent rhetoric.

· Building Institutional Understanding

The Salafi jihadists themselves can point Western strategists toward methods of bringing about their demise. The knowledge gained from the Terrorist Perspectives Project indicates that a critical capability in fighting the Salafi jihadists is understanding their thoughts and how these evolve over time. Former secretary of defense Robert McNamara, reflecting on America's misjudgment in the Vietnam War, came to a similar conclusion about that war and the broader Cold War. "We might have made similar misjudgments regarding the Soviets," he said, if not for experts who "spent decades studying the Soviet Union, its people and its leaders, why they behaved as they did and how they would react to our actions."[36] To reduce the chance for future misjudgments of Salafi jihadists, the United States should expand its long-term knowledge base of the Islamic world. Studying the lessons from the Cold War programs that enlarged America's understanding of the Soviet Union can help us determine how to expand our long-term knowledge base of the Islamic world.

One focus for enhancing understanding involves expanding the knowledge base of U.S. public servants. Military officers, intelligence personnel, diplomats, law enforcement representatives, and others who represent the United States should be expected to know foreign languages, to understand Islam, to understand foreign cultures, and to know how to operate in multinational and multicultural environments. The U.S. government owes these men and women proper training for their missions. Despite efforts to recruit and reward language skills, America's pool of foreign-language-qualified professionals remains inadequate for its mission.[37] The U.S. government lacks professionals with basic foreign-language skills and area knowledge, and even those with such skills often find that their training has not equipped them for the tasks they are asked to perform.[38] Beyond training these people, the departments and agencies of government need to address issues of rewarding career tracks, promotions, and assignments.

Another focus should involve expanding the knowledge base outside the government. Early in the Cold War, the U.S. government supported language and area studies in Russian (as well as Chinese, Arabic, Persian, and Turkish) through the National Defense Foreign Language program. The DoD established Centers of Excellence in Soviet studies (military, political, economic) in universities, in think tanks such as IDA and RAND, and with private contractors. Some of these "centers" were simply collections of people who met occasionally for conferences, such as the Dalhousie Seminar on Soviet Naval Developments, a group of American, British, and Canadian scholars interested in the Soviet Navy who read and discussed the Soviet technical literature on it. Representatives of the intelligence community and the Center for Naval Analyses attended Dalhousie's conferences but did not run them.[39] These programs trained and engaged a generation of American area specialists during the Cold War who took positions in academia, business, the intelligence community, the military, and the diplomatic service.

A third focus should involve supporting cultural and educational exchanges with knowledgeable academics, media, and nongovernmental organizations from around the world. While the Department of State would run the exchanges central to the effort, the DoD and the intelligence community would necessarily be involved. The Department of Homeland Security and the FBI need to ensure that academics, foreign-language teachers, journalists, and others can quickly get the visas they need to come to the United States to teach and study, without becoming entangled in a stifling immigration bureaucracy.[40]

Americans should not be deluded that the struggle against Salafi jihadism will be anything other than protracted. However, America and its allies prevailed in a similar war during the twentieth century. During the Cold War, the U.S. government and intellectual community studied communism; the Soviet Union; and Soviet military, political, and economic thought. It seems highly unlikely that the United States will surmount the threat of Salafi jihadism without similar study. The enemy has plenty of weaknesses. It is incumbent upon us to identify and take advantage of them if we are to prevail in the twenty-first century.

Notes

1. Jeff Jaworski, Ambassador John Limbert, and Joel Resnick made especially valuable contributions to this chapter.
2. These descriptions present a useful but not exhaustive list; there are undoubtedly others. The ones identified here are useful in that they can be exploited in America's fight against Salafi jihadists.
3. Harmony document folder AFGP-2002-600080; see also FBIS GMP20020108000 197.
4. Harmony document folder AFGP-2002-600005. Fear of penetration was evident in commentary posted to a jihadist Web site in December 2006 warning that another popular jihadist Web site, Al-Hisbah Net, was "infiltrated by spies" who had virtually taken over the forum. The posting warned that the Arab ruling "tyrants" sought entrée in order to influence al Qaida's thinking. See FBIS GMP20061210342007, "Mujahidin Suffer 'Setback' after 'Spies' Infiltrate Al-Hisbah Net," December 8, 2006.
5. FBIS SEP20041222000085.
6. FBIS GMP20040209000243001.
7. Harmony document folder AFGP-2002-600080.
8. The Salafi jihadists have at times had their own disagreements; for instance, al-Zawahiri's and bin Laden's numerous disagreements with al-Zarqawi exposed in the captured letter from al-Zawahiri to al-Zarqawi; see FBIS EUP20051012374001. Al-Zarqawi and al-Maqdisi, his former mentor, also had very few kind words for each other.
9. Al-Suri, *Call to Global Islamic Resistance*, OSC translation. See also al-Zawahiri's Knights under the Prophet's Banner, FBIS GMP20020108000197; and Naji's *Management of Savagery*.
10. Naji, *Management of Savagery*.
11. See document ICPVTR-14401 in the database of Rohan Gunaratna's International Centre for Political Violence and Terrorism Research, *Ansar al-Islam*, London, www.pvtr.org/coreprojects_pathfinder.htm ICPVTR-14401. Also see FBIS GMP2003 0929000003.
12. See FBIS GMP20020108000197; FBIS GMP20060106532004; FBIS GMP2006 0427538001.
13. FBIS GMP20041216000222.
14. Western analysts consider how the curriculum is taught to be more important than the curriculum itself and find little connection between school curricula and the propensity to carry out violent acts (see Sageman, *Understanding Terrorist Networks*, 74–77); however, there is evidence that religious schools may "foster conditions that are conducive to public support for terrorism." See also C. Christine Fair, "Islamic Education in Pakistan," United States Institute of Peace, March 21, 2006, http://www.usip.org/events/2006/trip_report.pdf, accessed October 27, 2007.
15. Al-Suri, *Call to Global Islamic Resistance*, OSC translation.
16. FBIS GMP20050601712006.
17. FBIS EUP20051012374001. In May 2007, a man claiming to be a member of the al Qaida–linked Islamic State of Iraq said in an interview that the beheadings were still being carried out and filmed but that there was an "order" not to show them; FBIS GMP20070516950026, 2007.
18. FBIS GMP20050308000220.

19. We differentiate here between Sunnis and Shia because Salafi jihadists do not consider Shia to be legitimate Muslims.

20. The Pew Global Attitudes Project, "The Great Divide: How Westerners and Muslims View Each Other," June 22, 2006, http://pewglobal.org/reports/display.php?ReportID=253, accessed September 22, 2007.

21. Maamoun Youssef, "Islamic Web Sites Criticize Jordan Bombing," *Washington Post*, November 15, 2005. "Prime Negotiator" was the alias of a contributor to a jihadist Web site.

22. FBIS GMP20040615000107.

23. FBIS EUP20051012374001.

24. FBIS GMP20031027000226.

25. See ICPVTR-14419.

26. FBIS GMP20040406000138. Bin Laden has also stressed the importance of winning in Iraq. See FBIS GMP20060427538001.

27. FBIS GMP20040109000138, "Interview with Nabil Sahraoui, Leader of Islamic Fundamentalist Salafi Group." See also FBIS GMP20040422000283, "Wanted Mujahid al-Awfi Defends Decision to Fight 'Crusaders' in Saudi Arabia," January 8, 2004.

28. In the United Kingdom's strategy "Countering International Terrorism" (July 2006), the discussion of the "Battle of Ideas," 13–16, describes a campaign analogous to rollback. In the French white paper "Domestic Security against Terrorism" (July 2006), the discussion of "Winning the Battle of Ideas," 113–22, also describes ideas and actions analogous to rollback.

29. A recent GAO report states: "No interagency public diplomacy strategy has been implemented that lays out the messages and means for government-wide communication efforts to overseas audiences. The absence of an interagency strategy complicates the task of conveying consistent messages and thus achieving mutually reinforcing benefits"; from GAO (GAO-04-1061T): U.S. Public Diplomacy (August 2004), 9.

30. USAID has provided $8.4 million for the creation of *Alam Simsim*; see "Arabic 'Sesame Street' Is a Hit in Egypt," *Telling Our Story*, www.usaid.gov, March 31, 2006.

31. "A Dramatic Change of Public Opinion in the Muslim World; Results from a New Poll in Pakistan," and "New Polls throughout Muslim World: Humanitarian Leadership by U.S. Remains Positive," both at *Terror Free Tomorrow*, accessed at www.terrorfreetomorrow.com (site no longer active).

32. By "communication" we mean nonoperational communications, such as discussions of military concepts, history, theology, and current events.

33. Yusuf al-Ayiri essentially argued, for example, that if Allah required certain actions, they must be undertaken even if they would certainly lead to catastrophe. See FBIS GMP20031211000267.

34. Her Majesty's Government, *Countering International Terrorism: The United Kingdom's Strategy* (2006), 13.

35. Center for Religious Freedom of Freedom House, "Saudi Arabia's Curriculum of Intolerance," May 23, 2006, 25, http://www.freedomhouse.org/uploads/special_report/48.pdf, accessed September 23, 2007.

36. Robert S. McNamara, *In Retrospect* (New York: Vintage Books, 1996), 322.

37. A recent GAO report says that "despite its efforts to enhance the language capabilities of its staff, State continues to fill language-designated positions with staff who do not meet the proficiency requirements. . . . Some officers believe that

State's assignment and promotion system hindered their ability to maintain their language skills over time." See GAO "Department of State: Staffing and Foreign Language Shortfalls Persist Despite Initiatives to Address Gaps," August 2006, www.gao.gov.

38. It normally takes an officer two years of full-time study to reach the proficiency level of "general professional" (S/3-R/3) in Arabic, one of the four "superhard" languages. Yet that level is just a beginning for an officer who needs to deal with counterparts in the subtleties of counterterrorism policy; understand the nuances of Arabic discourse; or engage with Arabic-language media to convey an accurate, literate, and culturally sensitive message to a suspicious and often hostile public.

39. We are grateful to Jacob Kipp for bringing this to our attention. The Dalhousie Seminar on Soviet Naval Developments engendered at least three edited volumes: *Soviet Naval Developments: Capability and Context* (1973); *Soviet Naval Policy: Objectives and Constraints* (1975); and *Soviet Naval Influence: Domestic and Foreign Dimensions* (1977).

40. When President George W. Bush announced the National Security Language Initiative at the State Department, university presidents in the audience criticized the role the Department of Homeland Security played in hindering international academic travel.

Acronyms and Abbreviations

AQ	Al Qaida
AQAM	Al Qaida and Associated Movements
AQI	Al Qaida in Iraq
ASG	Abu Sayyaf Group
CISR	Center for Islamic Research and Studies
COG	Center of Gravity
DoD	U.S. Department of Defense
DSB	Defense Science Board
EIG	Egyptian Islamic Group
EIJ	Egyptian Islamic Jihad
FBIS	Foreign Broadcast Information Service
FIS	Islamic Salvation Front
FLN	Front Liberation Nationale
GIA	Armed Islamic Group
GSPC	Salafist Group for Preaching and Combat
IDA	Institute for Defense Analyses
IED	Improvised Explosive Device
IO	Information Operations
JAWD	Joint Advanced Warfighting Division
JFCOM	Joint Forces Command
JuD	Jamaatud Dawa, Pakistani group affiliated with al Qaida
KO	Kinetic Operations
MEMRI	Middle East Media Research Institute
NSCT	National Strategy for Combating Terrorism
OSC	Open Source Center
SITE	Search for International Terrorist Entities

Glossary of Arabic Terms

Al-Ikhwan al-Muslimeen	The Muslim Brotherhood.
Allah	God.
Allahu akbar	God is great.
Al-tali'a al-Muqatila	"The Fighting Vanguard," a Syrian jihadist group of the 1970s and early 1980s that allied itself with the Muslim Brotherhood to fight the Syrian regime.
bayat	Oath of allegiance to a leader.
dar al-harb	House of war; refers to lands not under the governance of Muslims.
dar al-Islam	House of Islam; refers to lands under the governance of Muslims.
dawah	The call; proselytizing of Islam.
fard 'ayn	An individual duty. Salafi jihadists believe that in the present situation jihad is *fard 'ayn* upon all Muslims.
fard kifaya	A collective duty, often one performed by a state on behalf of the entire population.
fatwa	A religious legal ruling.
fitna	A difficult-to-translate word that has connotations of civil war, division, upheaval, and anarchy within the *ummah*.
ghazi	Warrior for the faith.

hadith, pl. *ahadith*	The sayings and practices of Muhammed as passed on through oral tradition for many years before being recorded in writing. Some are generally agreed to be authentic, others are generally agreed to be inauthentic, and others are disputed.
hizbiyah	Party-like or partisan; pejorative term used by some Salafis to describe other Salafis who engage in politics or political violence.
houris	The original meaning of the term is disputed. Salafi jihadists understand it to refer to dark-eyed virgins who await a martyr in paradise.
Ikhwan	Brotherhood.
jahiliyya	Originally the state of pre-Islamic ignorance in which Arabs lived before the time of Muhammed. In the twentieth century CE, Sayyid Qutb argued that the term could be used to describe the present condition of the ummah.
Jama'ah	Group.
jihad	Striving. The religious connotations of the word are disputed. Salafi jihadists understand jihad to refer primarily to combat. Under this interpretation, jihad can be seen as roughly comparable to the Christian idea of "just war." Many other Muslims say that the primary meaning of the word refers to the inner struggle to be a better Muslim.
kufr	Pejorative term for an unbeliever—a person who hides, denies, or covers the truth (i.e., Islam).
madrassa	An Islamic religious school.
mujahid, pl. **mujahideen**	A person engaged in jihad.
Qur'an	The sacred scripture of Islam. Muslims believe the Qur'an is the final and perfect revelation by Allah and that he delivered it to Muhammed.
ribaa	Interest, as on a loan.

Salaf al-saliheen Pious predecessors; referring to the first generation of Muslims who were the source of the hadith. Salafis view them as living a pure faith and seek to return to their understanding of the Sunnah, uncorrupted by some thirteen hundred years of intrepretation and extrapolation by Islamic scholars.

Salafi A Sunni Muslim who believes that the Qur'an and the Sunnah are the only legitimate bases for law. Salafis would like Islam to be practiced the way they believe it was practiced in its earliest days. Salafis are not, properly understood, followers of any of the major schools of Islamic jurisprudence.

shahid, pl. ***shuhada*** Martyr.

sharia Islamic law.

Sunnah Way of the Prophet. The words and deeds of Muhammed as known through the Qur'an and the hadiths.

taghut Idolatry.

takfir The practice of declaring that a person previously believed to be a Muslim is, in fact, a nonbeliever.

tawhid Unity, a reference to the indivisible nature of Allah.

ulema Islamic scholars.

ummah The community of all Muslims.

wahn Word used by Muhammed in a hadith to refer to "the love of life and the hatred of death."

Index

About the Authors

Mark E. Stout is a research staff member with the Institute for Defense Analyses in Alexandria, Virginia. He previously served in the Department of the Army, the Department of State, and the Central Intelligence Agency. He is coauthor of *The Iraqi Perspectives Report: Saddam's Senior Leadership on Operation Iraqi Freedom from the Official U.S. Joint Forces Command Report* (Naval Institute Press, 2006).

Jessica M. Huckabey is an adjunct research staff member with the Institute for Defense Analyses in Alexandria, Virginia. She has degrees in military history and war studies and is an information warfare officer in the Navy Reserve.

Dr. John R. Schindler is professor of national security studies at the U.S. Naval War College in Newport, Rhode Island. He previously served for nearly a decade with the National Security Agency as an intelligence analyst and counterintelligence officer. He has published widely on issues of terrorism, intelligence, and national security and is the author of two other books on al Qaida: *Unholy Terror: Bosnia, Al-Qa'ida and the Rise of Global Jihad* (Zenith, 2007) and *Agents Provocateurs: How Intelligence Can Defeat Al-Qa'ida* (Zenith, 2008).

Jim Lacey is a former U.S. Army infantry officer and IDA analyst. He and Stout were co-authors of *The Iraqi Perspectives Report* (Naval Institute Press, 2006).